rosemary laing

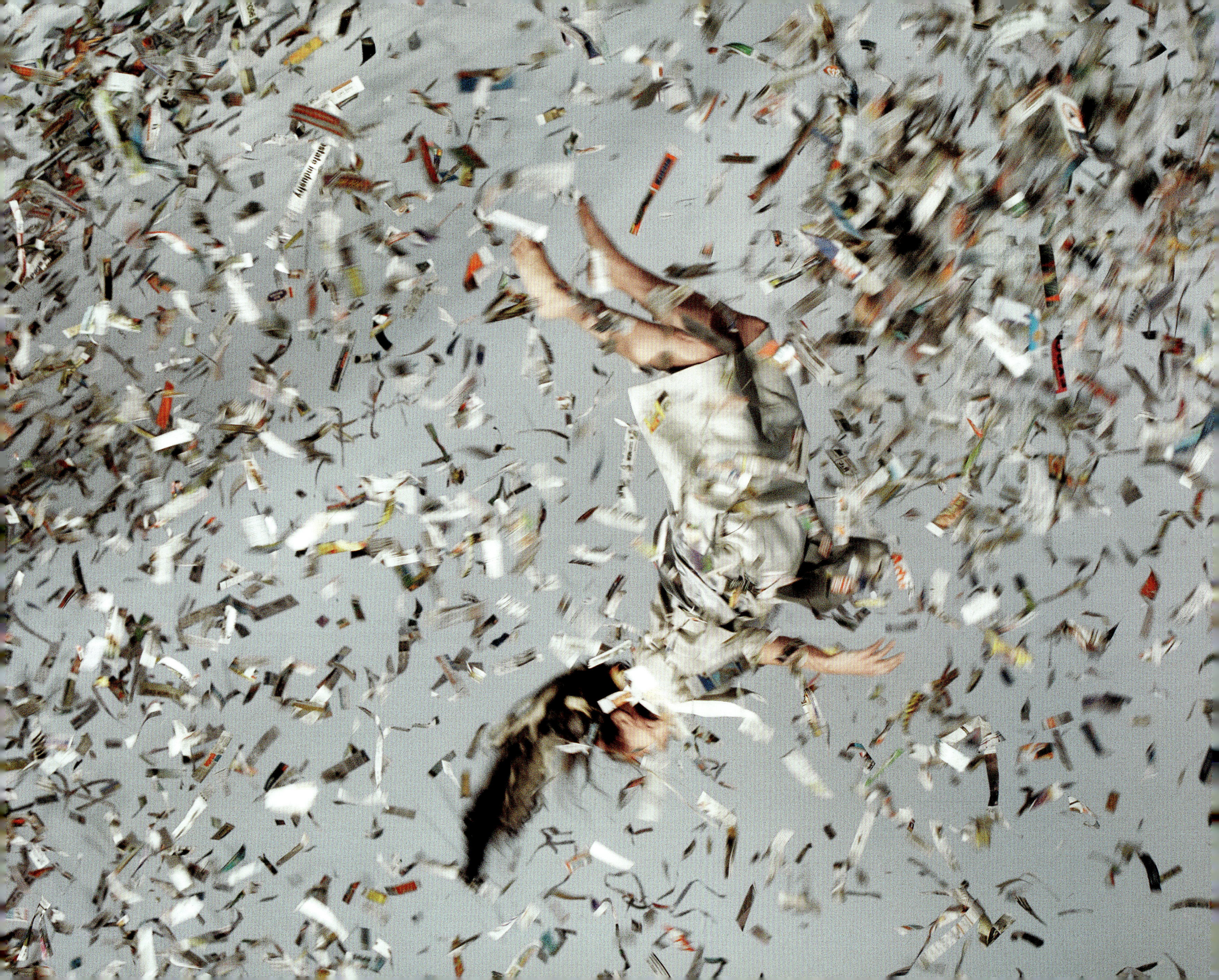

rosemary laing

essay by Abigail Solomon-Godeau

Prestel | Munich London New York

Prestel, a member of Verlagsgruppe Random House GmbH

Prestel Verlag
Neumarkter Strasse 28
81673 Munich
Germany
Tel. +49 (0)89-4136-0
Fax +49 (0)89-4136-2335

Prestel Publishing Ltd.
4 Bloomsbury Place
London WC1A 2QA
United Kingdom
Tel. +44 (0)20 7323-5004
Fax. +44 (0)20 7636-8004

Prestel Publishing
900 Broadway, Suite 603
New York, NY 10003
United States
Tel. +1 212-995-2720
Fax +1 212-995-2733

www.prestel.com

Prestel books are available worldwide. Please contact your nearest bookseller or one of the above addresses for information concerning your local distributor.

Library of Congress Control Number: 2012931845

Photography Credits
Sue Blackburn: page 18; Tim Marshall: pages 66, 68; Carl Warner: pages 38, 62, 63

This project has been assisted by the Australian Government through the Australia Council, its arts funding and advisory body.

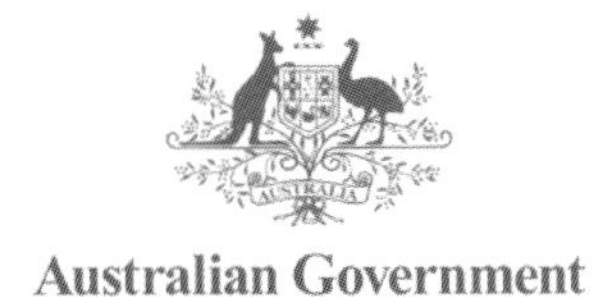
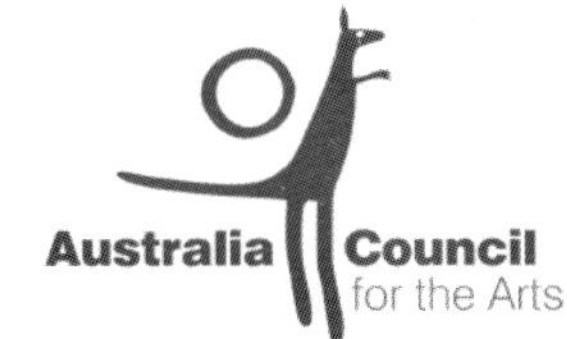

EDITORIAL DIRECTION: Ryan Newbanks
RESEARCH AND EDITORIAL ASSISTANCE: Tanya Peterson
COPYEDITING: John Farmer
PROOFREADING: Nicole Lanctot
DESIGN: Laura Lindgren, New York
PRODUCTION: The Production Department
ORIGINATION: GHP, Westhaven, Connecticut

Verlagsgruppe Random House FSC-DEU-0100
Printed on the FSC-certified paper 170gsm LumiSilk, produced by Stora Enso

ISBN 978-3-7913-4666-3

Front cover: *flight research #5*, 1999, detail (pages 86–87)
Back cover: *brumby mound #6*, 2003, detail (page 127)
Frontispiece: *weather #12*, 2006, detail (page 149)
Page 6: *groundspeed (Red Piazza) #5*, 2001, detail (page 102)

Contents

Preface   7

Chapter 1:   Rosemary Laing: An Australian Artist   8

Chapter 2:   Home/Lands   20

Chapter 3:   Disasters Natural and Unnatural   36

Chapter 4:   Altered States   50

Notes   58

PLATES   61

Selected Exhibitions, Projects, Publications, and Collections   170

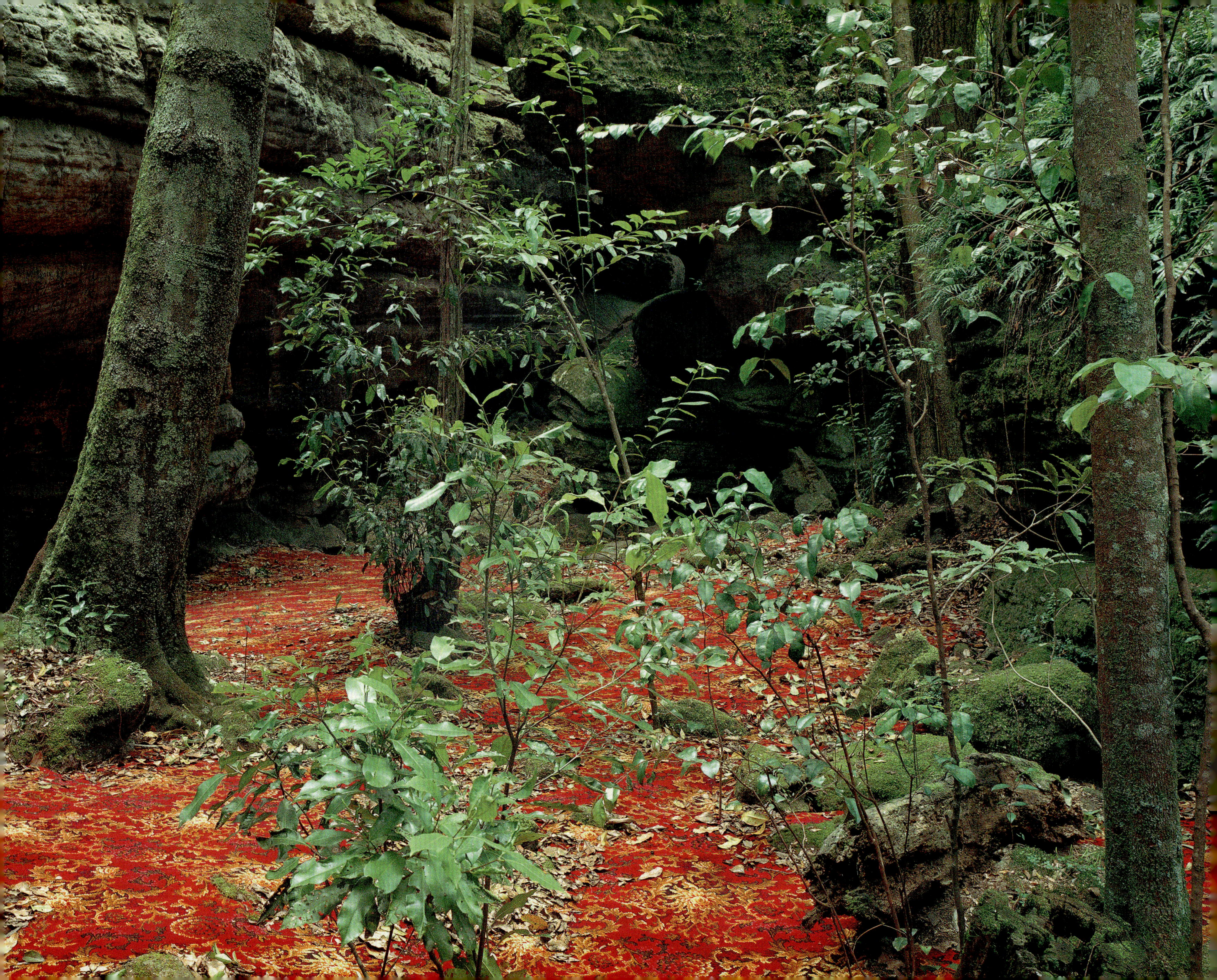

It is an art-critical commonplace these days to invoke the terms "nomad" and "nomadism," referring to the itinerant artist or intellectual, or, in a somewhat different sense, to site-specific artworks that artists may produce in places far from where they live or from where they are citizens. Some artists, of course, are literally "stateless" people, for example Palestinians; others may have refugee status in the countries where, provisionally or not, they make their homes. In terms of contemporary art, however, this more generalized usage might account for how I, as a US citizen, have come to write a book about Rosemary Laing, an Australian, whose work for nearly three decades has been fundamentally grounded in what I have described as both her location and her situation.

This is not without its own share of contradictions and, on my part, a certain discomfort, if not embarrassment. As a trained art historian of a certain type (feminist, materialist, etc.), I take for granted the importance of "context" in considering any form of cultural production. Which is not to say that even its most exhaustive plumbing yields a fixed or final meaning for any work of art. However, and as will certainly be evident to Australian readers, I have no particular expertise about, nor any profound knowledge of, the country whose historical and political specifics so significantly inform Laing's art. Working with Laing on this project, and aided by her wonderful research assistant, fellow art critic and art historian Tanya Peterson, I have learned a lot. From the writing of Australian critics and curators whose work I read with great admiration, I also learned a lot. Not enough, I hasten to add, but perhaps enough to serve as a mediating voice for those non-Australians who may be introduced to the body of remarkable work that this book presents.

As a US national writing about work so deeply moored in the histories of Australia—past and present—I have been constantly aware of the parallelisms between these two ex-colonial states. The "haunting" that I refer to throughout these pages has, in the first case, to do with the respective residues of violent expropriation, indeed genocide, enacted well before the word was coined. This history of violent conquest and settlement is officially—governmentally—acknowledged only in Australia, and however unachieved is the regeneration and redemption such an apology potentially enables, its absence from the agenda of my own country is cause for reflection.

My thanks go first to Rosemary Laing, who as someone with no pretensions to being a "scholar" of Australian history could certainly pass for one. As I have indicated in these pages, her artwork is not only of the highest quality, but her ethical and political convictions and ideals are a model of what it means to be a "responsible" image maker. In so generously opening to me her studio, her archives, her notebooks, and—by no means least—her library, she enabled this book to be written. Tanya Peterson was indispensable as an impeccable researcher, second reader, and much more. Any errors of fact are undoubtedly mine. I wish also to thank Ioulia Terizis, who facilitated the project's studio administration, from the most practical (bus tickets and food) to the most intellectually essential (books, articles, DVDs). To Mary Sabbatino, vice president of Galerie Lelong in New York City, is due my deepest gratitude for many things, but in relation to this book, for having been the first to introduce me to Laing's work (and later, Laing herself) in 2002.

November 2011

An Australian critic once characterized Rosemary Laing's work overall as "a visualization of a cultural predicament."[1] The immediate subjects of Graham Forsyth's brief but eloquent essay are two of her photographic series, *flight research* (1998–2000) and *spin* (1997–99), and the predicament refers both to Australia's overwhelming scale and the fraught identity of its white citizens, variously descended from a mix of convicts and colonizers, explorers and imperial administrators, indentured labor and adventurers, immigrants, exiles, and refugees. Unlike those descended from Australia's indigenous peoples, these historically recent residents confront (or fail to confront) the complexities of national identification, which are themselves contingent, volatile, and subject to changing historical forces. Thus, as he observes, "the recent re-emergence of white Australia's more ancient and atavistic suspicion of the foreigner and fear of being swamped by the incomprehensible masses to the north…demonstrates the precarious nature of white Australia's sense of their own belonging to the Australian landscape."[2]

In Laing's multipart project, *to walk on a sea of salt* (2004), the precariousness and ambivalence of this condition are powerfully conveyed.[3] One section of the work consists of large-scale photographs of the Woomera Immigration Reception and Processing Centre (IRPC), a facility in the state of South Australia, first opened in November 1999 to incarcerate asylum seekers and other undocumented refugees, many of whom arrived in the wake of the wars in the Middle East and elsewhere.[4] Originally inhabited by the Kokatha people, by 1947 it was employed as a British rocket range for weapons testing; later, in the 1960s, NASA developed a nearby site to operate a deep-space-tracking station. Built to contain 400 people, by 2000 the IRPC held nearly 1,500 men, women, and children. Conditions at Woomera—severe overcrowding,

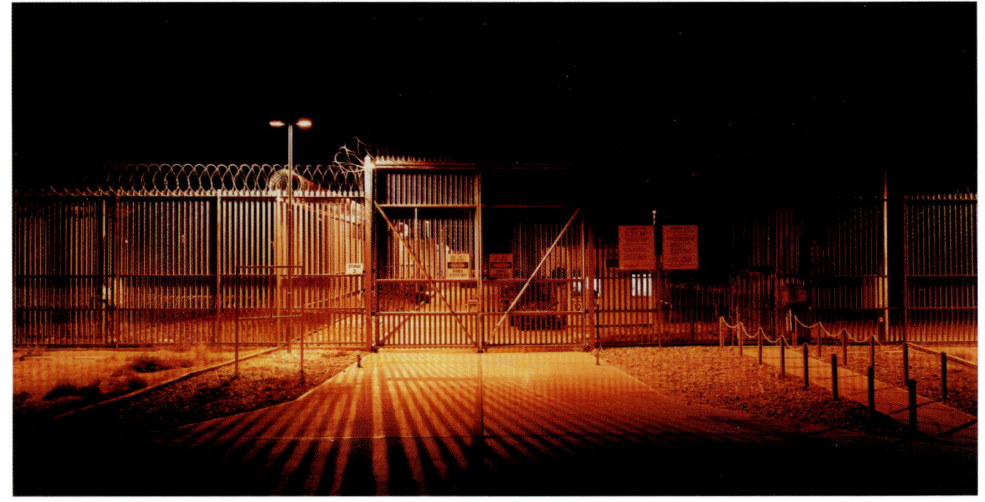

5.10 am, 15th December 2004, 2004 (page 140)

which spawned riots, civil rights abuses, and suicides—created enough public protest to compel the government to shut it down in 2003. Laing's stark and unpopulated photographs were taken after its closure, from outside the steel perimeter fence, still topped with coils of razor wire. "Classically" composed, the photographs' dimensions emphasize the horizontality of the flat arid land and the length of the one-story structure. *welcome to Australia*, shot as the fading light has lost its intensity, provides an oblique viewpoint, the angle of the fence bisecting the middle of the frame; the same vantage point is used for *8:40 pm daze past* (2004–07), when dusk has fallen and the security lights illuminate the fence and its periphery. In *and you can even pay later*, the viewpoint is directly frontal, shot at midday in blazing sunlight. Its title refers to the 1992 Migration Reform Act and other bills holding internees responsible for the cost of their detention.[5] The strip of land, the fence, and the building thus compose three lateral bands constituted by the deep cerulean of the desert sky, the grays of the fence and building, and the dusty beige of the sandy earth. It is, however, the fence that is the

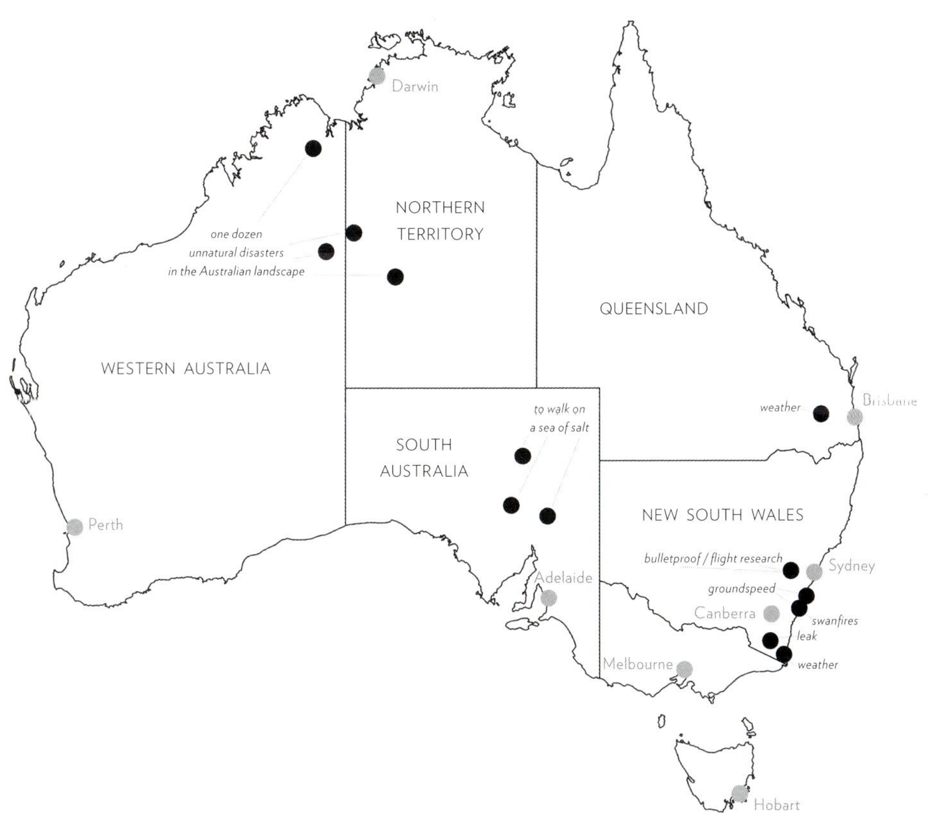

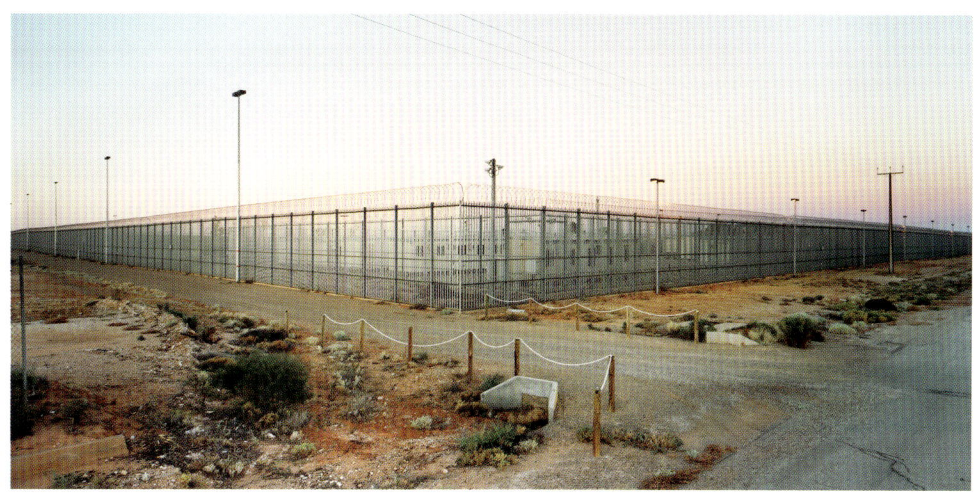

welcome to Australia, 2004 (page 139)

central element in both pictures' composition, blocking the views of the horizon from all directions and providing its own mute statement about the closing of Australia to unwanted immigrants. For Australian viewers, the meanings of these understated and nonrhetorical photographs are unmistakable: "Fences, prisons, borders, containment and exclusion extend deep into the Australian psyche. Non-indigenous Australia's origins as a penal colony and the subsequent taking of land from Aboriginal custodians have left a legacy of anxiety about demarcating, fencing, ownership and belonging. The barrier at Woomera is a zone between inside and out, belonging and not belonging."[6]

Into the carceral imagery of the detention center Laing has integrated two other thematic sections whose meanings circulate between and among the individual pictures.

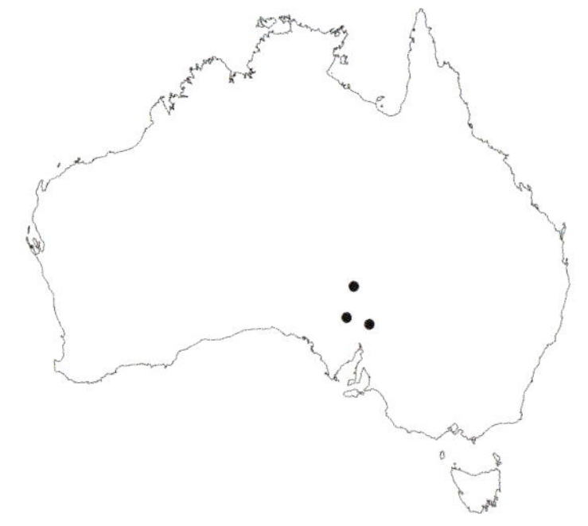

The photograph that provides the series' title, *to walk on a sea of salt*, was made on the surface of Lake Eyre. About 800 kilometers north of Adelaide, in the state of Southern Australia, it lies on the lowest point of the continent, about 15 kilometers below sea level. It is the largest lake on the continent, although shallow even in the rainy season. But large parts of the basin are a salt pan, quite literally a sea of salt; in summer, temperatures reach 40 degrees Celsius in the shade. Like many of the areas Laing has worked in, Lake Eyre, named for Edward John Eyre (the first European to sight it), possesses its own storied past, one of intrepid explorers and doomed quests for what was desired, but was never there. In this respect, Charles Sturt's near-fatal search for a phantom inland sea in 1845 is evoked in Laing's title. Here, the subtlety of the picture's pale blues and whites belies the blinding glare and heat of the actual environment; indeed, the crusted texture of the dry salt surface could well be ice. The horizon line bisects the image, as it does in *and you can even pay later*, signaling its symbolic linkage, the unbounded landscape of the Australian imaginary, grimly paralleling the bounded space of incarceration.

In one of the photographs comprising the third thematic section of the work, Laing "revisits" the tradition of Australian landscape painting—literally, insofar as the pictures were made in the Flinders Ranges, hundreds of kilometers from both Woomera and Lake Eyre—and iconographically, restaging the landscapes of Hans Heysen (*after*

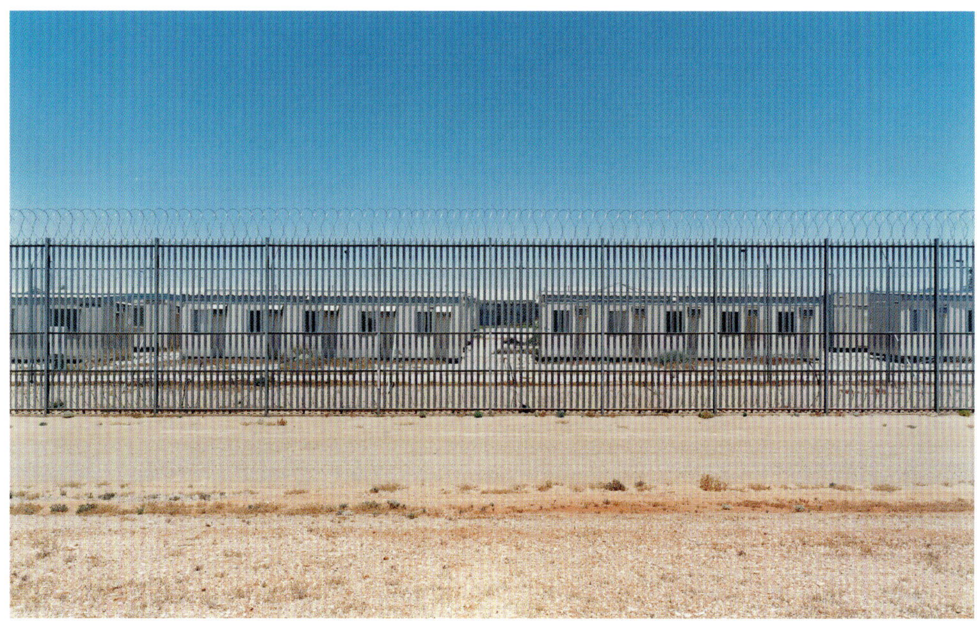

and you can even pay later, 2004 (page 138)

Heysen). Born in Germany, Heysen (1877–1968) emigrated to Australia and became one of its most renowned artists. His landscapes featuring gum trees and other native vegetation were of major importance in constructing a domesticated (and nationalist) view of the beauties of Australian "wilderness," especially the Flinders Ranges area. Laing's pallid, unsaturated chromatics mimic the tonalities of the delicate watercolors to which they allude, but they also suggest a leaching out of original meaning through layer upon layer, generation after generation of the work's reproduction.

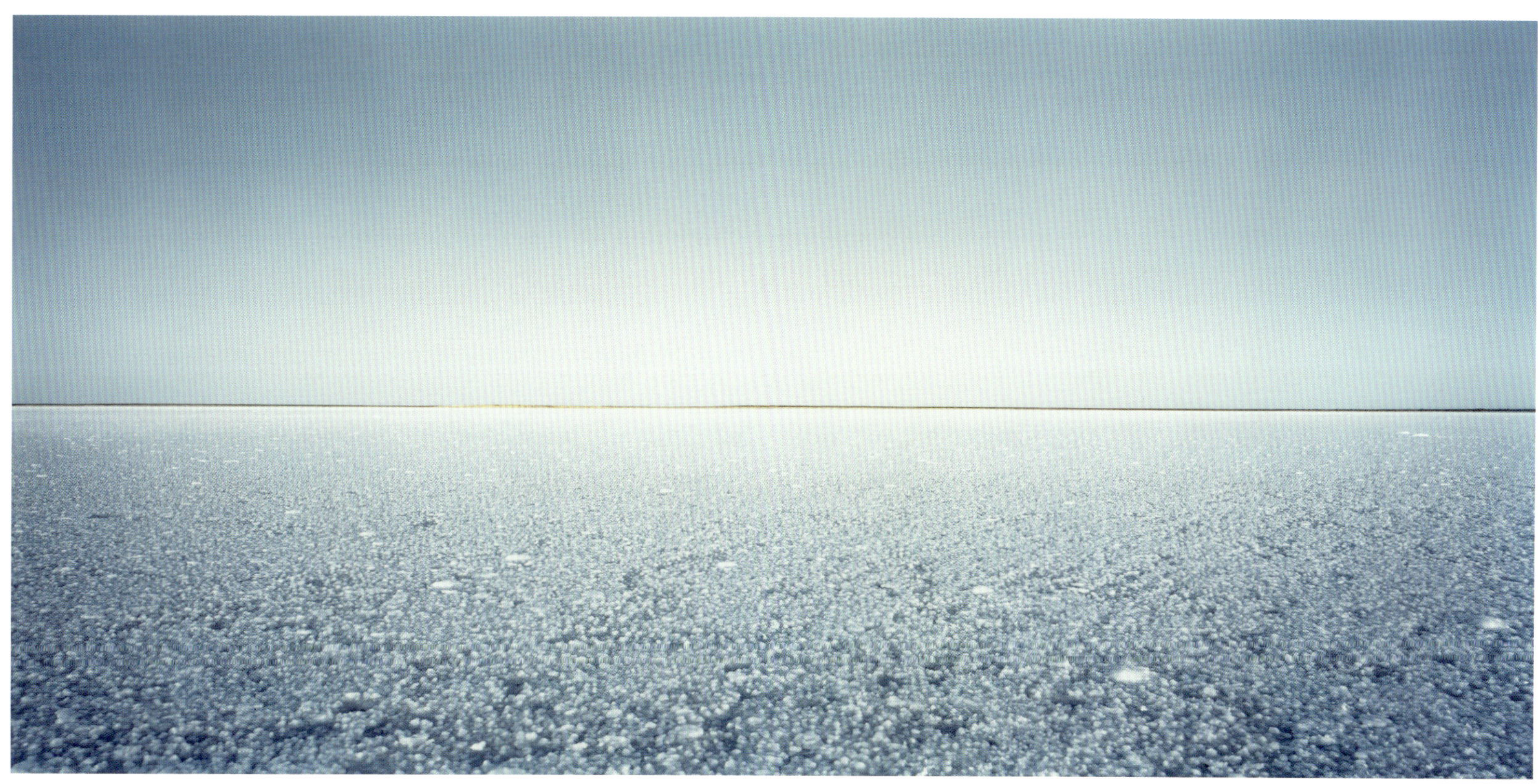

to walk on a sea of salt, 2004 (page 134)

All of which is to say that the art of landscape, in Australia and elsewhere, does its ideological work inflected by the particularities—historical and geographical—of a given place. As Tanya Peterson has remarked, Laing's quotational strategies serve not only to signal the "already-represented" status of the image, but gesture also to the cultural imaginary that underpins such expressions and to which they contribute: "While this reference to Heysen's earlier work evokes an Arcadian image of the Australian bush, Laing's bleached out interpretation straddles the shift in his work, and of the times,

which had embraced the scorched regions of the outback as a new symbol of hope. Yet Laing's revision does more than merely reiterate the sentiments of the past. The bleached effect of overexposure in *after Heysen* serves to screen points of pictorial information, leaving the ambiguity of nostalgia unfiltered by the lens of colonialism."[7]

As *to walk on a sea of salt* attests, the cultural predicament Forsyth evokes in his essay encompasses past and present, incorporating issues that are simultaneously spatial and temporal, broadly political, but also environmental, social, and indeed, racial. But here I would suggest that Laing's thirty-odd-year artistic investigation of this predicament encompasses an even more expansive set of issues, not all of them specific to those that shaped, and continue to shape, the Australian nation and its inhabitants. By this, I do not mean to suggest that as a significant artist with an international reputation, Laing "exceeds" or "surpasses" her identity as an Australian artist or that her work, by virtue of its quality, "transcends" the local. On the contrary. While the mechanisms and apparatuses of the contemporary art world can easily create the illusion that an artist exhibited in numerous art-world capitals, or featured in large international exhibitions and collected by museums in many countries, is by definition an "international" artist, there is reason to question what such a label actually signifies. In fact, all artists come from somewhere or other, and an artistic formation in New York does not make an artist more "international" than one from Sydney. Or elsewhere. It may be that the "international" artist is the postmodern but no less mythical avatar of the "universal"

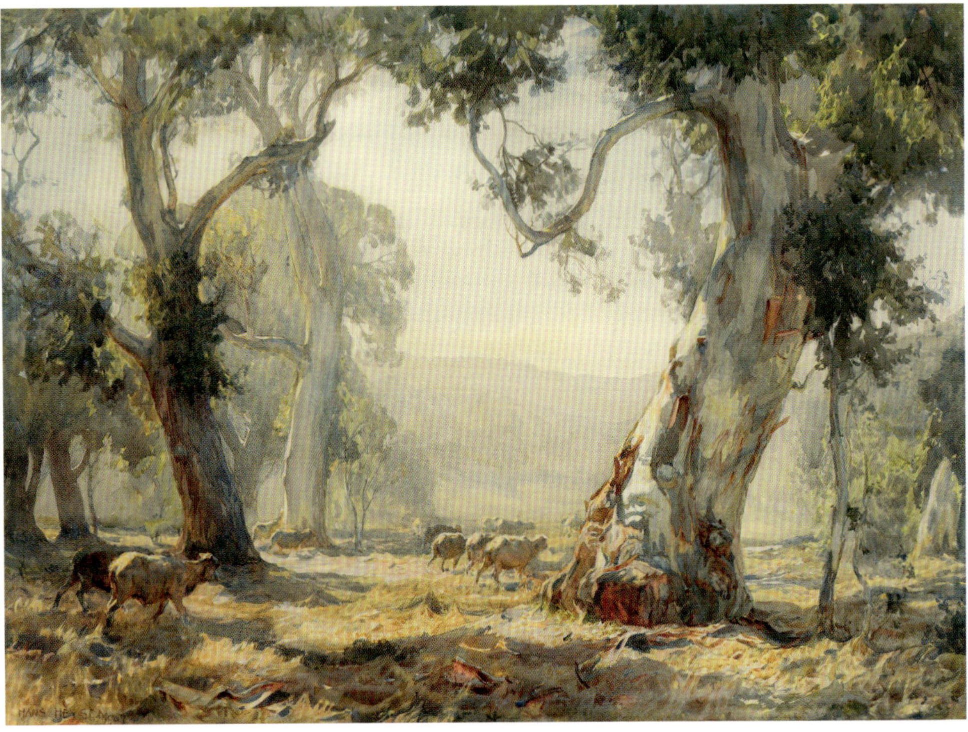

Hans Heysen, *Summer*, 1909. Pencil, watercolor on ivory wove paper, 22$^{1}/_{4}$ x 30$^{7}/_{8}$ in. (56.5 x 78.4 cm). Art Gallery of New South Wales. © VG Bild-Kunst, Bonn 2012

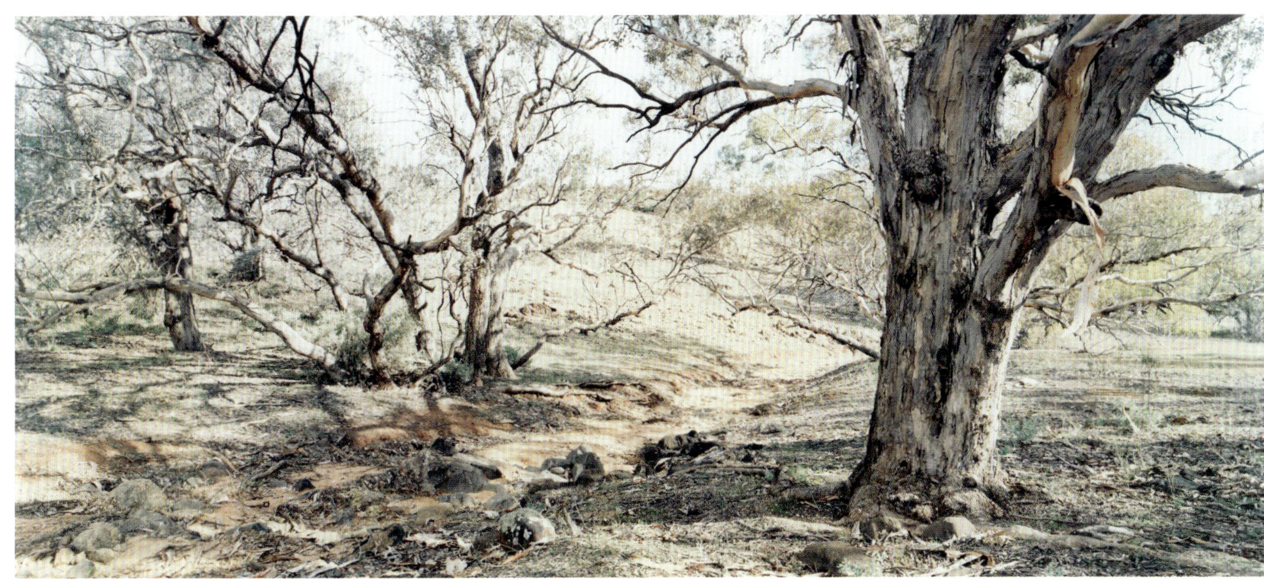

after Heysen, 2004 (page 137)

Louvre, for example, organizes its collections and catalogues. But in its mythic incarnation, the figure of the "universal" artist—Michelangelo, Poussin, Rembrandt, van Gogh, Picasso—has long been conceived as a (male) artist who while incorporating the finest artistic traditions of his culture or nation, is understood to break out, so to speak, into the empyrean of universality. This is why his work (there are no "hers" in this lineup) is said to speak to "us" at all times and places. And while there are historical periods and ideological configurations during which the "national" characteristics of an artist or "school" are privileged—typically right-wing nationalism, fascism, or newly minted colonial or postcolonial identities—these rarely, if ever, require that the honorific of universality be repudiated.

In the particular instance of Australia, this embrace of the "national" character of its art has its own rationales that are inseparable from its history. Obviously, Aboriginal art, historical or contemporary, is uniquely Australian, although it was not elevated to the status of art (or to aesthetic commodity) until well into the 1970s.[8] With respect to the traditional, i.e., European forms of the visual arts, notably painting, landscape played an especially important role in the creation of a white Australian national identity, just as it did in other colonial "new worlds" such as the United States and Canada. But nationalism has many guises and many avatars (we might think here of Clement Greenberg's celebration of "American-type painting").

one. It hardly needs mentioning that among other things, both categories operate as exclusionary devices, consigning women and other "others" to the margins of art history, when not to actual oblivion.

However, it is also the case that premodernist, even modernist, art history is very much concerned with national identity. Classificatory terms such as Renaissance, Baroque, Classical, Romantic, and other stylistic categories are still organized art historically according to this logic of identity, which may, or may not, conform to existing nation-states (e.g., Dutch, French, Italian, Spanish, or British "Schools"). This is how the

These explicitly nationalist discourses are for all intents and purposes now trumped by the descriptive and critical terms of contemporary art, although there remains an *implicit* distinction between the artist "outside" of any national or geographical mooring and those who remain identified with a particular place.

It is, therefore, within these particular artistic categories, ideologies, and discourses that shape the binaries universal/national or, more contemporaneously, international/local that I want to initially consider the place of Laing as an Australian artist. This question of national identity, or better, national belonging, is, to be sure, an overarching issue in Australian cultural as well as political life. As the novelist George Alexander has written, "For non-indigenous Australians, Australia may be our first home, but it is also our first elsewhere."[9]

To Laing's national identity, however, may be added two additional markers: race (Laing is white; her ancestors came to Australia from the United Kingdom and Germany in the nineteenth century) and gender. These could be extended: class is not irrelevant (crudely, let me say she is of a "middle-class" background), insofar as this is a determination of whether anyone is likely or able to become an artist in the first place. As would be the case with most contemporary artists, these categories collectively do not in and of themselves predict, explain, or account for the kinds of artworks she makes, her changing procedures, the works' material and formal elements as they have been developed from project to project, nor even, in most cases, their nominal subjects or themes.

On the other hand, and as I will argue throughout this book, Laing's art is fundamentally rooted in, informed, and mobilized by these specific conditions, understood precisely as *conditions*, not essences. As such, they constitute only one "set" of determinations, among many others. (Had Laing been born, for example, in the 1920s or the 1970s, her art would be different.) Thus, while all artists are variously formed and influenced by their respective locations and situations, not all of them choose to draw from these the material, if not the subject, of their art.

These two terms—location and situation—seem particularly apt in approaching Laing's oeuvre. Where "location" is a spatial term, designating first of all the literal physical space of Australia (as geographical land mass, continent, ex-colony, nation-state, Antipode), "situation" includes existential as well as spatial meanings ("The position in life, or in relation to others, held or occupied by a person," OED). For Laing, therefore, location is both a given of who she is (citizen of the Commonwealth, one of many components of her civic identity) and to a greater or lesser extent, a source for themes and subjects that figure in her work. "Location" has another vector in Laing's artistic production, for many of her works are indeed produced "on location," in various places on the continent, whose local histories are seamlessly integrated into the thematic or visual infrastructure of the projects. Where, however, Laing has produced work in a studio (as, for example, in certain pictures in the *weather* series or in *a dozen useless actions for grieving blondes*), this too is a location. Accordingly, the "no place" of the studio, in which the photographs are staged and photographed, is as significant an element in the aggregate meaning of these pictures as are those in which the location, such as the Aboriginal community of Balgo in Western Australia, or the Cooma-Monaro district of *leak*, have been produced. This site specificity, to describe it more in keeping with art-historical as opposed to cinematic language, suggests that just as Laing in her position as Australian citizen and as artist is subject to her national, geographical, and spatial location, so too is location reciprocally a subject of her art making.

For this and other reasons, small thumbnail maps are inserted into the body of this text. On the most obvious level, they represent the actual places where Laing has produced certain of her works. Especially for the non-Australian, they immediately provide some sense of the minute scale of particular sites in relation to the immensity of the continent. They track her movement through space, often very distant from the eastern littoral (especially Brisbane, her place of origin, and Sydney, the metropolis where she now makes her home). Of course, and as famously aphorized by Alfred Korzybski in 1931, "the map is not the territory," and Laing, whose relation to any given site she works in is anything but casual, is also aware that the technologies of mapping are inextricable from the histories of colonial conquest and appropriation. That said, another purpose of these thumbnails is to suggest through graphic means a movement through space that is also a movement in time. Laing's projects are long in gestation and long in production—often two years in the making—and when they are photographed in various locales, these are the result of numerous previous sorties or exploratory road trips, sometimes accompanied by friends for whom these places were, or are, "home."

Laing's journeys through the far-flung spaces of the continent accrue yet another level of meaning, given one of the quotations she underlined, decades ago, in a book by Paul Virilio, an important intellectual influence for her in the 1980s: "According to George Sand, the woman artist is first of all a voyager, a wanderer."[10]

This definition anticipates Laing's own later wanderings as an artist, but it further reminds us that "woman artist," unlike "artist," is a marked term. As such, and even now, the woman artist operates in a more or less alien territory, which is, after all, the symbolic order of patriarchy itself. The choice of photography as medium is not without its gendered implications either; until recently, the photographic mapping of colonial or wilderness areas was predominantly a masculine preserve. Like the intrepid explorer, the topographical or survey photographer (e.g., Francis Frith, Timothy O'Sullivan, Samuel Bourne) is an accomplice of empire, visually mastering the spaces before him.

This particular territory belongs more properly to that of "situation," a more complex word and concept than location. For while it too designates specific spaces ("The place, position, or location of a city, country, etc., in relation to its surroundings," OED), it could be said to encompass other markers of Laing's identity—*white* Australian, *woman* artist. So too does "situation" include Laing's ethical and political affiliations and commitments, many of which are variously, often very subtly, integrated into her art. Certain of these, as we have seen, are grounded in the current political landscape of Australia, in its treatment of and policies toward its indigenous peoples, its policies on immigrants and asylum seekers, the mechanisms of class as well as racial inequality, and the stalled project of republicanism. While certain of these are specific to Australia (although there exist analogies to other nations, such as the United States and Canada), Laing's work engages issues that also overarch national boundaries, including the radical psychological dislocations of postmodernity and the devastation of the environment. But "situation" takes on a further meaning here, for while one of Laing's continuing preoccupations is indeed the legacy of Australia's colonial history and its catastrophic consequences for its indigenous peoples, this history relates to her own position as citizen as well as artist.[11] Accordingly, Laing has never produced work "about" the situation of Australia's Aboriginal population, but rather how her own situation as a white Australian is informed and marked by these other histories. In fact, when human subjects appear in her work, they are always hired models or stunt people, never the unwitting subject of a photographic gaze. Laing's extreme sensitivity to the appropriative, indeed aggressive, aspects of photographic "capture," is, I would suggest, an example of how feminist ethics shape the ways she produces her work no less than the issues dealt with in her individual projects.

Throughout Laing's work there is a recurring tension between the couplet "belonging/unbelonging" with respect to Australia—as site and situation—that is acknowledged as an inescapable component of her own identity. Notions of "birthright," "homeland," and "home and country" are therefore highly complex and ambivalent, for the doctrine of *terra nullius* (from the Latin, meaning no man's land or land belonging to no one) that provided the legal fig leaf for the expropriation of indigenous lands was only legally overturned in 1992.[12] One central feature of this cultural predicament is therefore rooted in the recent past; the other, in present circumstances: on the one hand, in two hundred years of the construction of what Benedict Anderson famously described as "imaginary communities"; on the other, in the belated collective reckoning with Australian history (settlement or conquest?) that accelerated with the Bicentennial celebrations of 1988 and the intensifying pressure of

the political claims (and militancy) of that nation's dispossessed. "The past," as William Faulkner observed, "is never dead. It's not even past."

In light of these "situations," one can better understand Laing's recurring references (textual and iconographic) to Australian landscape painting, counterpointed with subjects such as detention centers for asylum seekers, burning pyres of cheap imported furniture in ancestral homelands, the surreal placement of floral carpets in the national parks of New South Wales, and hopelessly weeping blondes.

In these senses, and notwithstanding the overly narrow meanings of what is generally (and simplistically) understood by the term "political artist," or, for that matter "Australian" artist, Laing's political understandings of her country and culture integrally inform the substance of her art. Not, to be sure, such that any given work is "illustrative" of them, much less tendentious, but rather, that in their formal structures, their poetic inventions, their imaginative expressions of a time out of joint—even in their considerable visual beauties—they give visual form to what is our shared state of emergency, disavowed or not.

That photography has been Laing's chosen medium since the late 1980s requires some further discussion. Laing's art-school training was as a painter. As was the case in art schools (and art worlds) everywhere, painting and sculpture occupied the pinnacle of the hierarchy in the visual arts, and there existed in Australia as elsewhere a considerable divide between what might be called contemporary-art-as-such and the far more modest enclave of art photography. Helen Ennis has summarized the situation in Australia, and it is not especially different from the positioning of photography elsewhere: "Photographers had been producing self-conscious works of art in Australia since the late nineteenth century but their public profile waxed and waned during the first half of the twentieth century…by the 1950s art photography was mostly confined to a medium specific realm, rarely penetrating the larger art world. A strict hierarchy operated in which the traditional art forms of painting, and to a lesser degree sculpture, were regarded as most important, followed by drawing and printmaking.…Furthermore, for much of the twentieth century a distinction was made between the fine arts and the applied arts which encompassed design, different branches of the decorative arts (ceramics, furniture, textiles), as well as photography."[13]

That Laing was by the end of the 1980s making her work exclusively with the camera, but outside the aesthetic and institutional precincts of art photography in Australia, is therefore by no means a unique or idiosyncratic evolution. The "turn" to photography (but outside the framework or aesthetic dicta of modernist art photography) by that generation of artists we now routinely classify under the sign of the postmodern (or under related terms such as "postmedium" or "poststudio") is not only an international phenomenon, but one in which women artists—also internationally—have been especially prominent. As I have argued elsewhere, this is a massively overdetermined development, and Laing's having become an artist whose primary medium was photography is, as I have indicated, not unrelated to her gender.[14]

In the context of contemporary Australian art, and because her work has been exclusively camera-based since the late 1980s, Laing has been exhibited under the medium umbrella of "photography," as well as that of contemporary art *tout court*. For example, works of hers purchased by the Art Gallery of South Wales have been purchased by the photography department. Within the same institution, however, her work is also exhibited, singly or within group shows, under the rubric of contemporary art. Laing's own artistic affiliations with Australian artists of her generation are mostly linked to this latter category. These affiliations are grounded not in shared "stylistics," much less shared formal procedures, but in shared political identifications and concerns. Thus, positioning her with artists such as Destiny Deacon, Tracey Moffatt, and Judy Watson, as has occurred in certain exhibitions, might be along the lines of a shared political and artistic identification with feminism, or the artistic investigation of the meanings of alterity. Other artistic affiliations, such as, for example, with the artist Susan Norrie, might be made along the lines of shared environmental concerns. Still others could be allied with respect to their explorations of the media-ization of subjective or visceral experience, reflections on Australian political actuality, and so forth. Many of the most provocative and thoughtful exhibitions assembled by Australian curators in recent years are structured by this awareness that it is the nature of the conceptual and analytic preoccupations of artists that link them more profoundly with one another than do their respective methods, procedures, or even media. But equally important, many of Laing's well-known contemporaries—Moffatt, Deacon, Norrie, but also Richard Bell and Bonita Ely—with whom she has also been shown in group and thematic exhibitions—may themselves employ photography in their work, but often in combination with other media. Indeed, if one looks at the entire spectrum of contemporary practice, especially video and performance, the list is far longer. The title of a 1996 exhibition at the Sydney Museum of Contemporary Art, *Photography Is Dead! Long Live Photography!*, perfectly encapsulates this disintegration of older paradigms of medium specificity, while wittily signaling the eclipse of formalist paradigms and the efflorescence of contemporary hybridized usages. Moreover, in any number of recent exhibitions, books, and catalogues, including the 2009 *Twelve Australian Photo Artists* (the term "photo artists," as opposed to either "photographers" or "art photographers" is itself suggestive), curators and scholars have implicitly or explicitly acknowledged that purist notions of medium specificity are entirely inadequate to describe the protean and hybridized procedures of contemporary practice.

Laing has observed of her own artworks that the resulting pictures are but the last and concluding element of the work, not the work itself. From her initial formulation of an issue, a question, a problem, to the final realization of the given project, there is a complex series of practical and logistical activities, often involving collaborators, assistants, and those with special skills. Along the way, she produces sketches, diagrams, and plans; accumulates research; and, where the work is predicated on a particular site, travels extensively. As a number of critics have remarked, many of the works involve a process similar to cinematic preproduction (made invisible in the resulting film). As Vivienne Webb has observed, "By recording the events in process, the images often resemble film stills, or moments excerpted from a larger durational narrative that continues outside of the frame."[15] This is especially the case with *a dozen useless actions for grieving blondes*, where the movement from image to image approximates a cinematic sequence of frame to frame. Nevertheless, even where Laing's works have explored speed and motion (particularly in *greenwork, TL*, 1995, where the "*TL*" stands for "time lapse"), they must be located squarely in the realm of the photographic. By this, I do not mean with respect to any investment in the aesthetics of "straight" photography, much less the adherence to the protocols of formalist modernism (or modernist formalism). Rather, their rootedness in the fundamentals of analogue photography is related to what Laing calls their identity as "distillations of time." And the "time" that Laing has consistently engaged throughout her artistic career is not the split-second or instant that the click of the shutter immobilizes, commemorating the appearance of an object in that discrete moment. Instead, one might think of it as an attempt to invent an equivalent for historical time that is still potent and active in the present moment of our contemporaneity, the time of the subject whose very subjectivity, whose location and situation, is invisibly imprinted by equally invisible histories that shape and haunt the present.

It goes without saying that many of Laing's most elaborate and sensational special effects could now be easily produced with a computer. Although she is reticent about the details of the complex machinery of the works' creation (whether on site or in the

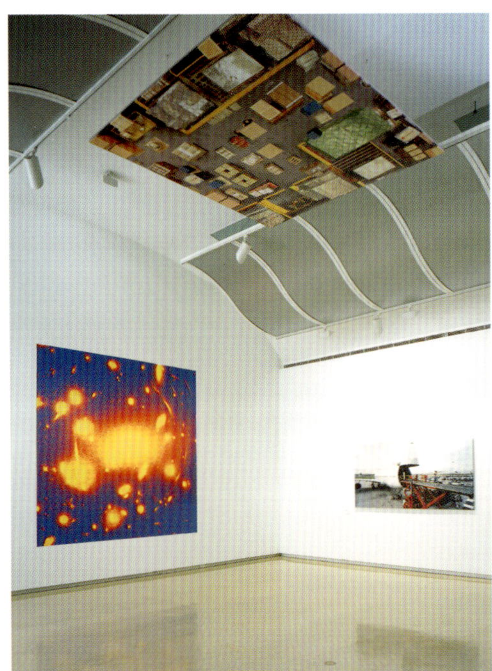

Installation view of the series *brownwork* from the exhibition *Photography is Dead! Long Live Photography!*, at the Museum of Contemporary Art, Sydney, 1996.

studio), this is meant to downplay or de-fetishize both the labor and the technologies involved in any given shoot.

For Laing, therefore, the task of finding a representational and expressive language that encompasses both invisible or repressed histories and complex contemporary social realities has long been a central concern in her art. With the exception of a few earlier individual works, Laing's photographs are infrequently the product of digitalized imaging. Even the most stunningly improbable of her images (e.g., the carpeted beach and forests of *groundspeed*, the flamboyantly oneiric images of *flight research*, the whirlwind-tossed woman of *weather*, and so forth) have been painstakingly fabricated and performed in order to be photographed. For this reason, certain of her critics have called them "tableaux," but this is not the term that best describes them. A tableau is, in the first instance, a picture, a painting, a scene; as such, the emphasis is on the material distance between the signifier and what it purports to represent. Laing's artworks, even when produced in a studio, even in her deployment of a medium that freezes time forever, are concerned with critically mobilizing the history of the present, as it were, with more distant histories that are, as Faulkner aphorized, not even past.

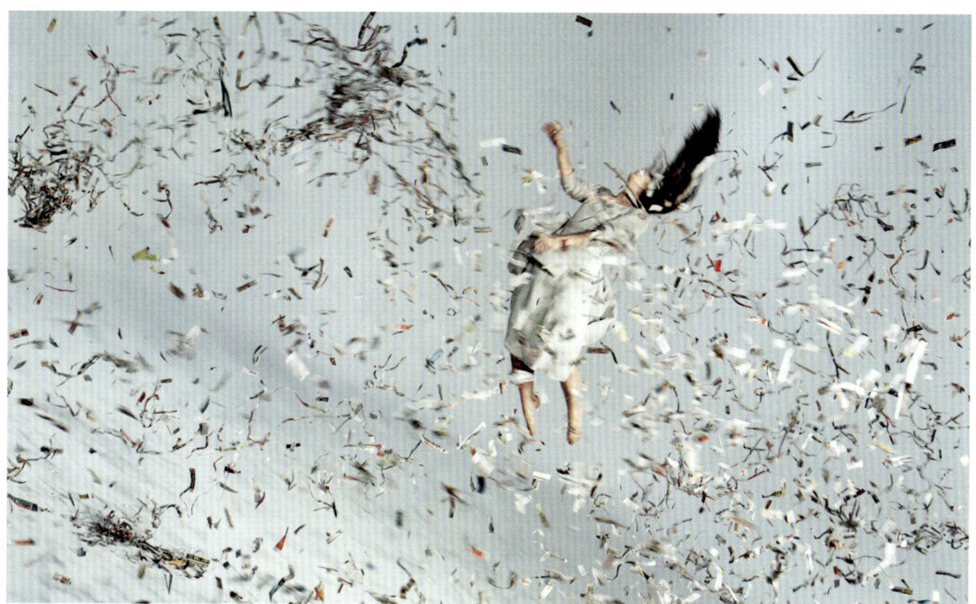

weather #4, 2006 (page 151)

At this stage of history, the Australian landscape shimmers in the collective

consciousness as a mirage-like environment phasing in and out as sign.

Ross Gibson[1]

There are clear parallels between the history of the colonization of America's frontiers and that of Australia's. For that matter, so too are there parallels to the histories of Canada, Southern Africa, and all the other "new" worlds conquered by white Europeans.[2] The extremities of climate, the daunting immensity of the land, its resistance to its newcomers, its deceptive, that is, fantasized emptiness (*terra nullius*), its very intransigence to European notions of civilization, agriculture, and domesticity: all these features shaped the psyches of their early settlers and those successive waves of immigrants who succeeded them. Equally at work in the formation of the newcomers' subjectivity, even if subliminally, was the haunted history of these newly colonized spaces, marked as they were—as they are—by their violent legacies of expropriation, genocide, displacement, and the crimes of colonization against whom Canadians call the First Peoples. This sense of Australia as a haunted nation is an omnipresent motif in the work of Australian writers, intellectuals, filmmakers, and artists; the term recurs almost obsessively in literature and criticism, and furthermore, as Ross Gibson observes, "This 'haunting' is not only metaphorical. It is a way to name a perturbance that lingers in the Australian consciousness."[3]

For Australian artists, those who are the descendants of the settlers, including those who arrived as convicts or indentured labor, or those whose forebears arrived more recently, the haunted history of the country (including those parts popularly referred to as the "outback"), as well as its geographical specificity, meant that the relation to the continent was in marked contradiction to the Old World's notion of "landscape." As an artistic genre, and from its inception, the concept of landscape was more closely allied to the garden than to the bush, the outback, the prairie, the veldt, the jungle, or the forest. Considered, however, from a more critical perspective, the landscape genre, as it evolved from its origins in sixteenth-century Europe, is inextricably bound to the mechanisms of possession, property, capitalism, colonialism, and nationalism. Nevertheless, nineteenth- and twentieth-century Australian painters retained—and sought to refashion—the various landscape schema produced by their European and American predecessors or contemporaries. This process of visual translation was largely focused on content, as successive generations of painters adapted European styles in romantic, picturesque, naturalistic, or impressionist modes to the actual flora and topography of the Australian continent.

Where beautiful or picturesque notions of landscape often include the trace of human presence (evident in much of the work of Australia's first landscapists), the depiction of the sublime was another matter. Although Edmund Burke's founding theorization of the concept did not consider it an aesthetic category (much less a genre of visual production), it swiftly mutated into one; fueled by romanticism, it was soon assimilated into painting practice. In its artistic manifestations, the sublime was associated, alternatively, with wilderness vistas, especially mountainous or "extreme" environments, for the sublime wilderness, by definition, was unmarked by cultivation, pasturage, or human intervention. But with the possible exception of polar regions, few if any places are without history, without the traces of human presence. In this respect, modern touristic, nationalist, or scenic photographic imagery of the sublime, imagined as "uncharted" or pristine wilderness of the sort associated with *National Geographic* magazine or conservation organizations, typically denies or represses this history. In so doing, nature becomes figured as a spectacle, outside of time as well as history, a spectacle fabricated for various forms of consumption.[4]

This "spectacularization" of nature and the repressions and elisions that structure the representations of Australian "wilderness" and "outback" are explicitly engaged in Laing's landscapes. Where certain of these make reference to the sublime, others are in dialogue with the more prosaic conventions of the Australian landscapists of the previous two centuries. Wilderness in Australia, however, is not an uncontested category. Recently, it has pitted conservationists and environmentalists against Aboriginal peoples.[5] But one of the particularities of Australian landscape art in the nineteenth and early twentieth centuries was the evident precariousness of the bucolic or Arcadian vision. Given the omnipresence of its "other," the expanse of a continent whose arid spaces resisted agricultural exploitation or even habitation, the inherited model of landscape required retooling. Thus, however tenuous the embrace of the beautiful or the picturesque, the sublime did not initially generally offer an alternative. Perhaps because the qualities of awe and terror with which Burke associated it were only too close to the physical realities that colonial Australia struggled to master.

The first generation of Australian landscapists—most prominently, John Glover (1767–1849), Eugene von Guérard (1811–1901), Conrad Martens (1801–1878), and Louis Buvelot (1814–1888)—had been trained in Europe, and even where the specificities of Australian flora and fauna were depicted—gum trees, kangaroos, even indigenous people in the case of Glover and Guérard—formal composition, lighting effects, *staffage*,

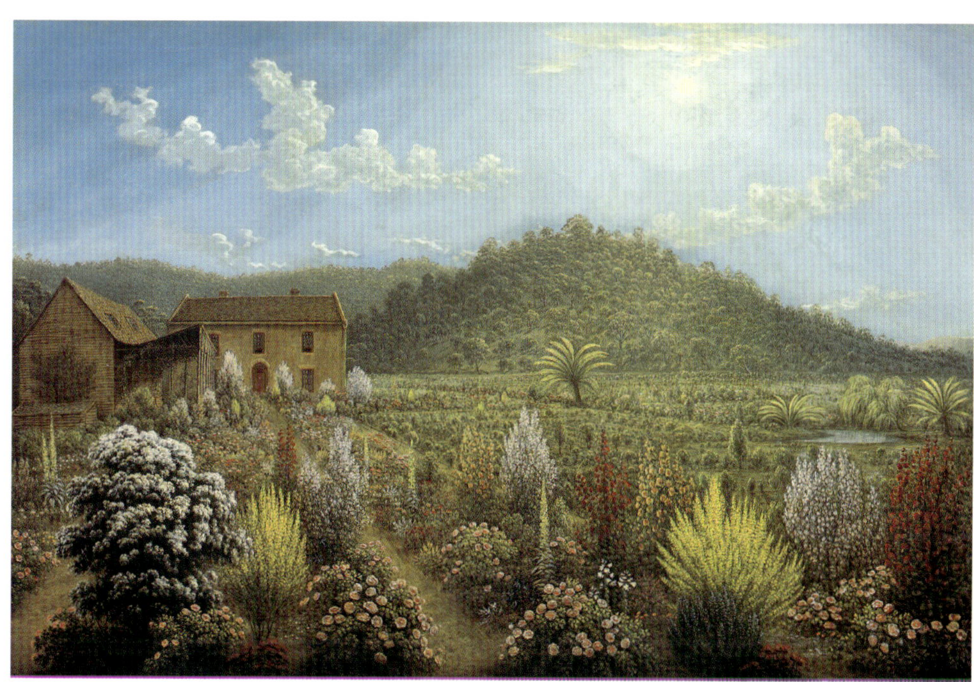

John Glover, *A View of the artist's house and garden, in Mills Plains, Van Diemen's Land*, 1835. Oil on canvas, 30⅛ x 45⅜ in. (76.4 x 114.4 cm). Art Gallery of South Australia, Adelaide. Morgan Thomas Bequest Fund, 1951

and other pictorial structures were, in effect, made in Europe. (Glover is especially significant in this history, and his much-reproduced 1833 depiction of his house and garden in Van Diemen's Land (now Tasmania) is a talismanic reference in Laing's work.) Thus, for them, the very notion of landscape required the reassuring sense of human

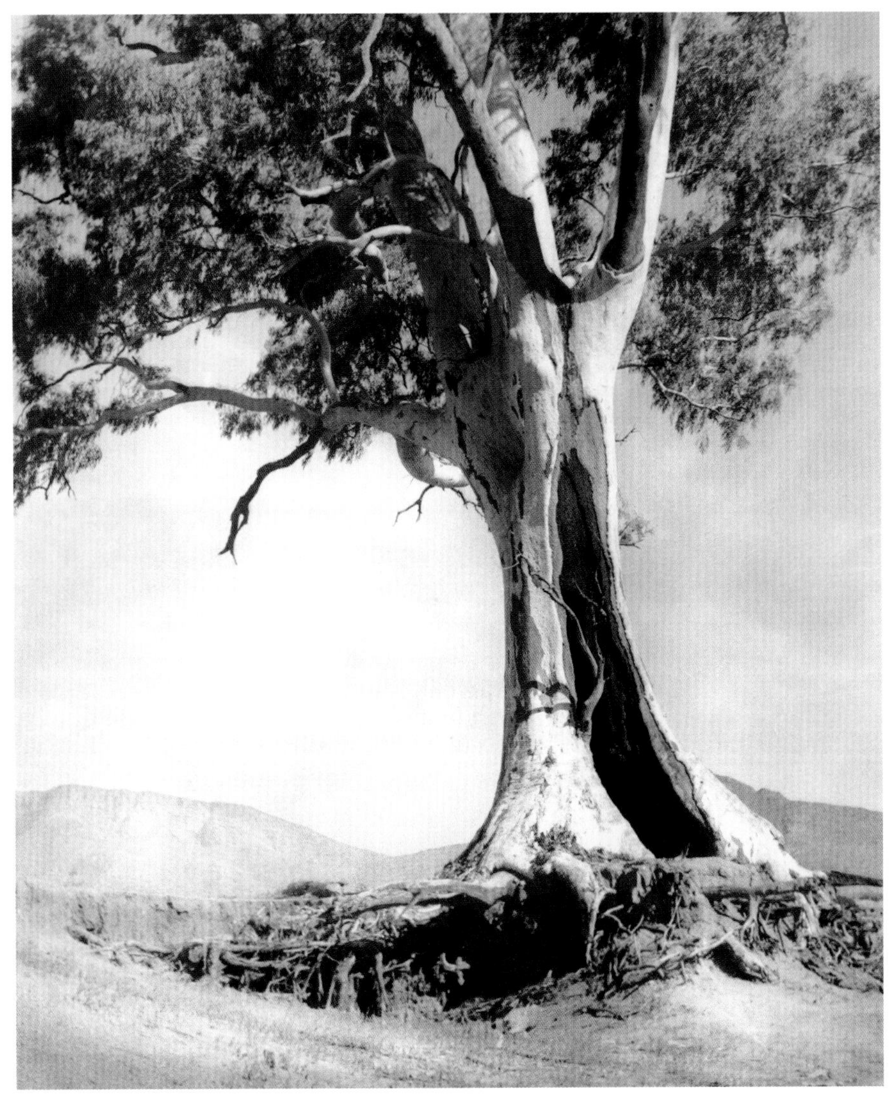

occupation, even in its literal absence. (Aborigines, significantly, rapidly disappeared from within the frames of easel painting.)

A second generation, the so-called Heidelberg School, whose major figures were Tom Roberts (1856–1931), Arthur Streeton (1867–1943), and Frederick McCubbin (1855–1917), were Australian-born (except Roberts, who emigrated at age 13), but here too geographical and cultural difference was secondary to the formal influence of contemporary British or French landscape practice, and concomitantly, they too sought to effect an imaginary resolution of the conflicting aspects of nature and culture.[6] Even the paintings and watercolors of Hans Heysen (1877–1968), which represent the "typically" Australian trees and vegetation of South Australia, were nonetheless pastoralized, domesticated by light, atmospheric effects, signs of husbandry, or other signifiers of colonial presence. Consequently, when art photography emerged as a discrete genre, as exemplified in the pictorialist work of Harold Cazneaux (1878–1953), the representation of Australian nature was effectively "acculturated." One of Australia's most widely recognized and revered photographs, Cazneaux's 1937 black-and-white image of an individual eucalyptus tree, its roots exposed, its trunk split and fissured, is intensively allegorized, if not anthropomorphized. Originally titled *Giant Gum from the arid land of the North, Wilpena, S.A.*, it was renamed by him *The Spirit of Endurance* in 1941 during the Second World War.[7]

"Wilderness," however, in Australian photography only became iconographically available as an alternative to the humanized versions of landscape when settlement

Harold Cazneaux, *The Spirit of Endurance*, 1937. Gelatin-silver photograph, 12³/₄ x 10¹/₂ in. (32.4 x 26.7 cm). Art Gallery of South Australia, Adelaide. South Australian Government Grant, 1978

was sufficiently established to inflect wilderness with positive if not euphoric values. Nevertheless, as Helen Ennis observes in her invaluable survey of photography in Australia, similar to the history of landscape painting, "wilderness" never became a significant part of the Australian version of photographic landscape: "The predilection has been for the settled, humanized landscape above all else, and inland areas rather than those of the coast. The modes of representation used most widely have been generally undramatic: the picturesque…and a more prosaic approach that emerged in the 1890s and persisted for decades."[8] And, as she further remarks, within the conceptual and material determinations of Australian visual culture, the sublime was, in a sense, out of place: "the sublime, which flourished in early nineteenth century [European] painting, had little sway on photographic practice, perhaps because of photography's utilitarian emphasis and the focus on documenting compelling proof of the successes of colonization."[9]

In Laing's career-long engagement with the concept (and genre) of landscape in Australian culture, both traditions have been variously engaged. To the degree that particular visual traditions, or even particular works, are evoked in her art, they are chosen because they function as nodal points in the Australian visual imaginary. For Laing, however, the landscape genre is taken not as a given, but as a problem with which her artwork engages critically, as a form of interrogative investigation. As a pictorial genre that posits a relationship of artist and spectator to a *topos*, a place, it poses questions of what that relationship is, was, or might conceivably be. In photography, that most emphatically and self-evidently "visible" of media, one that so potently provokes the illusion that the visible world speaks itself, her works prompt such

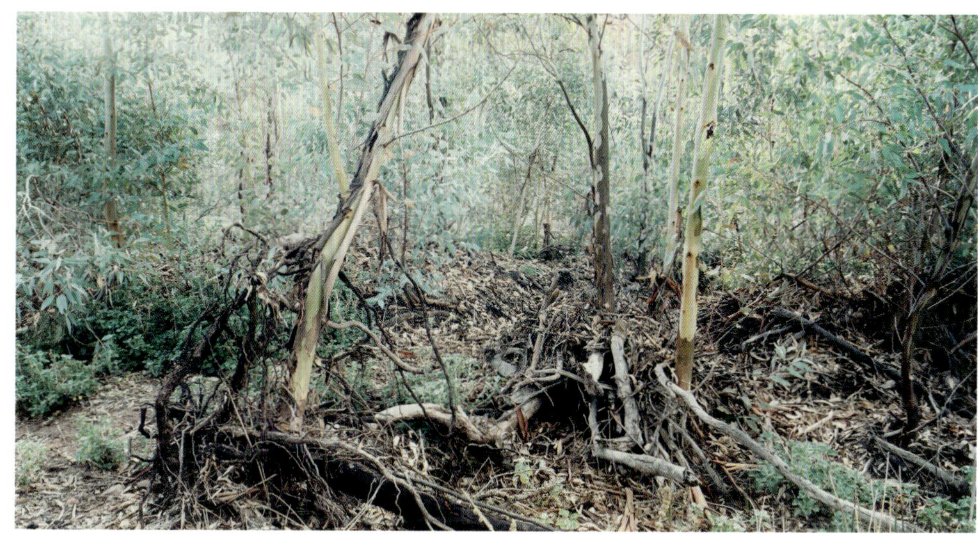

opposite Cazneaux, 2004 (page 136)

questions as, What do we not see? What is occluded, repressed? What is not present? Through what filters (ideological, psychological, phantasmatic) do we view what is in the picture?

Although the visual language of the sublime landscape is, as Ennis indicates, somewhat marginal to Australian visual culture (especially in the elite form of easel painting), Laing has nonetheless made work in which it is an unmistakable referent. However, where it has been featured, for example in such series as *from Paradise work* (1990–92), *greenwork* (1995), and *groundspeed* (2001), it is approached through the recognition of its overlapping mediations. In other words, what has received visual

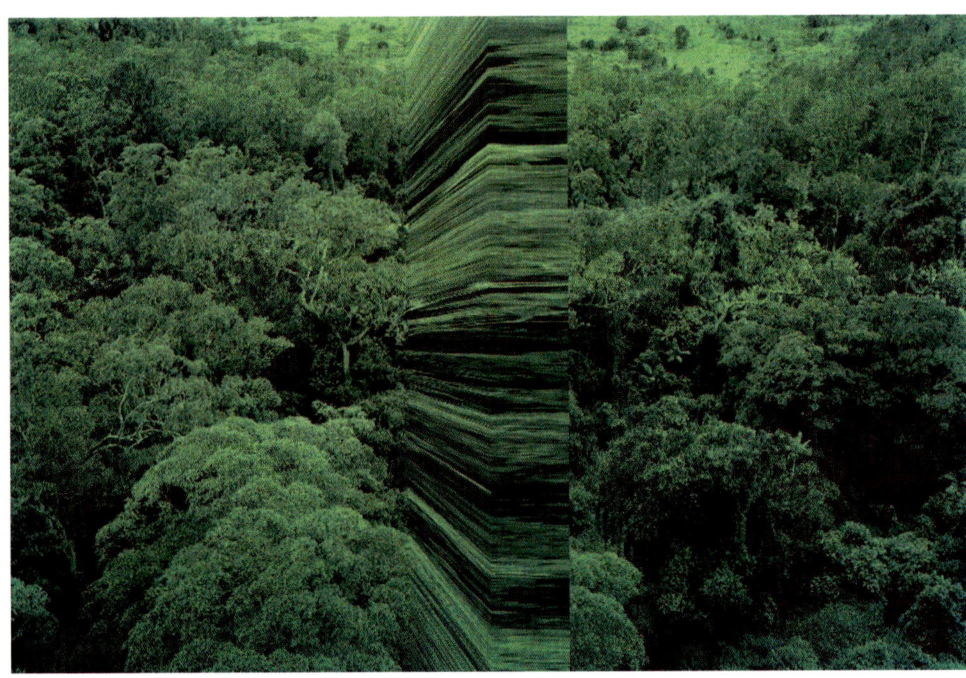

greenwork, aerial wall, 1995 (page 70)

expression as the sublime is taken by Laing to be always and already conventionalized and the product of particular discourses. In this respect, accretion over time has enabled various representational practices to signify precisely as the sublime. Moreover, in its Australian articulations, there exist effaced traces of what was there before; ghostly residues of history are overwritten by artistic conventions like landscape itself.

Mediation, therefore, in all its meanings, is a conceptual *a priori* in Laing's art. In *greenwork, aerial wall*, for example, the aerial view of the forest canopy of the Nimbin Valley in northern New South Wales provides the point of departure, a view that assumes advanced technology for its transcription. The view's "origin," however, is located in a black-and-white photograph by the well-known landscape photographer Peter Elliston appropriated (with permission) by Laing as a form of conceptual ground of and for the resulting images. Digitally transformed into an intense, highly saturated green, and converted to a slick vinyl surface, "nature" is not only the aggregate product of technological apparatuses, but has become radically de-naturalized, materially plasticized. (Such a demonstration of the Baudrillardian simulacrum is also the subject of Laing's *from Paradise work*, whose digitalized imagery of chillingly "perfect" roses, use of hyper-saturated colors, and laser-etched surfaces are elaborate orchestrations of pixilated artifice and artificiality.)

In her studio notes for this project, Laing recalled having been struck by the optical effects of roadside billboards depicting landscape imagery seen while driving. "I had been considering green landscapes as exterior, as opposed to interior spaces (like the inside of my car, laced with technological prostheses)."[10] When she stopped to examine the billboards more closely, she observed how their surfaces optically decomposed, an effect imperceptible from a moving car or from a distance. "These billboards," she continues, "seem like the inversion of the time-lapse trick—an optical illusion. In time-lapse photography you...slow the coupling of eye and motor (camera), de-accelerate the film to catch the object (the image to be formed) within its space (vector) of motion. For viewing billboards, you couple mobilised speed (acceleration—and the distances of its vectors) with the eye to bring an image (the object) into a field of recognition (to create the illusion of form—for the subject)."[11]

As with other work of this period, Laing was preoccupied with the psychological and perceptual consequences of the acceleration of time, motion, and speed (of communication, transmission, and informational and image economies), but also with what could be called "prosthetic vision." In this regard, the increasingly sophisticated and complex modes by which the real is both perceived and rendered have led to its radical dematerialization and desubstantialization. The natural world, our encompassing material "home," is as *greenwork* suggests, not merely disenchanted, but increasingly mirage-like, replaced by simulation and simulacra. Accordingly, the dense opacity of the computer-painted vinyl prints extends throughout the highly detailed surface of the visual field, from edge to edge, without horizon or spatial-perceptual anchor other than the aerial viewpoint. Such a viewpoint is itself the product of advanced technology, but concomitantly the bird's-eye (or god-like) prospect echoes other, older photographic perspectives that provide the impression of a commanding relationship to what is given to see.

In *greenwork* the relationship of speed, mobility, and technology is the opposite to that of the *TL* works. While the *TL* works are contrived to slow down visual information as well as its optical perception by the viewing subject, *greenwork* inverts these processes inasmuch as the coherence of the billboard imagery conversely depends on the viewer's speed. In these works, mounted on the wall, the spectator's viewpoint is therefore one in which the conventional mastery of the visual field is variously complicated or contradicted by the digital manipulations imposed on the image. Thus, in *greenwork, aerial wall*, a rectangular sector composed as a striated green blur zooms out from the treetop canopy; in *treewallstretch*, two block-like horizontal sections of green reprise the picture's dimensions, with a central band of pixels zapping laterally across the surface between them, as though registering accelerated motion. In her notes on this work, Laing stresses its cybernetic artifice as well as its alienation effects:

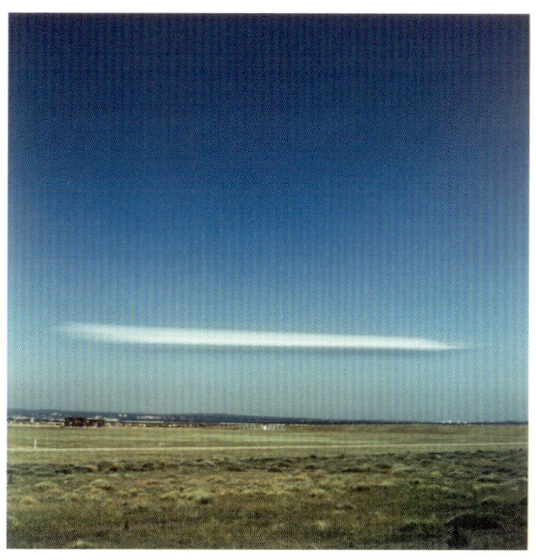

greenwork, TL #8, 1995 (page 75)

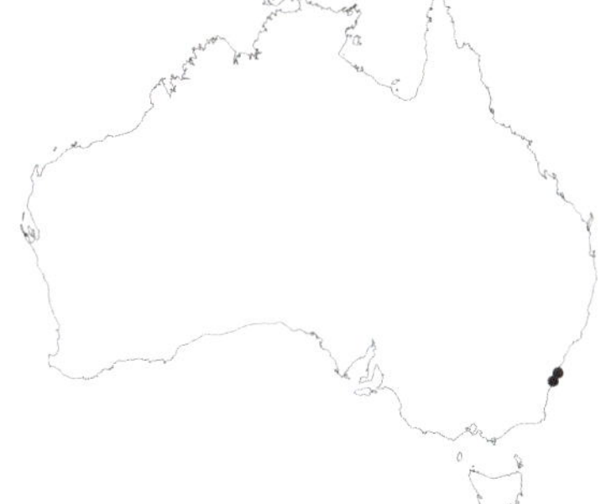

The familiar landscape view in the large *greenwork* vinyls is ruptured, aerialized and re-translated as thousands of points of electronic information. It pictures a terrain flown over by aeroplanes and punctured by invisible passages of information-in-transit. It is emblematic of our shifting perceptions of time and place, and these works consider the experience of the distant "real" place as it is brought closer via accelerated transportation and its transmitted image.

However what also interests me, is that in flying at great speeds "real" places are paradoxically bypassed completely—increasing their distance from our experience.[12]

Where certain of the pictures in *greenwork* gesture to the sublime (as concept or as vicarious experience) only to signal its dematerialized, desubstantialized status through its pixilated matrix, the generously scaled photographs that make up *groundspeed* perform a different kind of critical work. Photographed in various sites in New South Wales (Swan Lake, George Boyd Lookout in Morton National Park, Kiama on the southern coast), wilderness is in these prints quite literally colonized by mass-produced, flower-patterned carpets made by Feltex. A *tour de force* of site specificity, in certain of the series (*Red Piazza #2, #3, #4, #5*; *Rose Petal #15, #16, #17*) Laing has had the carpet carefully trimmed to encircle and isolate each individual tree trunk, rock, and foliage clump, just as one would normally cut it around the radiator or door jamb of the living-room floor. (The titles of the works are the manufacturer's names of the three carpet styles.) In *groundspeed, (Harrogate Flower) #10*, however, the rug is a perfect oval, laid down on the rocky surface of the beach, a former quarry for bluestone. Industrially abandoned since 1940, the quarried bluestone was used for fences and buildings in the Kiama district and later to build roads in Sydney and New South Wales. It is now registered as a geological heritage site.[13] But the coastline itself has other meanings; navigationally treacherous, it has been the site of about two thousand shipwrecks, narratives of which abound in Australian literature and folklore.[14]

Under its lowering sky, with its crashing surf and tower-like rock formations, the spectacle of nature (in panoramic perspective format) is thus startlingly interrupted by the perfect, centrally positioned oval of Harrogate carpet, signifier of middle-class taste and the comforts of home. In her notes on the project, Laing has remarked that the domestic associations of floral carpets were central to her conception; indeed, she notes that the working title for *groundspeed* had earlier been *to lay to rest my weary eyes*. In this respect, a floral-carpeted living room might well be imagined as additionally adorned with reproductions of Australian landscape paintings or photographs. Laing thus stages a surreal collision of Anglo culture with its wilderness other, each with its associational baggage, each with its histories, each with its significance in the Australian imaginary.[15] This "clash of codes," as George Alexander has characterized the series, disrupts the very notion of landscape, of wilderness, indeed, of the sublime.[16] But, as with other of her landscapes, the allusion to the historical past of the Europeans' arrival and conquest of "virgin" territory refers as well to the present. In this case, we are prompted to examine how wilderness as a given site is variously spatially contained (in national parks and preserves, within protected boundaries); mediated as a sight (in the photographic imagery of wilderness); and, like everything else, packaged and commodified, as part of global as well as national economies of tourism and leisure.

Where *greenwork* and *groundspeed* make reference to the photographic conventions for depicting the wilderness sublime, other of Laing's works engage the artistic ancestry that collectively forged the iconography of "Australicity" itself, here as part of the colonial project of "civilization." In these projects, Laing makes reference to the more conventional forms of painted landscape. With respect to the Heidelberg School

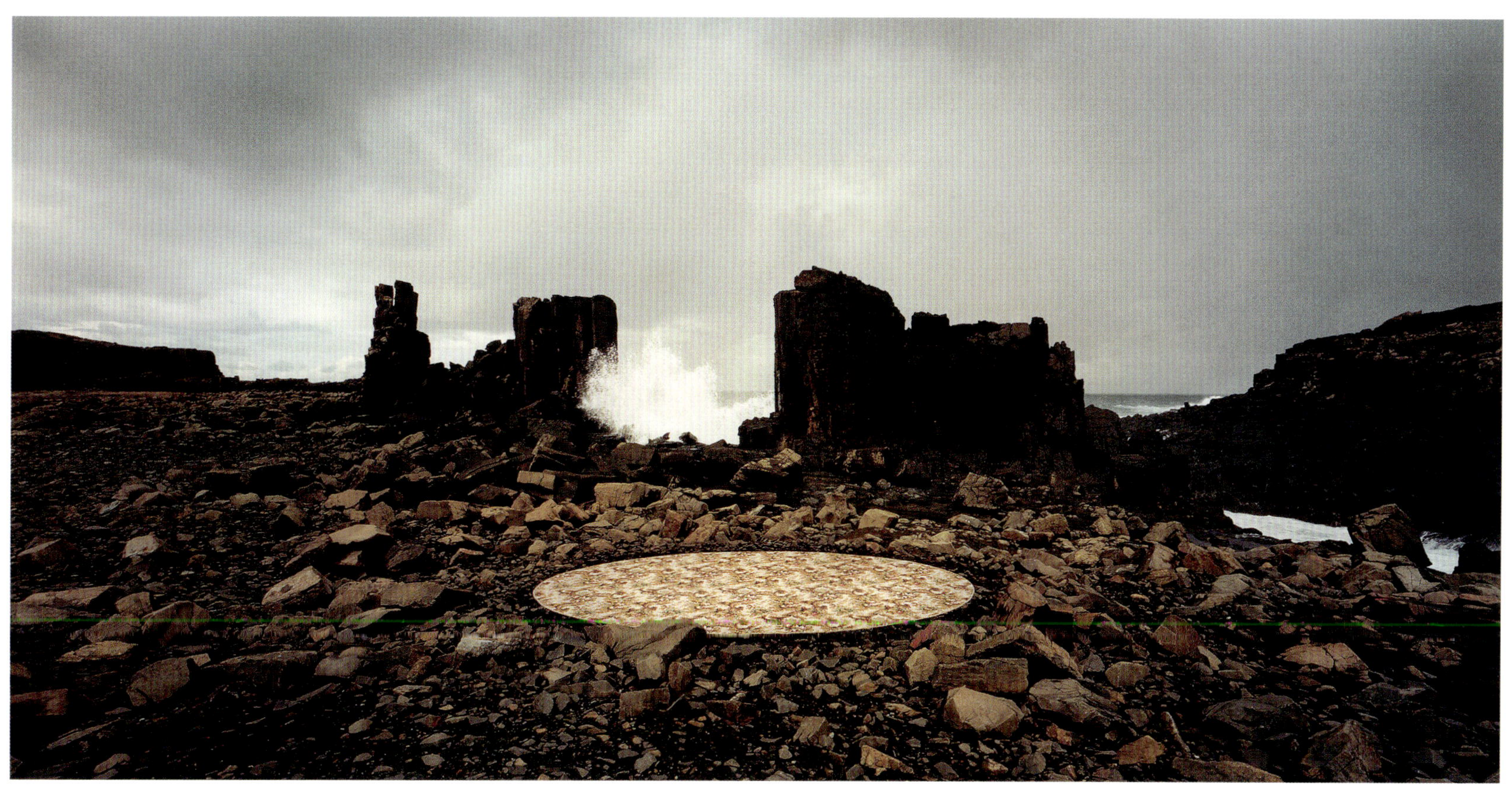

groundspeed (Harrowgate Flower) #10, 2001 (page 98)

artists, many of whose paintings have attained emblematic status, Laing has even conscripted some of their titles—for example, in the *Natural Disasters* series of 1988 as pictorial quotations, as in *to walk on a sea of salt* (2004), discussed in the previous chapter. References to these antecedents are also made through formal structures, such as emphatic horizontality, with its associations to the vista and the panorama, and of course, to the actual horizon line in landscape painting and photography. These compositional devices, commonplaces in the painted landscape tradition, like other pictorial structures such as perspective, are themselves ideologically charged, constructing a pre-established position of mastery and command for the viewing subject. With the invention of photography, these framing and viewing structures were integrated into camera optics, just as photographers duplicated, or found equivalents for, the formal structures governing easel painting. But Laing's references to these icons of Australicity are neither nostalgic nor made in the spirit of respectful art-historical homage. As quotational tactics, they make unmistakable reference to the iconicity of the originals, but primarily to make visible the ideological "work" that made them function as effective icons of colonial domination in the first place.

"Place," one of Laing's overarching preoccupations, thus refers to actual geographical locations as well as one's relation to them.[17] It also includes one's identity, one's place in a place. For Laing, one's place as a white Australian artist is inescapably a locus of contradiction and difficulty insofar as the indigenous people have historically been displaced. Or re-placed. Laing's various sorties into the continent are provisional, tactful, and always self-conscious investigations of her own imperfect or unachieved "belonging" to her homeland. In each location where work is produced, she takes great pains to efface any traces of her temporary presence. This follows from her acknowledgment of the problematic relation of the contemporary white Australian to "the land"—itself an abstraction—a relation manifestly different from that of indigenous people. It is they who belonged to the land, a very different relationship than that of physical possession or even civic inheritance. Place is therefore of the utmost significance in Laing's work; the history and meanings of her various locations determine the contents of the pictures and the aggregate meaning of each project. Fully aware that she inherits, as do we all, the burdens of our histories, Laing's is therefore an artistic practice that seeks to invent formal and symbolic languages with which to produce, as she herself defines it, "a proper accounting," one that must "also include the consequence of corrupted histories within which belonging attempts to place itself."[18] Such concerns, questions, indeed predicaments, make her emphasis on or investigation of landscape (albeit in reconceived formats and iconographies) a fundamental axis of much of her production.

This question of the relation of white Australians to the land they inhabit is, needless to say, an omnipresent theme in cultural production spanning all media. It cannot be overemphasized how recent is Australia's putative discovery, settlement, and emergence as a nation-state—slightly more than two centuries old. This means that processes of settlement, conquest, and agricultural and industrial development that developed over centuries elsewhere have occurred in Australia with stunning rapidity. Similarly, the myriad violences underpinning its evolution as a modern nation-state are far closer to collective memory—indeed in many cases, to living memory. Australian fiction endlessly returns to the overlay of populations and cultures, to the spectral traces of often now-invisible histories that have collectively forged the haunted spaces of the continent. Where few Americans, especially those in urban metropolises east of the Rockies, feel much connection to the history or fate of its indigenous inhabitants (although the last chapter in the Indian wars occurred in the early twentieth century), this is not necessarily the case in Australia. Accordingly, the question of the constitution of an inclusive national identity, the possibility of its citizens belonging universally to a shared place, has distinct valencies in a culture where this remains precisely an urgent, unresolved, and perennially contested political and legal question. It was only in 1949 that Aboriginals (with a service record in the armed forces) were able to vote in federal elections, and only in 1962 that the Commonwealth Electoral Act enabled all indigenous people to vote in federal elections. It was only in 1993 that the Native Title Act was passed, which restored much but not all ancestral land, and only in 2008 that the Rudd government made its formal apology for the past policies and treatment of indigenous Australians, including the tragic fate of the Stolen Generations. The legacies of this history remain active in the present.[19]

For artists like Laing, who assume their historical burden as a form of ethical acknowledgment and symbolic restitution, the production of culture can be considered as a collective activity of reconciliation, even redemption. As George Alexander observes, "The mix of belonging and not belonging that underlies so much of Australian art and culture accounts for much of its fraught energy. Orphaned from Mother England and without the birthright entitlements of the indigenous people, we have to make do with a synthetic identity. Only in the act of making art, art as a combination of belonging and not belonging, can we make up Australia."[20]

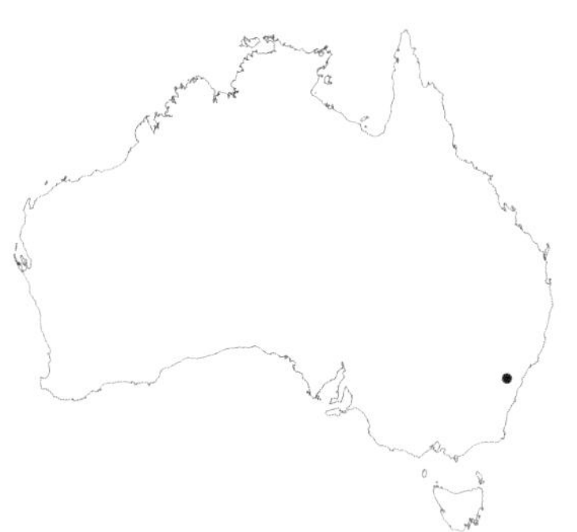

Laing's artistic commitment to a revisionary practice of landscape has, among other things, to do with her refusal of its typically celebratory or euphoric implications. If "disaster" figures as a recurring thematic, it not only involves the actual extremity of Australian climate and environment, but the disasters of colonialism and imperialism that shaped Australian history and the culture it forged. Thus, if *Natural Disasters* references the recurring cataclysms of drought, flood, fire, and cyclone, the *unnatural disasters* project evokes the alien presence of white settlement, the exhaustion or poisoning of the environment, and hardly least, the "homelessness" and alienation of white intellectuals, such as Laing herself, incarnated in their disembodied and rootless heads, floating mid-air or in salt-encrusted bores.[21]

Disaster, however, is not the only thematic that runs throughout Laing's revisionary landscapes. A pessimist of the intellect and an optimist of the will (Gramsci), Laing has produced work on at least one occasion suffused with the exhilaration of heightened hope and renewal. I refer here to one of her most well-known (and most reproduced) series, the Type-C photographs that collectively comprise *flight research* (1998–2000).

The series was conceived on the cusp of the millennium, around the time of the Republic Referendum debates, the vote on which occurred in 1999. The referendum asked voters to decide whether Australia should become a republic and whether a preamble should be inserted into the Constitution. Both proposals were defeated, having

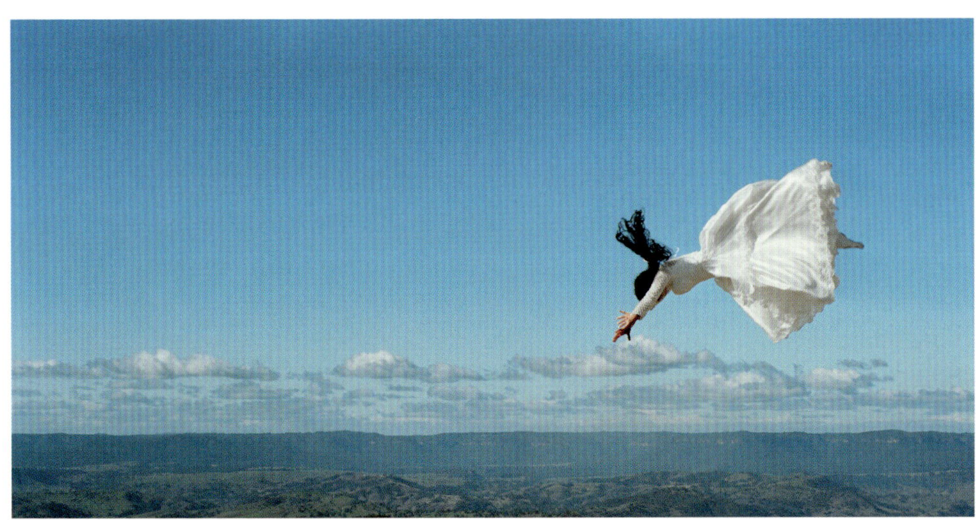

flight research #6, 1999–2000 (page 94)

for liberation and are entirely escapist. On a possibly banal level they are an embodiment of the desire for a better state of existence in the world—unhindered and unfettered by the stymie of necessity and cultural condition. I wanted to unfetter the body from the trappings of the technical prostheses of flight…and place the body in flight (in suspension) between the earth and oblivion (the sky) and all that can be out there."[23]

Photographed in the Blue Mountains in New South Wales (the mountains are visible in the distant horizon of #5, #6, and #9), the series returns to Laing's preoccupation with flight and movement explored in the *greenwork TL* pictures and the *brownwork* series. But where the subject of the earlier series developed out of her (not unambivalent) fascination with the advanced technologies of flight, of extreme speed, of the collapse of space/time that features so importantly in the work of Paul Virilio, *flight research* expresses a vision of transcendent freedom.

Here, as Laing has described it, is the incarnation of an ecstatic state (from the Greek: to be put out of place, OED), the dreamworld of free flight, the body weightless and airborne. In this series, Laing endows the white-gowned bride, that

failed to achieve a majority overall and a majority in any State. Such a formal separation from Commonwealth status (and the crown) has great symbolic resonance for many Australians on both sides of the political divide. For progressives, cutting the colonial tie implies more than affirming the values of democratic republicanism (i.e., no hereditary monarchy, no aristocratic titles, no individualized sovereign, no established church, no curtsies).[22]

In her studio notes, Laing reflects on the optimism that infused the euphoric pictures that make up the earlier series: "I made *flight research* in 1999—at a time of great optimism for the new century. The photographs on one level…resemble a desire

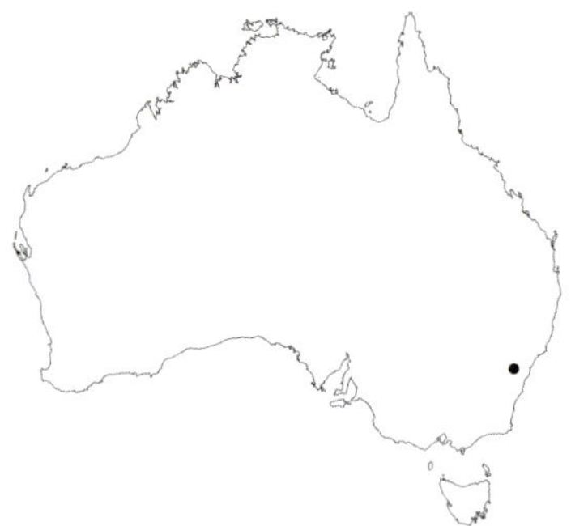

most clichéd if not kitsch symbol of transition, with new life, for indeed the flying bride is the hoped-for incarnation of a redeemed homeland. Swooping, leaping, falling without fear, in skies that range from intense cerulean to the gold and pale azure of sunset, the black-haired bride is an emblem of unshackled liberty, of giddy liberation from earthly dross. Despite their extraordinary appearance, these are analogue photographs in which the stuntwoman Gillian Statham performs the flight of the bride. But the series of the bride is prefaced by one in which she is suspended midair over a verdant forest canopy, ascending a stick ladder, presumably linked to an unseen plane or helicopter. This momentary suspension between earth and air is not magical, and thus its drama, aside from the activity, is the less sensational one of the photographic seizure of an action in time and space. As such, it heightens the make-believe real of the following pictures. In five of the series, including *#2a* and *#2b*, a diptych that Laing has had installed in both vertical and horizontal pairs, the bride is isolated in square frames against the sky. In *#5*, however, she is fully frontal, like a presiding angel, arms extended over the panoramic landscape as though performing a ceremonial and enveloping embrace.

Such a transfiguring vision was, needless to say, ephemeral, both in terms of the failed referendum and Laing's own recognition of the shortcomings and disappointments of the Howard government, as well as in the far more somber tenor of her work. Moreover, just before she would begin the shooting preparations for her *bulletproofglass* series two years later, New South Wales was again struck by devastating brushfires, including the area where Laing has a home. (See the discussion of *swanfires* in the following chapter.)

In the *bulletproofglass* series, Laing returned to the airborne bride, this time to choreograph her assassination. In the prints that constitute the series, against no less extravagantly beautiful skies the bride reels or recoils from a bullet wound in the chest, falling downward, backward, frontward, and sideways, accompanied (in *#3*, *#4*, *#7*, and *#8*) by fluttering pigeons. These are not fundamentally "realistic" simulations

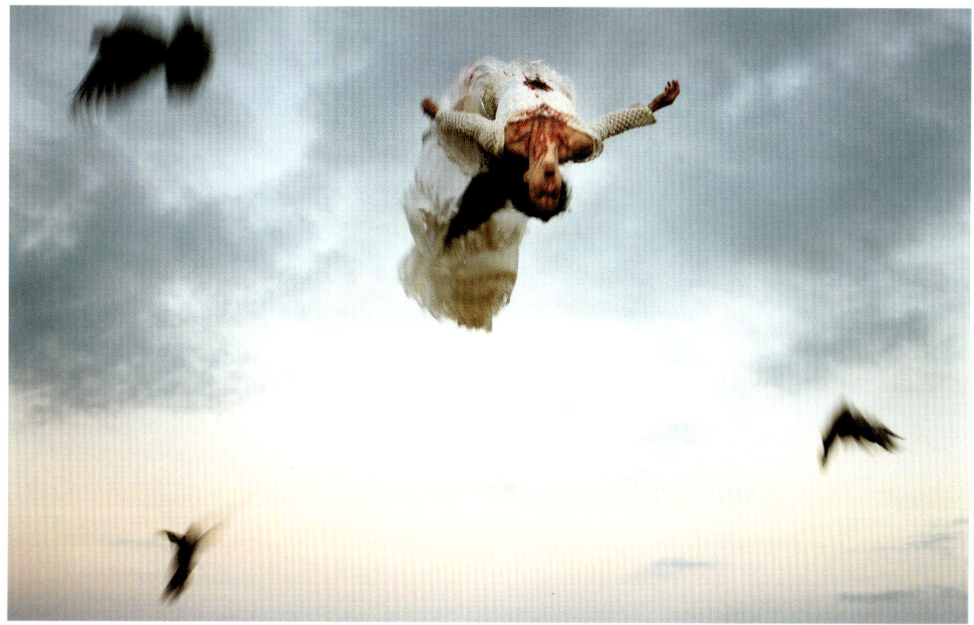

bulletproofglass #3, 2002 (page 112)

of slaughter, notwithstanding the bloody wound and the flailing gestures. Their staginess, or better, their theatricality, is in keeping with Laing's often-allegorical visual language. Nevertheless, they seem meant to instill an element of shock—reality biting, as it were—signaling the dashed hopes and heightened expectations of the previous years.

bulletproofglass is highly theatrical in its rhetorical effects and cinematic in its formal ones because, first of all, the violence is metaphorical. Laing has contrived to produce a figurative articulation of events and conditions that are not visual as such. In news or documentary photography, a political referendum or the act of voting can only be metonymically represented by such images as a queue of voters, a politician speaking, etc.; it cannot represent a socio-political climate or individual or collective situations. Only physical disaster—its representation also innately inadequate to the real—is photogenic.

Laing's practice is therefore predicated on an acceptance of the limits of visual representation in its indexical and transcriptive capacities. The artistic task confronted in each of her projects requires that she integrate her own situation as individual subject, as artist, as photographer, with conditions or events that are spatial, temporal, material, and political and historical, and vastly exceed the particular or the individualized instance.

In the project that became *leak*, Laing signaled the correspondence between the "local" and the "global" as they intersect within a specific geographical locale. "Leakage between things," she wrote, "between past, present, and future…leakage between the

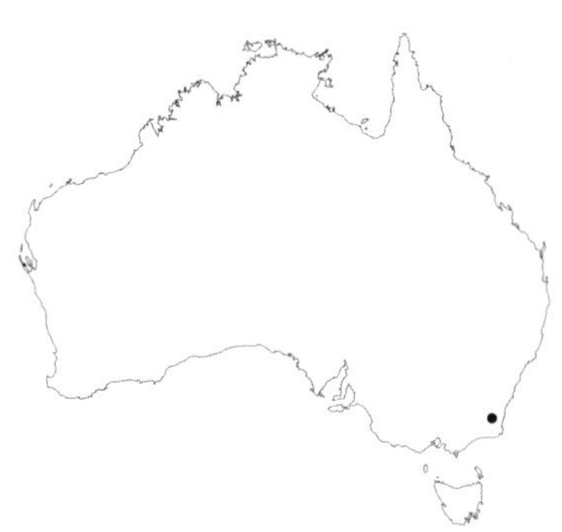

past of the idyllic pastoral landscape and, very broadly put, surburban-to-global leakage."[24] The site she chose for the project was the Monaro district of New South Wales, a high plateau close to the area demarked by the Great Dividing Range. Encompassing a swathe of territory of approximately 20,578 square kilometers, bordered on the west by the Snowy Mountains, it had by the

mid-nineteenth century become a region of relatively small-scale farming and cattle and sheep raising.[25] Its settlers had begun their westward migrations from coastal whaling stations and fishing communities such as Eden, the town from which Laing made her initial forays into the region. (Eden figures in *weather #1* and *#2*, discussed in the following chapter.)

Characterized by rolling hills and open grassland, the district lies in the rain shadow of the Monaro mountain range. In Australian art history, it was the subject of landscape paintings by George Lambert and Hilda Rix Nicholas following the First World War. As Samantha Littley notes, Lambert's *The Squatter's Daughter* (1923–24), painted at Michelago in the Cooma-Monaro Shire with its blue sky, gum trees, and sloping hill, is also one of the works recalled in Laing's *Aristide*.[26] But, as she further remarks, "Rather than giving us a lesson in art history, though, Laing gives us cause to think about how our visual and cultural histories collide and affect our understanding of the landscape, now."[27] In any case, the associations of this area are, if anything, more significant in Australian literature. It features, for example, as the locale of Miles Franklin's 1901 novel *My Brilliant Career*, where the novel was actually filmed. More recently, it serves as one of the settings in Patrick White's *The Twyborn Affair* (1979). Laing's titles for the individual photographs that make up *leak* are in fact drawn from White's characters; Eddy/Eudoxia is a sexually and morally ambiguous character whose identity is tenuous, mobile, and subject to change; Aristide Pelletier, whose surname is that of a famous castaway, is coincidentally the character who recognizes his/her ambiguity. Within the Australian cultural imaginary, however, the district possesses its greatest resonance as the region represented in Banjo Paterson's 1890 poem "The Man from Snowy River,"

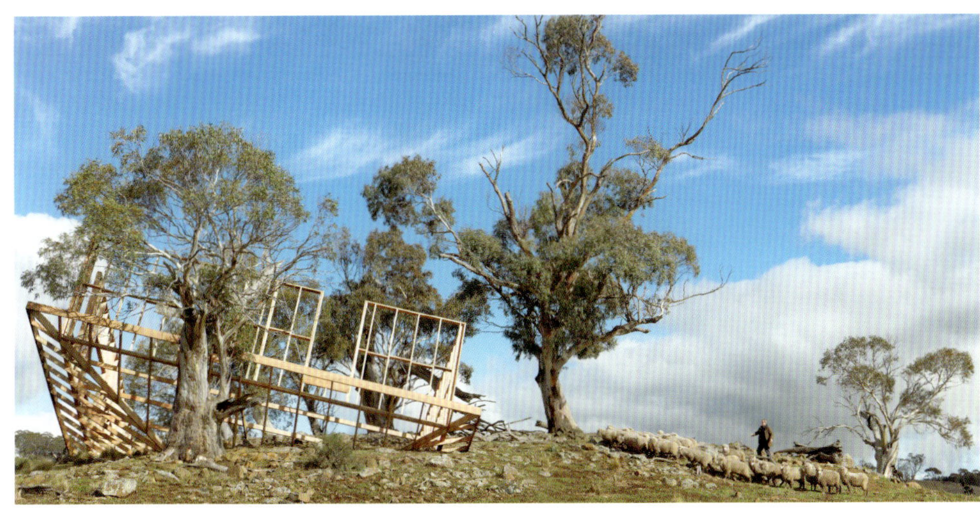

Aristide, 2010 (page 162)

which as early as 1920 had already been made into a silent film (two later films were made in the 1980s, an Australian television series in 1993–96, and a musical spectacle in 2002). As one of the "origin" myths of Australian nationhood, the poem recounts the daring rescue of an escaped racehorse by the eponymous horseman, who seeks the animal among the wild brumbies in the rough terrain of the Snowy Mountain ravines and escarpments. Paterson's effigy and microprinted excerpts of his poetry are inscribed on the Australian ten-dollar banknote.

Like all of Laing's chosen regions, settled or not, domesticated or wild, Cooma-Monaro is densely textualized. That is to say, it is overwritten by narratives that even before Federation sought to establish and secure a notion of "Australia-ness." What such narratives attempted, with greater or lesser success, was to forge an intelligible entity encompassing a collective (white) identity, encouraging political, nationalist cohesion, while fostering a discursive mapping of the immensity of the land mass itself. The cultural work of such narratives was, and is, as complex and often as ambivalent as it is symptomatic of Australia's plural histories. Among their various functions, such narratives had necessarily to navigate the fissures and conflicts of class (including those whose ancestries descend from convicts and indentured persons), diverse ethnicities, and national origins, all of which were, and are, imperfectly contained within the simplistic binary of white/black or colonial/Aboriginal.

Due west of Eden, on the coast, from whence she initiated several exploratory road trips in July 2009, Laing eventually chose as her site a farm in the hilly sheep country of the Monaro, on a hilltop on which grew a stand of old (and partly shattered) gum trees. By the time she had decided on the particular site, Laing had formulated the "subject" that would be constructed for the photographs: the wooden skeleton of a standard suburban house, of conventional single-family design, whose measurements would be slightly enlarged (using a scale of 1:6) over its ordinary dimensions. This typical wooden structure, however, would be moored in the earth upside down, as though it had dropped from the sky, from nowhere, resting on its site like a hallucination, a mirage. A house, therefore, was conceived as not (yet) a home, nor even possible of becoming one, given its reversed position. In keeping with her thematics, and notwithstanding more than two centuries of white possession and occupancy, the concept of an unproblematic "homeland" remains perpetually unrealized.

But also, in Laing's material and visual realization, and as the critic Robert Nelson has aptly observed, the resulting images are the literal expression of the "world upside down," an expression whose venerable ancestry in early modern European culture included carnivalesque sexual and social reversals (i.e., woman on top, horse mounting rider, etc.).[28] Here it serves to literalize our time radically out of joint, including the consequences of environmental destruction and global warming. And as Nelson also remarks, the single-family suburban dwelling, a voracious machine of resource consumption, is a powerful symbol of environmental abuse: "The beautiful idea of the house amid bountiful space…is an ecological nightmare. On top of the most inefficient footprint in the world, the archetype of the suburban house also entails social isolation and disempowerment for anyone who doesn't drive a car."[29]

Laing's invention of an architectural (and spatial) metaphor for the upside-down world of heedless consumption/destruction, as well as its evocation of the mythic location of the Antipodes, has multiple meanings. As a complex feat of construction and engineering, it required the skilled labor of four builders and other workers, requiring fourteen days for constructing, rigging, and securing the structure. Midway through its construction, the region was struck with powerful rain- and windstorms; the ground was flooded, although the wooden house frame remained securely anchored, and the gum trees suffered further damage, some of their limbs snapped from their trunks by the force of the winds. (The highly destructive Queensland floods occurred shortly afterward, from late December 2010 to early January 2011; three-quarters of the state was declared a disaster zone, recalling the epochal floods of January 1974—an historical event Laing witnessed as a child growing up in Brisbane). Given her recurring

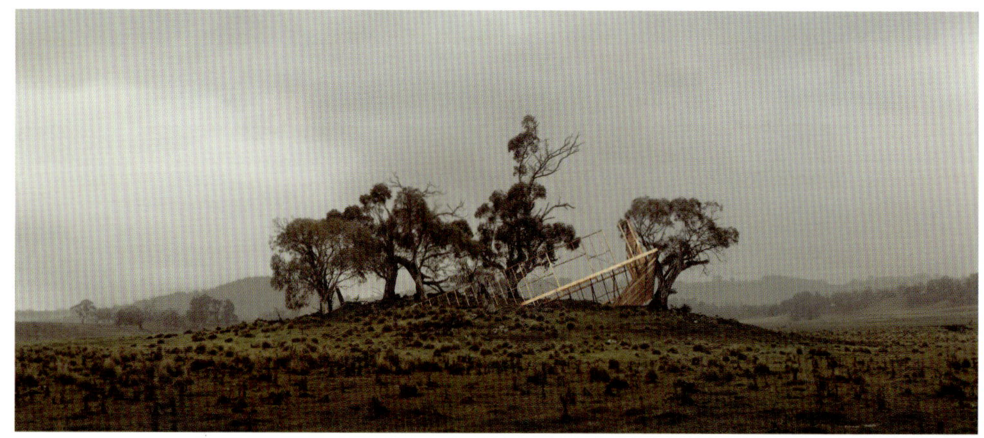

Eddie, 2010 (page 168)

evocations, as well as personal experience, of flood and drought, there was a certain irony in the storm's occurrence in the midst of the project.

Be that as it may, among the prints that constitute the ensemble of *leak*, the leaden sky of *Eddie*, with its misty gray background hills, provides a telling contrast to the brilliant azure sky and cirrus clouds of *Aristide*. Chromatically, moreover, the somber tonalities of the former, with its metaphorical as well as literal depiction of stormy weather, is evocative of those seventeenth-century Dutch landscapes in which large expanses of gray sky occupy much of the pictorial space. Similarly, *Aristide*'s herdsman and flock adjacent to the house frame recall the *staffage* conventions of the pastoral landscape. Although these are European pictorial motifs, Laing's landscapes in all their diversity and regional specificity appear to refer to these historical precedents. But where the tradition of Dutch landscape (and classical landscape in general), expresses the harmonious cohabitation of nature (sky, earth, water, vegetation) and culture (distant church spires, villages, boats, tillage), Laing's are disruptive icons of the unnatural, landscapes of disturbance, disinheritance, and dis-ease. The radical dislocation of spatial orientation in *leak*, wittily alluding to Australia's Antipodal designation and emphasized when *Eddie* is exhibited upside down, challenges the viewer in her own perceptual orientation.

In her project notes, Laing remarked that one of her preliminary working titles had been the *Mutant Chronicles*, a reference to a punk sci-fi movie featuring aliens and mutants. Both categories, needless to say, are operative figures for the other—the other of the human being, to be sure, but more complexly, the projection of what is ostensibly repudiated, disavowed, expelled from the human self. In the *Mutant Chronicles* version, the alien colonizes the human by means of viral metastasis. But for Laing, the ongoing mutation of particular geographies, terrains, ecosystems—here instanced in the suburbanization of the rural economy of Cooma-Monaro—is the result of human activity that is likened to a virus, endlessly reproducing itself, eradicating difference in the service of the same.

In *leak*, however, Laing, is not implying that the Monaro district is more prone to urban sprawl than other rural areas, or that it should be seen as a specific symbol for such development. Nor is there any suggestion that these ongoing economic and environmental transformations constitute a violation of a once-pristine Arcadia. Indeed, the agriculture or livestock of rural economies were themselves the imposition of successive waves and layerings of colonial settlement. Consistent with her refusal of sentimental nostalgia for a mythic and undespoiled past, Laing's critical work on the historic genre we still recognize and persist in calling "landscape" assumes no simple solution to the consequences of development or overdevelopment, whether specific to Australia or elsewhere. *leak*'s reversal accordingly speaks to more fateful and overarching ones, and in this respect, it can be linked to those broad concerns that run throughout Laing's career and that charge it with political and ethical meaning. These are, preeminently, the lived consequences of reversals of socially responsible values and priorities, among them, the custodianship of our earthly home, without whose health and ability to sustain our human presence the very notion of homeland is meaningless.

Most unnerving of all was the knowledge that, just three years back, the very patch of earth you were standing on had itself been on the other side of things, part of the unknown, and might still, for all your coming and going over it, and the sweat you had poured into its acre or so of ploughed earth, have the last of mystery upon it, in jungle brakes between paddocks and ferny places out of the sun. Good reason, that, for stripping it, as soon as you could manage, of every vestige of the native; for ringbarking and clearing and reducing it to what would make it, at last, just a little bit like home.

—David Malouf[1]

In December 2001, and continuing through the month of January, a series of fires, collectively named the Black Christmas bushfires, broke out in the state of New South Wales. For a month they burned, consuming 750,000 hectares, producing a fire-front 4,360 kilometers in length. On the night of January 3, fire destroyed large tracks of land at Sussex Inlet, about 200 kilometers south of Sydney. Laing and her partner, along with their neighbors in the district, were safely evacuated and their own house was spared.

Like many Australians, Laing has grown up with the phenomenon of periodic bushfires (in American English, these are called wildfires), especially severe during long periods of drought—for example from 1997 to 2009 ("The Big Dry" in southeastern Australia). Bushfires are part of the natural cycle of destruction and regeneration, and the deliberate burning of certain areas is a traditional—and also regenerative—aspect of Aboriginal culture. However, and in the context of climate change, global warming, and more frequent and lengthier periods of drought, the incidence of fire increases, and as a consequence of expanding real-estate development, more people and property are put at risk. The management of bushfires is in Australia and elsewhere a source of controversy; there exist ongoing debates about managed burning, back-burning, and housing development in at-risk areas, issues that encompass ecology, real-estate development, and government policy.

Laing shot the project that became *swanfires* (2002–04) in the wake of the fires at the Sussex Inlet Waste Transfer Depot, on the south coast of New South Wales. She made the photographs at the local dump that had serviced a small number of scattered coastal hamlets and villages punctuating the bushland and national parks of the region. (These fires dramatically affected certain of the nearby *groundspeed* locations, the project she had completed the previous year.)

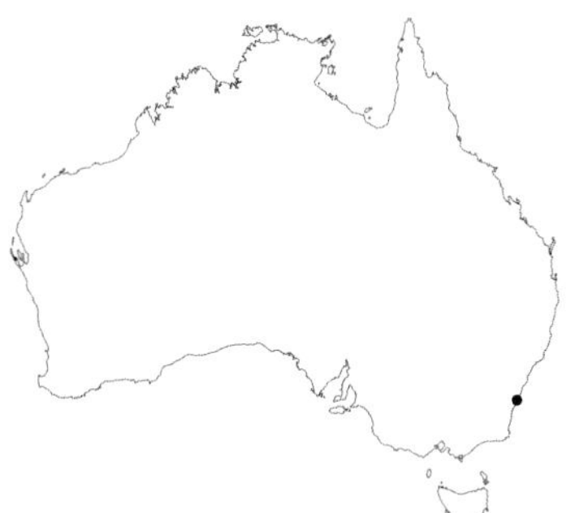

In her project notes, Laing remarked that among those affected by the fires, including friends and neighbors, were people who had

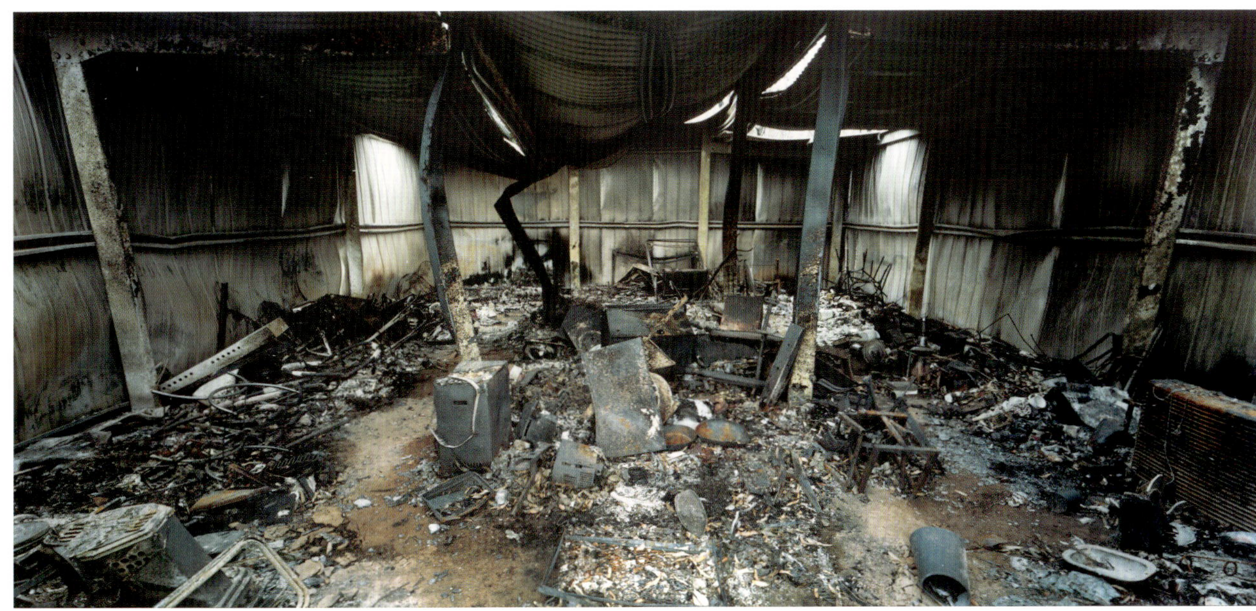

swanfires, Chris's shed, 2002–04 (page 110)

The theme of disaster that features so prominently in Laing's work, no matter its visual beauties, and despite its frequently allegorical articulations, is never abstract. It has marked her lived experience as it has marked that of so many other Australians. But the distinction between cycles of "natural" disaster (fire, flood, etc.) and "unnatural" ones (the internment of refugees, injustice toward indigenous people, environmental destruction) is anything but hard and fast. Between these ostensible polarities of nature and history play out the still-resonating effects of successive traces and overlays of settlement and human migration, constant remaking and reshaping of the terrain on which policies and politics produce their own transmutations.

Laing has chronologically organized her artwork for this book to officially begin with the 1988 project *Natural Disasters*, a title (and subject) that resonates throughout her subsequent production. Although she had been producing a wide range of works in various media since her art-school years and after, she considers that with this project her conceptual, aesthetic, thematic, and critical preoccupations were effectively integrated and given formal and material resolution. Viewed retrospectively, it is by no means difficult to see its obvious continuities with her later work, but what is retrospectively striking is its formal realization as an object, not an image.

Of course, photographs in their actual material substance are also objects, but one salient characteristic of the medium pivots on how photographic images are optically,

worked with her on *groundspeed*. In *John and Kathy's auto services* and *swanfires, Chris's shed*, both part of the series, she photographed the aftermath of the fires: the collapsed sheets of corrugated metal and surrounding debris that had once been an auto shop; the blackened incinerated interior of a shed. These are somewhat unusual works for Laing. Soberly straightforward, colors subdued, they are detailed registrations of the destruction she viewed as she made the exposures. "I would say," she wrote, "that one's body is marked by such events."[2]

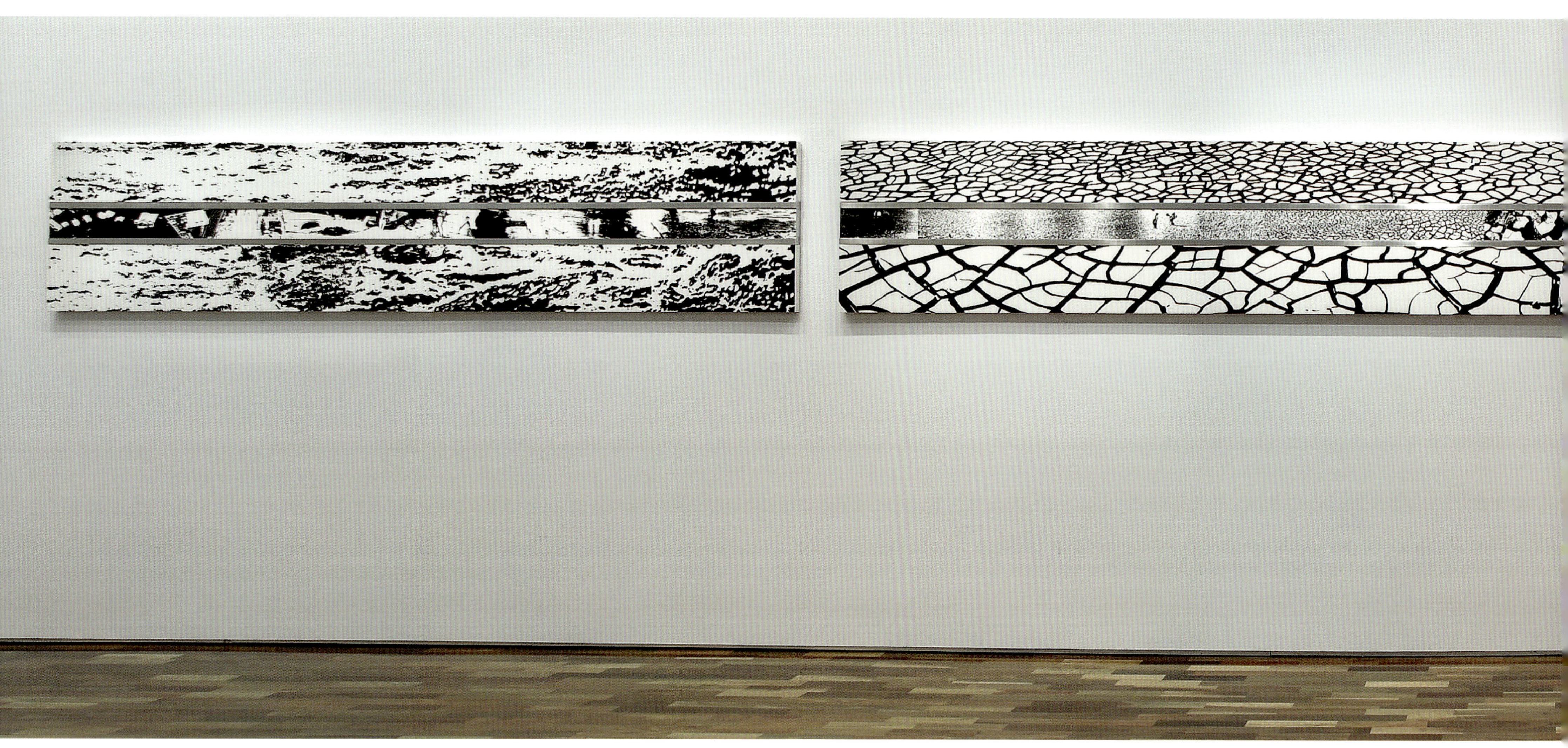

Installation view of the series *Natural Disasters* (1988) from the exhibition *prostrate your horses: weather and then some — Rosemary Laing*, at the University of Queensland Art Museum, Brisbane, 2009.

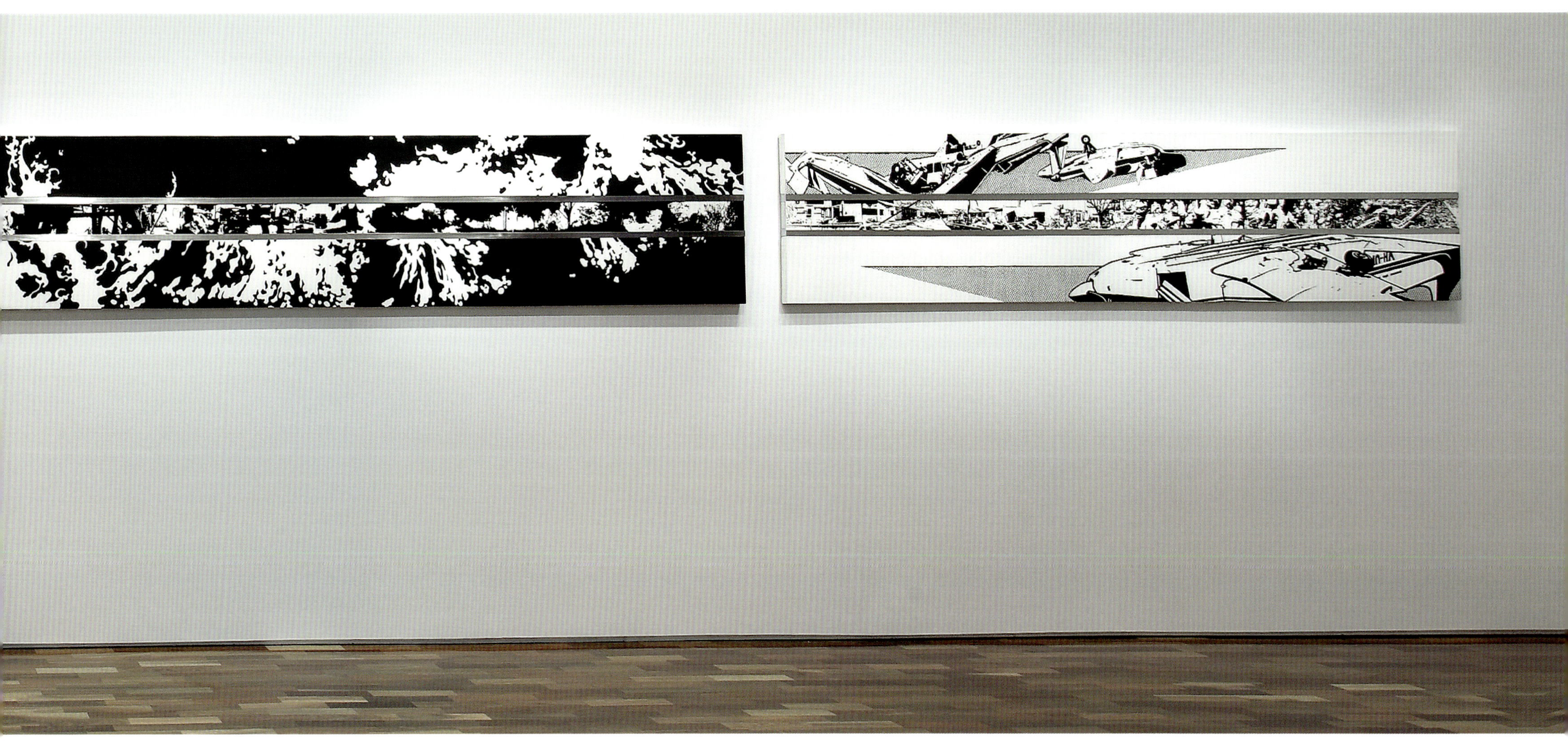

and indeed psychologically, perceived. In their patent flatness, and because of their photomechanical generation, photographic images normally generate a powerful illusionism, such that we rarely perceive the image as something superimposed or overlaid upon its paper support. Thus, image and support cannot be readily distinguished from one another. If, historically speaking, one of the goals of certain types of easel painting, especially landscape, was to provide the fiction of a window through which the world presented itself, the advent of photography established a new benchmark: the *ne plus ultra* of such illusionism. This aspect of the camera image holds good irrespective of physical scale, and like other image technologies, such as film or video, the image itself subsumes, renders imperceptible, its material substrate. By contrast, the physical components and materials, as well as the commanding scale, of *Natural Disasters* affirm its materiality, its status as a concrete, physical object. Its horizontality, emphasized by the steel strips that separate the visual fields, refers to the visual form of the panorama (painted or photographed); but suppressing any distinction between earth and sky, it fails to deliver to the viewer the sense of spatial mastery that these compositional forms conventionally affirm. Unlike most photographic imagery, it operates against the effect of stasis. The length of its panels requires physical as well as optical movement, and the metal strip dividing its graphic components produces the illusion of a moving point of light paralleling the viewer's own lateral movement in space. It is, moreover, a painted object, if not in any conventional sense a painting. The more or less abstracted imagery depicted on the horizontal sections is derived from black-and-white news agency photographs, which are intensively manipulated: cut up, montaged, rephotographed, graphically

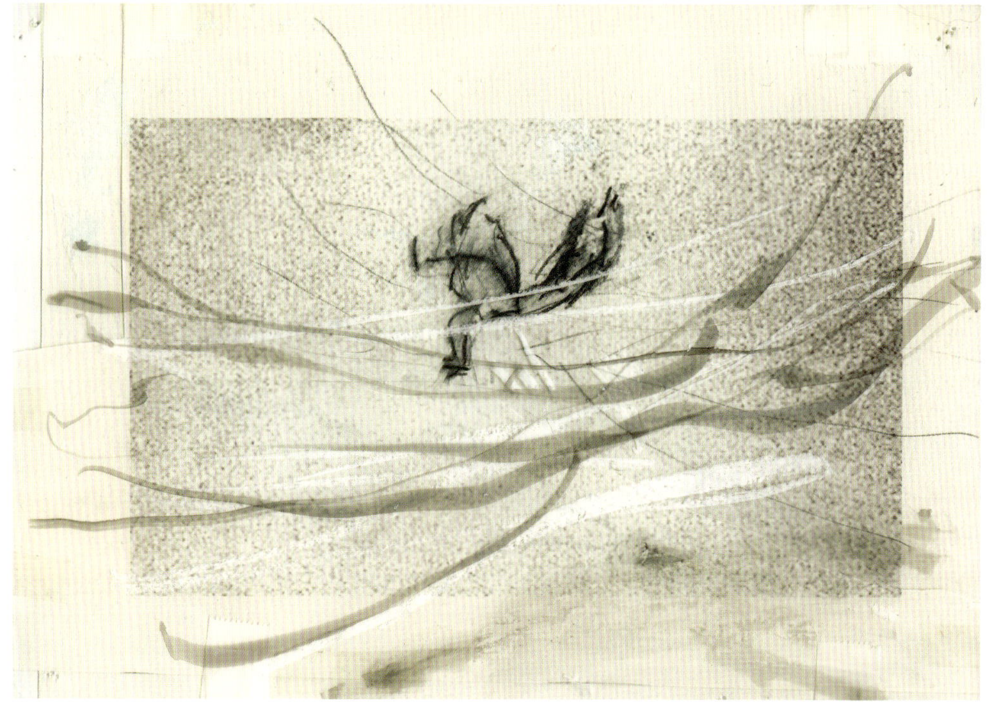

weather drawing #8, 2006. Ink, paint, pencil on paper and acetate, 8¼ x 11¾ in. (21 x 29.7 cm), irregular

stylized. Laing painted the top and bottom elements on gessoed surfaces from highly mediated photographic source materials. In this respect, the work marks her last use of painting as her medium and anticipates her subsequent work produced exclusively with the camera. It might thus be considered as a coda to her youthful artworks and a prelude to what in art-historical parlance is generally termed her "mature" production.

(It should be noted, however, that Laing has always made large numbers of sketches and studies around her various projects, and in fact, has included graphic works in exhibitions of the 2006 series *weather*.)

The year that Laing undertook *Natural Disasters* is itself an integral aspect of the work's conception. Its fabrication occurred following the year-long Bicentennial—an official all-media extravaganza that celebrated the First Fleet's raising of the flag in 1788, in honor of Captain James Cook's 1770 putative "discovery" of Australia and the establishment of the nation. The political and cultural significance of this Bicentennial was enormous. Under the Labor administration of Prime Minister Bob Hawke (and fully in keeping with analogous ritual spectacles in other former colonial nations, such as the United States, Canada, and South Africa), its ideological work was rooted in mythologies specific to the Australian nation. But its intensely self-celebratory and patriotic tenor was also instrumental in bringing to the foreground the contradictions, not to mention the repressions, obfuscations, and indeed injustices, that underpinned the nation's foundation and settlement. Consequently, its unfolding served to quicken and animate a range of oppositional and dissident forces, from Aboriginal land rights to renewed demands for a republic, from a revivified acknowledgment of structural racism(s) to the call for official acknowledgment of the expropriation and destruction of Australia's indigenous peoples for whom the ostensible "discovery" by Europeans constituted the beginning of their dispossession and devastation. As a response to

the official celebrations, the Bicentennial and subsequently "Australia Day" became renamed—and thus re-signified—as "Invasion Day."

The disasters that feature in Laing's 1988 project, with its highly abstracted photographic traces, are, however, all "natural" ones. The cyclone, fire, and drought are, as indicated, recurring phenomena in Australia, given its geographic, environmental, and climatic conditions, but in this project Laing chose very specific examples. Cyclone Tracy, which devastated the city of Darwin in the Northern

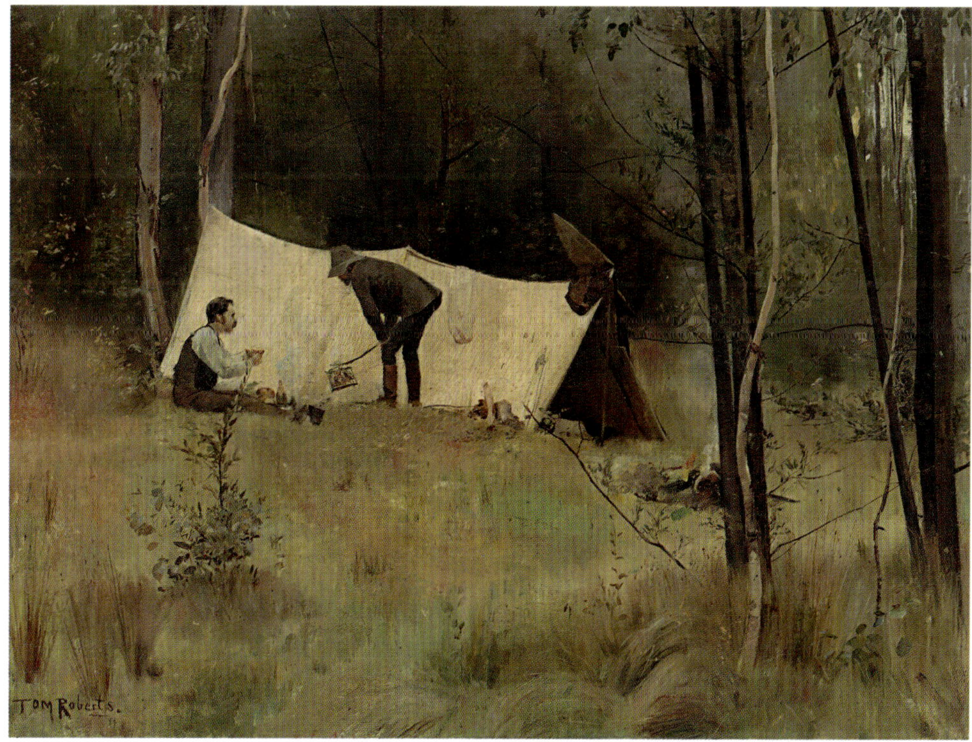

Tom Roberts, *The Artists' Camp*, 1886. Oil on canvas, 18¹/₈ x 24 in. (46 x 60.9 cm). National Gallery of Victoria, Melbourne. Felton Bequest, 1943

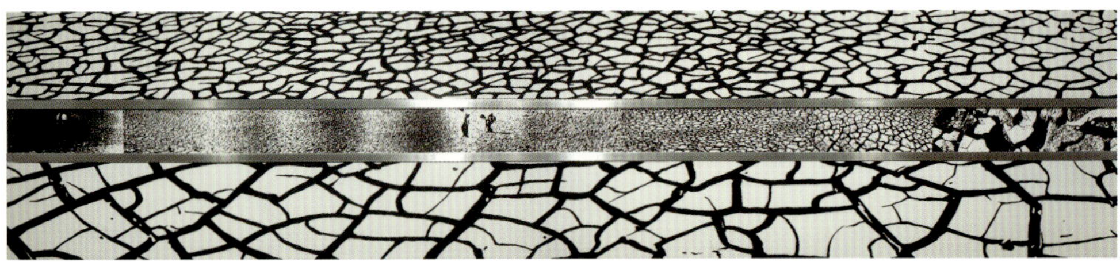

above: *Still glides the stream and shall forever glide (droughts)*, 1988 (page 62)

right: Arthur Streeton, *Still glides the stream, and shall for ever glide*, 1890. Oil on canvas, 32½ x 60¼ in. (82.6 x 153 cm). Art Gallery of New South Wales, purchased 1890

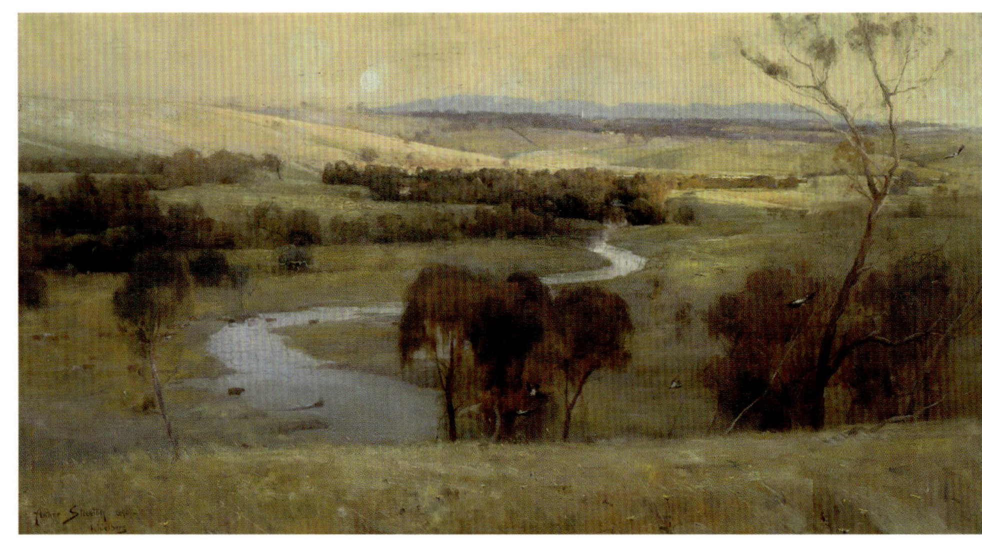

Territory on Christmas Eve and Christmas Day in 1974, has mythic status in the cultural imaginary, much like Hurricane Katrina in the United States.[3] For fire, Laing selected the Ash Wednesday bushfires that struck the states of Victoria and South Australia in February 1983. Following years of extreme drought, within twelve hours 180 fires killed 75 people and hundreds of thousands of livestock, as well as wild animals, destroyed over 3,700 buildings, and consumed vast areas in the stricken states. For drought, Laing chose the one that had furnished the conditions that had contributed to the Ash Wednesday bushfire, a drought that had afflicted most of the continent since 1982. Finally, for flood, she selected the one that devastated Brisbane in January 1974, which she experienced, killing 14 and flooding out almost 7,000 homes and businesses.

The four panels were given titles taken from late nineteenth-century Australian landscapes from the Heidelberg School. The cyclone panel is entitled *The Artist's Camp* (Tom Roberts, 1886); the fire, *How We Lost Poor Flossie* (Charles Conder, 1889); the flood, *Departure of the Orient, Circular Quay* (Charles Conder, 1888); and the drought, *Still Glides the Stream and Shall Forever Glide* (Arthur Streeton, 1890). Collectively, these paintings represent the development of the Australian landscape painting tradition drawing on the French introduction of *plein-airisme* (painting outdoors, not in the studio) and seeking to render the specificity of the Australian environment, both rural and urban. Collectively too, the artists who made these works, along with their contemporaries, established many of the topoi of the cultural and ideological coordinates of Australia-ness as they would be continuously manifest in elite and mass visual culture. Notwithstanding the stylistic differences among these artists and their work, the only "loss" depicted in these works is that of a pet dog on a rainy day in Sydney. It is, therefore, the yawning gulf between the artistic renditions of the landscape or cityscape and the grim realities of climatic and other environmental disasters to which Laing alludes. Like the disjuncture between the meaning of a celebratory Bicentennial and that renamed Invasion Day, so too the rift between wish-fulfilling representations of a luminous and harmonious Australia in which white colonials are "at home" and recurring cycles of disaster.

As Laing has described, *Natural Disasters* emerged from her concern with the manifest dissonance between the actual, visceral experience of events and their representation in mass-media incarnations. Insofar as the mechanisms of media-ization require compression, fracturing, distillation, and often metonymic symbolization, these were the formal procedures she adapted for the making of the work. Hence, the abstraction and stylization of her photographic sources, especially that relating to the bushfire; the running steel strips that bisect the elements of the work; and the resulting transformation of the spectacle into a laconic and abstracted object/panorama. These processes are one of Laing's continuing preoccupations, for they constitute central issues within the condition of postmodernity, a condition whose diagnosticians, from Jean Baudrillard to Paul Virilio, contributed greatly to Australian critical theory and to Laing's own intellectual formation.

In contrast to the virtualized no-place of the already-photographed, already-represented sites of *Natural Disasters*, Balgo in Western Australia, the place Laing chose for her project *one dozen unnatural disasters in the Australian landscape* (2003), is both an identifiable site and one charged with significance. An enormous landmass, the state of Western Australia extends over 2.5 million square kilometers. Being predominantly

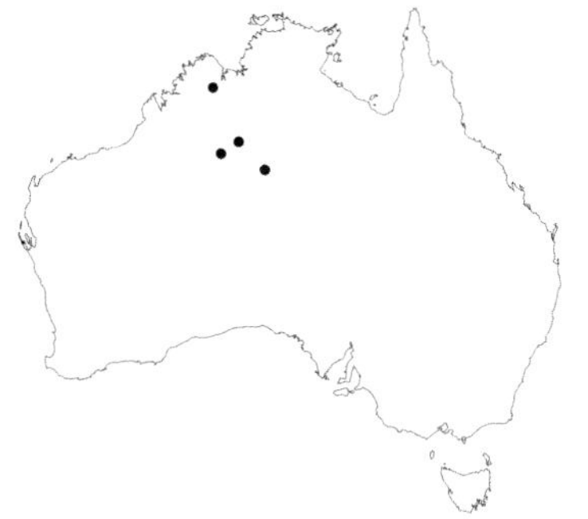

desert to semiarid, it is sparsely inhabited. The Balgo (Wirrimanu) community site is a small, fluctuating community of about 400 people, bordered by both the Great Sandy and the Tanami Deserts, and is part of the 2.6 million hectares of the Balwina Aboriginal Reserve. This is the meeting place of the Kukatja, Walmajarri, Jaru, and Pintupi language groups (or tribes).

Balgo Hills's present settlement began in 1964–65 "as a Catholic Mission Station for the nomadic people, mainly Kukatja speakers, from the remote areas south and south-east of Sturt Creek."[4] The Balgo Hills Mission operated between 1939 and 1975 as a residential facility for girls and boys of indigenous descent sponsored by the Catholic Pallottines. *The National Directory of Records of Catholic Organisations Caring for Children Separated from Families* states that the mission was set up in the area covering the Rockhole and Billiluna Stations.[5] Such stations, established near waterholes, created conflict between their Aboriginal populations and pastoralists, inasmuch as large herds of livestock put great pressure on existing water resources. The renowned artists' cooperative Warlayirti Artists at Wirrimanu, controlled and managed by a Committee of Aboriginal artists, was established in 1987 and includes well-established painters such as Eubena (Yupinya) Nampitjin and Helicopter Tjungarrayi.

Laing's choice of this particular area within which to stage her *unnatural disasters* was influenced by these factors, as well as its geographical location. With respect to Balgo's artistic production, notably paintings informed by what is popularly known as

Aboriginal traditions of "dreaming" their land, Laing's choice of this site reminds us that Aboriginal culture was and is integrally shaped by this existential relationship. As such, their relation to place constitutes an authentic birthright, a relation effectively foreclosed to the descendants of settlers, or to those aware of the histories and consequences of white colonization.

A mythologized entity in the Australian imaginary, the "outback" has been paradoxically constituted as both "empty" and as vivified and animated by the "populist" aspects of its sparse settlements. In this latter version, it is conceived as a place of aggressive masculinity, hardscrabble towns, and beer-drinking bushwhackers. Such commercial and cinematic packaging is familiar to non-Australians in the form of the Crocodile Dundee or Mad Max franchises. These associations are by now thoroughly mythic themselves, and as always, mythic representation masks complex social realities. Distinct from its frontier-like myths, as Laing observes, the outback was originally considered "out back," somewhat like the idea of "where's that?" or "nowhere." Like the Wild West of the American imaginary, its narratives and myths are ways of managing historical contradictions.

In its broadest sense, and as consistently apparent, Laing's work investigates the complexities and contradictions that attend the notion of "non-belonging," or "un-belonging." In certain works, such as *flight research*, it attempts to imaginatively envisage how this condition might be redeemed through a reconstitution of Australia as an authentically and fully democratic republic. If Laing's places—the places chosen for her staging of Australian reality—are those that sometimes turn on various claims to geographical and cultural belonging, as in Balgo, or its failure, her point of view

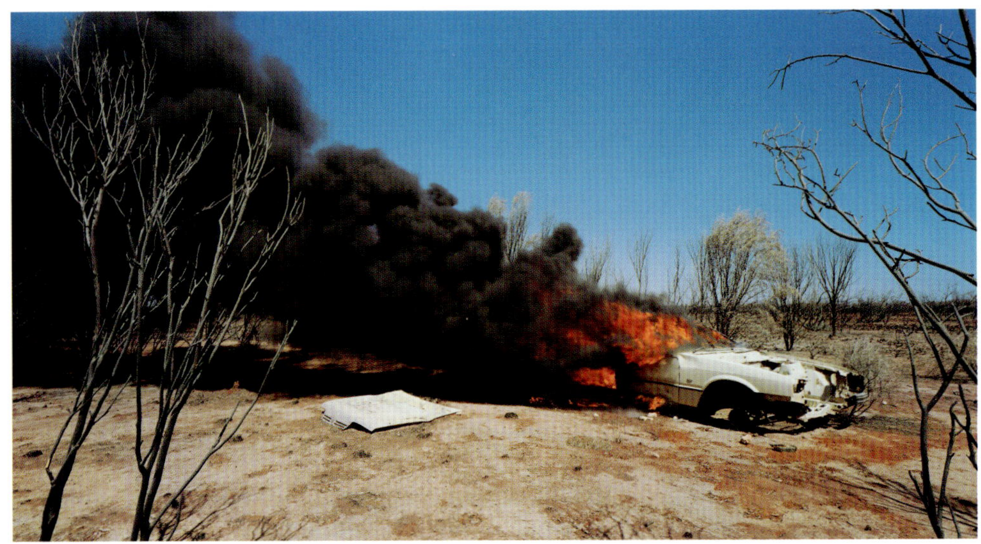

one dozen unnatural disasters in the Australian landscape #2, 2003 (page 120)

acknowledges her current place as always outside and apart from the legitimate claim of indigenous people. In formal terms, this acknowledgment is sometimes enacted in her physical, material vantage position—as, for example, in the bird's eye view from a small plane seen in the series' prefatory image, *third day of a five day muster*, the disembodied I/eye scanning the field of vision. The visual equivalent of the omniscient narrator, Laing "looks" with a camera at what *isn't* a landscape, notwithstanding the efforts of generations of Australian painters to impose such a vision on its resistant geographical reality. In its failure to conform to this domesticating endeavor, which is implicitly a possessive ethos, and given her physical and enunciative position above and apart from

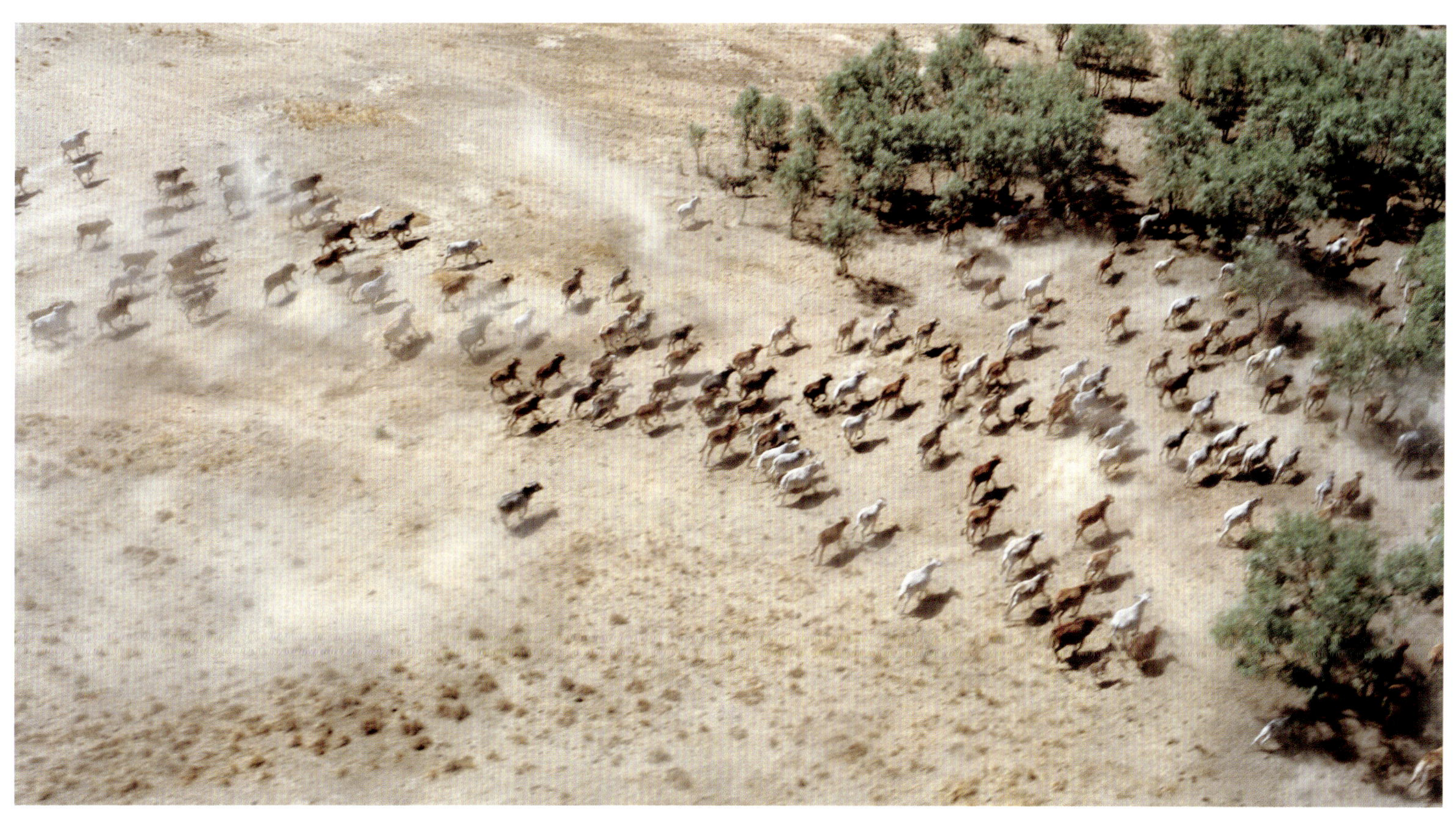

third day of a five day muster, 2003 (page 122)

it in this image, the recalibrated (shifted) viewpoint prompts questions of how, on what terms, and under what conditions Laing might convene a renewed "conversation" about the nature and terms of "belonging" in and to Australia.

The bird's eye view, however, also functions to literally depict the constant transformation of the country. Thus, the aerial view of herded cattle churning up dust alludes to the physical marking of the country produced by the grazing of livestock that accompanied the progression of European settlement across the continent. Nevertheless, the view from plane or helicopter from which the exposure is made is as much a technologically determined "look" as is that of the altered appearance of the now highly populated areas of the continent. Laing's unsentimental acceptance of her own cultural situation, in both its existential and physical senses, forecloses the possibility that empathy, political correctness, or even ethical awareness transcends one's politico-historical situation, which is always a given. "Whiteness," in Australia and elsewhere, is a privilege of birth, acknowledged or not. Such a range of associations and meanings, real and imaginary, subjective and historical, are transformed by Laing into fully materialized scenarios of disaster that are not only ecological, political, or historical, but psychological, even spiritual.

This theme is pervasive in Laing's collaborative series produced with Stephen Birch (1961–2007). A subset of *unnatural disasters*: *between heaven and belonging*; *between a rock and a place with no fish*; and *remembering Babylon* (*#5*, *#6*, and *#7*) are made with disembodied heads that Birch cast from life. In this respect, the bleached and disembodied cast heads of artists, including Laing's, that float in the salt-poisoned bores or are eerily suspended in mid-air suggest something of the psychic burden of historical

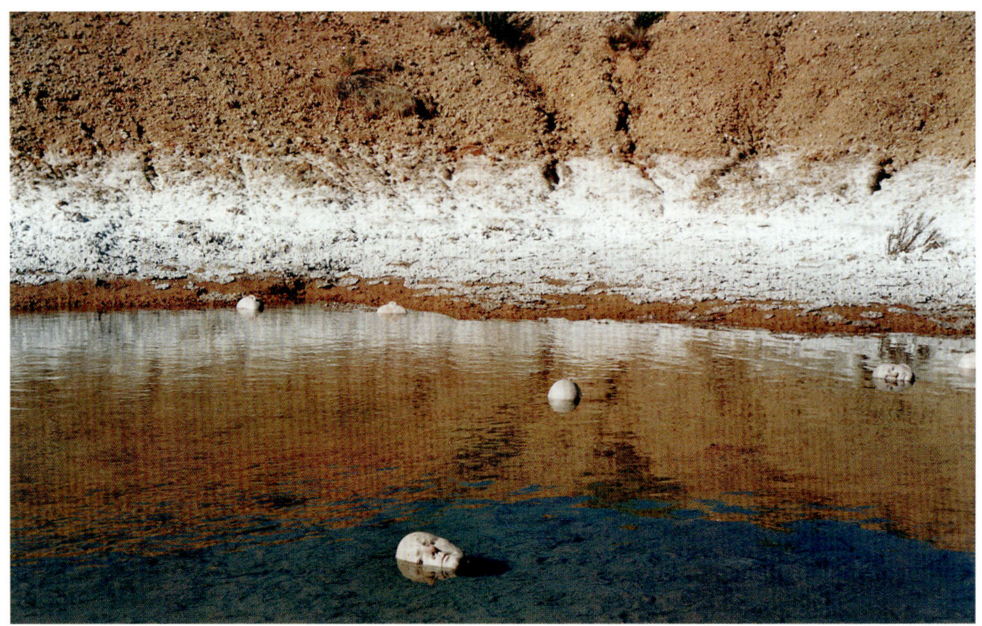

remembering Babylon #6, a collaboration with Stephen Birch, 2003 (page 132)

violence for white Australians within their own complex historical present. More broadly, they suggest the environmental and spiritual costs of modern Australian civilization itself. These mournful heads are perhaps less powerful in effect than the other photographs that constitute the series, for despite their undeniably surreal and uncanny effects, it is perhaps the blank impersonality of the other pictures that is more unsettling.

Laing's umbrella title for the project inevitably evokes the *Disasters* series of Andy Warhol, those ferocious but deadpan silkscreens of car wrecks and mangled victims that are now part of modern art history. And certainly, the burning car wreck that figures in *#2* of *unnatural disasters*, or the furniture Laing assembled on the desert floor only to be spectacularly consumed (*burning Ayer #6, #7, #12*), are familiar objects of modern consumer societies. In two of the locations used in the series, the *brumby mound* and *burning Ayer* photographs, the props employed are IKEA-type furniture: tables, swivel chairs, couches, floor lamps, and the like. The poor relation of Bauhaus design, such furniture, now ubiquitous worldwide, possesses genealogical links to the populist modernism (or perhaps modernist populism) that the Bauhaus sought to disseminate. But where the socialist ideals of the Bauhaus have long vanished from such inexpensive modernist-style furniture, its appearance, even in remote sites like the Balgo Hills, is a testament to a kind of fast-food model of habitation: instant domesticity, instant mass-produced modernity, instant Western-style habitation.

Variously disposed—heaped, clumped, or dispersed—on the arid surface of the ruddy desert earth, Laing had these artifacts of "affordable design" entirely encased in red earth or pigment (i.e., the local soil itself), as red as Uluru. She and her crew painted each article of furniture with a mixture of earth and glue, encrusting each imported object with the material of its setting among the dirt and scrub. When contrasted with the hallucinatory blueness of the sky, the heaped-up furniture, reddened by the setting sun, seems like a relic of a lost civilization or a site-specific artwork. De-natured and de-cultured, far from their European origins, these frail talismans of civilization are presented as almost camouflaged in the landscape (e.g., *brumby mound #5, #6,* and *#9*); barely illuminated in the enveloping blackness of night (*brumby mound #2*); arranged as though an abstract sculpture (*burning Ayer #1*) or consumed in sacrificial fire (*burning

Ayer #6, #7, and *#12*), alluding to the less mysterious flames of the blazing car wreck, belching black smoke against the cerulean sky.

Western Australia also borders the Northern Territory, the location of Uluru, previously known as Ayers Rock, perhaps the most famous icon of the Australian landscape. Restored in 1993 to its Pitjantjatjara name, Uluru, it signals restitution to those for whom the rock was sacred for millennia. (Ayers was only "discovered" in 1873 by the surveyor William Gosse, who named it Ayers Rock in honor of the Chief Secretary of South Australia, Sir Henry Ayers.) The Aboriginal name "Uluru" was first recorded by the Wills expedition in 1903. The contest for meaning with respect to place is thus also about the power to name, or to rename, just as "Invasion Day" re-signifies Australia Day. Like the founding of the Balgo Hills art and community itself, the return of Uluru is about an ethical claim of /to belonging, a claim that is part of Laing's conception of her work as an "accounting, an art practice akin to a restitution of sorts."[6] Visually, and especially given the absence of cues for internal scale, these pictures suggest disasters beyond themselves, referring retrospectively to the natural disasters emblematized in the earlier work. Those photographs in which the furniture burns in the distance might be taken for towns ablaze; distant perspective and lack of scale, especially in *#6* and *#7*, contribute to its drama. In his essay on this series, George Alexander remarked on the ritualistic elements of its production:

What to make of these burnt offerings? And how to explain this strange economics of destruction and restoration, of gaining and losing? We almost laugh at this mad expenditure because we seem to stand on the brink of seeing the economic order (indeed the logical order) entirely overthrown. In a series of striking images we witness the fierce joy of fire, and dense matter achieve release into other forms. Fire which is at the heart of an ancient burning continent.... With this work it as if Laing is trying to escape from the circle of the historical misalliance between city and country, Indigenous and non-Indigenous, and in its excess flirts with the violence of the sacred. Allowing for a return of freedom through the paradox of losing it, of giving it away, of burning and rejuvenation.[7]

The scale of many of these pictures are heroic, a deliberately orchestrated spectacularization that is nonetheless intended to counter—"homeopathically"—the conventional spectacle of Australian landscape painting, the touristic landscape photograph, the spectacle of nature purveyed as its official self-representation.[8] Laing's intent, however, is not to make an easy demonstration of an "aesthetic" or even environmental violation of country (which is not to say that such despoliation is not evident, as in the toxic bores), but rather to evoke the contradictions of settlement and culture provisionally, imperfectly achieved on the terrains of historic dispossession and expropriation.

   The pictures assembled in *unnatural disasters*, like so much of Laing's work, are the end result of a historically informed reflection on social reality as such can be grasped and artistically articulated, however partially or imperfectly, in the present. It is the demands of this reflection that determine her preliminary researches, her commitment to collective endeavor, her receptiveness to the knowledge of each "situation," and her adherence to an ethics as well as a politics of representation. This

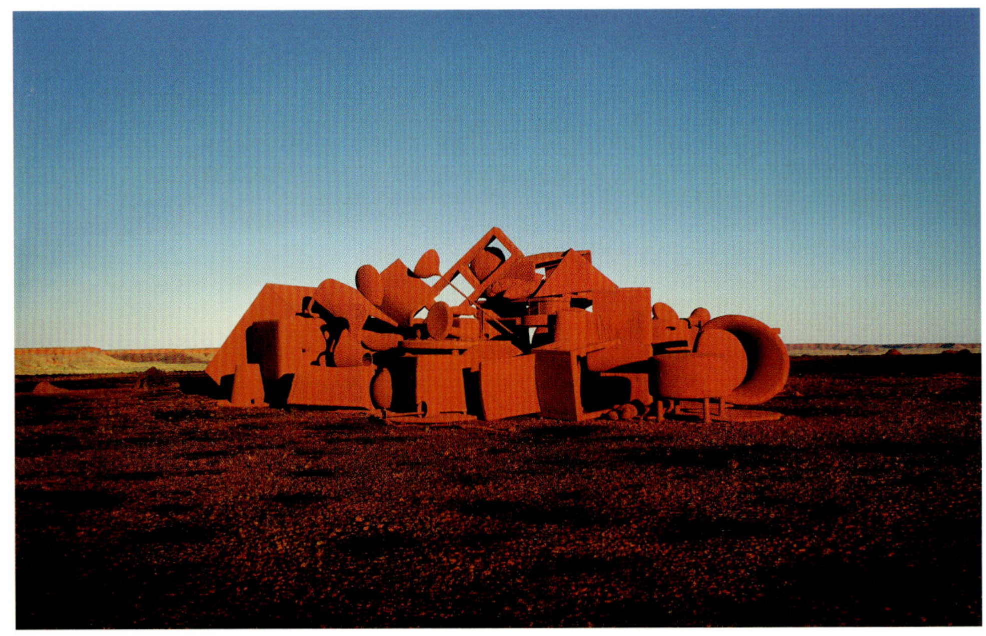

burning Ayer #1, 2003 (page 130)

includes her engagement with the Wirrimanu community and Art Center, whose places she effectively "borrows" for her work. As with other of her projects, the choice of site involves the consideration of the overlaying of historical events with their consequences in the present. That the pictures, which are the physical realization, the terminus, of her projects are formally beautiful should not be taken as the end to which she artistically aspires, but rather as the means by which we should be prompted to reflect on our own relationships, our own haunted histories "out" back.

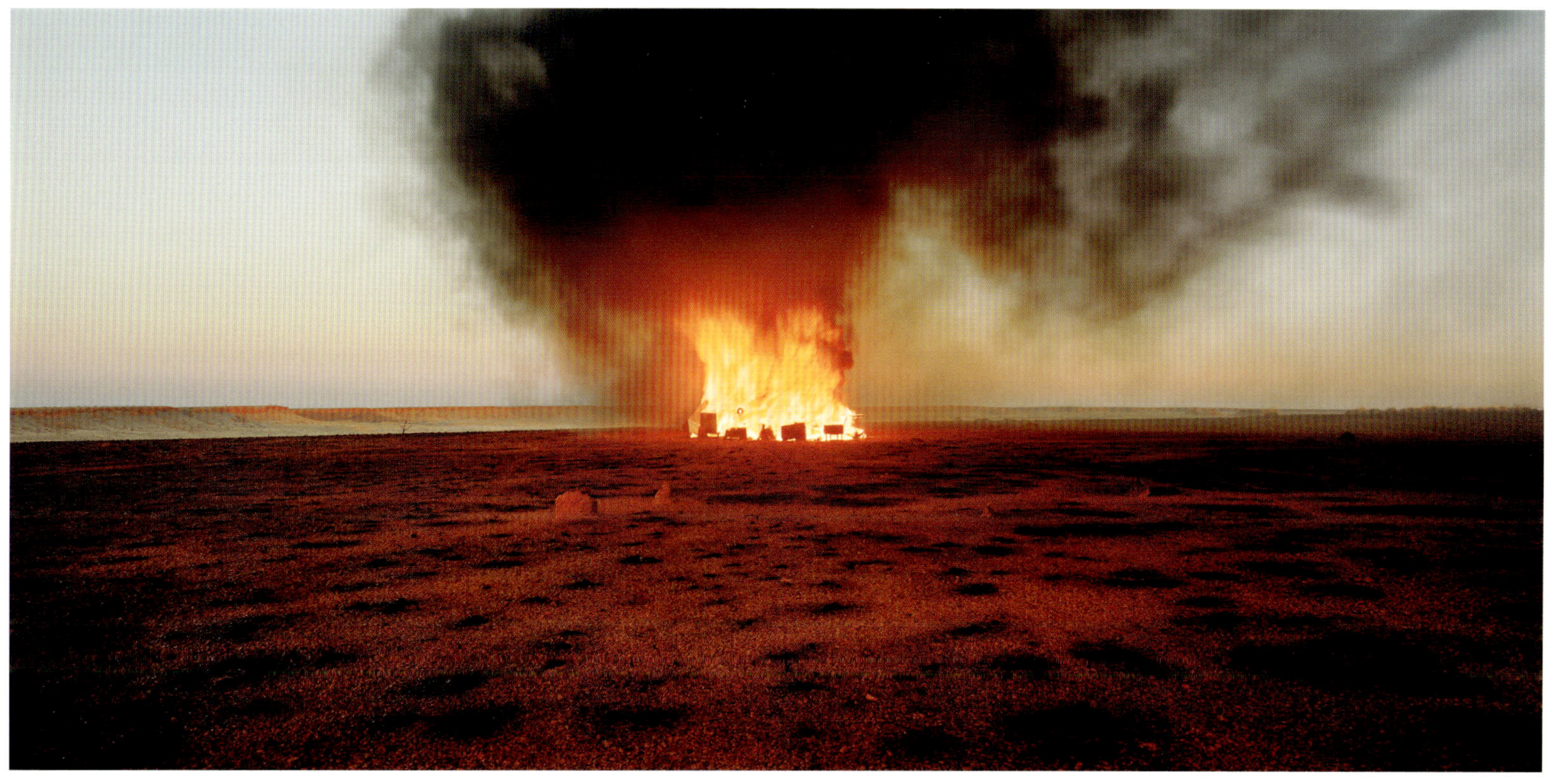

burning Ayer #6, 2003 (page 131)

The time has now come for the nation to turn a new page in Australia's history by righting the wrongs of the past and so moving forward with confidence to the future.

We apologise for the laws and policies of successive Parliaments and governments that have inflicted profound grief, suffering and loss on these our fellow Australians.

We apologise especially for the removal of Aboriginal and Torres Strait Islander children from their families, their communities and their country.

For the pain, suffering and hurt of these Stolen Generations, their descendants and for their families left behind, we say sorry.

To the mothers and the fathers, the brothers and the sisters, for the breaking up of families and communities, we say sorry.

And for the indignity and degradation thus inflicted on a proud people and a proud culture, we say sorry.

We the Parliament of Australia respectfully request that this apology be received in the spirit in which it is offered as part of the healing of the nation.

—Prime Minster Kevin Rudd,
excerpt from the address to the nation

On February 13, 2008, Prime Minister Kevin Rudd, representing the newly elected Labor government of Australia, made a public speech, broadcast on television and radio throughout the nation, whose reverberations continue through this day. What many Australians, such as Laing, had not expected to see in their lifetimes had come to pass, with the suddenness of a thunderclap. This formal admission of collective guilt forever changed the political and social map of the country, and its enormous symbolic import should not be underestimated. (It might be here observed that the United States has never seen fit to offer its apologies either to its indigenous peoples or for the crimes of slavery.)

What made Rudd's speech such an epochal event was its recognition that absent the acknowledgment of responsibility, reconciliation and regeneration are forever blocked and deferred. "The histories of most nations founded on violence," writes Ross Gibson, "suggest that an inability or refusal to acknowledge the past will produce evermore confusing and distressing symptoms in the body politic."[1] And while Rudd's apology was not uncontested, and has not resolved the omnipresent problems of indigenous people, it constituted an historical benchmark toward achieving social and economic justice.

a dozen useless actions for grieving blondes, which Laing completed in 2009, is

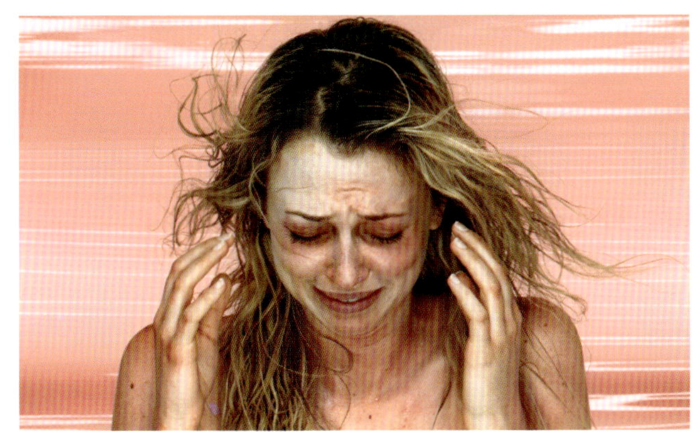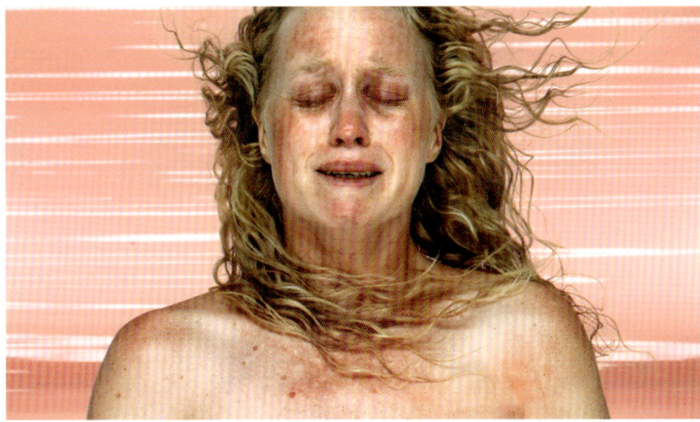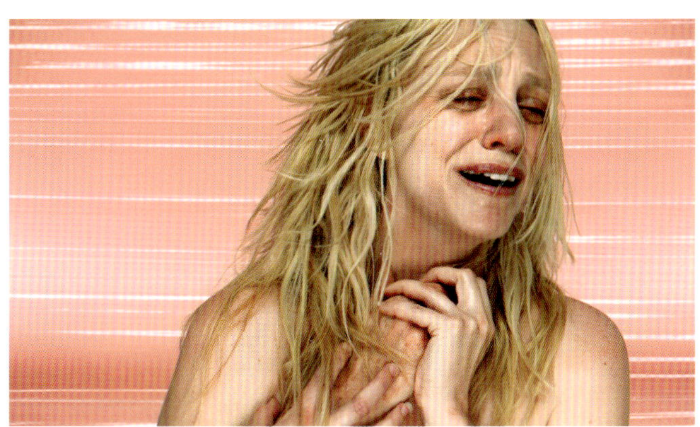

a dozen useless actions for grieving blondes #2, #3, #5, 2009 (pages 155, 156, and 157)

not, of course, "about" what has come to be known as Sorry Day. Initially formulated in late 2007 and early 2008, neither does it directly index the devastating brushfires that ravaged Victoria in January and February 2009. This, however, is not to say that contemporary events do not here, as in other of her projects, operate as one of its conceptual armatures. Like heating ducts concealed within a wall, Laing's projects are animated from within, and hers, as I have indicated, is essentially an allegorical mode of artistic thought. Similar to the photographic image itself, which in its analogue form registers the imprint of light on a sensitive surface, Laing's projects register the imprint of real events—political, social, and environmental—but transposed into a visual language that invites a form of decipherment, to be read in relation to (not behind or in strict parallel with) the events that shaped them.

grieving blondes is perhaps one of Laing's most explicitly feminist works. Although the human protagonists that figure (infrequently) in her projects have always been women (notably Gillian Statham, a professional stuntwoman), the three actresses she chose for this work were cast to represent the most stereotypical form of (white) feminine desirability: fair-haired, slim, even-featured, pale-skinned, youthful. So similar are their physiognomies that they initially suggest that they are the same woman. As Laing has remarked, "Blondes seem to me to have been the most over-imaged white women in the media and perversely, I was interested to put this grouping to another kind of work."[2] Laing therefore typecast her women according to this family resemblance, possibly a kind of composite surrogate for herself as a morphologically similar Australian. That their features are distorted by extreme sorrow, their skin blotched and mottled, their hair stringy and unkempt, their gestures histrionic, does not necessarily annul their underlying prettiness; this is as much a given of the project as is their impassioned, uncontrolled grief, simultaneously individualized and collective.

Cropped tightly from bare shoulders to the top of their heads, the background of each picture is identical: a rose pink backdrop striated with horizontal white lines connoting speed and movement as though seen from a speeding car, an effect accentuated by their wind-whipped hair. (This illusion of propulsive acceleration is, as noted earlier, a feature of projects such as *greenwork*.) In terms of its photographic syntax, Laing here contrasts the manifest stasis within which each weeping woman is individually cropped and frozen with a simulation of temporal velocities, an arrested tempest of feminine excess. Smaller in scale than much of her other work, *grieving blondes* displays a serial organization that suggests something like a series of cinematic stills from which the narrative has been perversely withheld.

That it is women who mutely weep and howl, who gesticulate so helplessly or clutch at others' hands, who abandon themselves wholly to their anguish, is not without its parodic implications. So too the blush-pink hues, archetypically associated with femininity, the rosy backdrop repeated in reddened noses, flushed cheeks, and inflamed eyelids. We are here squarely in the spectacle of "female trouble," a well-trodden terrain of the patriarchal imaginary. But to whatever degree one might identify a satirical subtext operative in the spectacle of sorrowing blondes, this is hardly to exhaust their meaning. When asked by a young writer for the secret of his literary success, Alexandre Dumas *fils*, the nineteenth-century writer, reportedly responded, "torture the heroine." Apocryphal or not, this reply encapsulates one of most durable conventions (or recipes) in Western culture, high and low. From Richardson's Clarissa to Puccini's Mimi, from Hollywood "weepies" to Lars von Trier, the sufferings of young women have never lost their capacity to fascinate and entertain, notwithstanding its causes, varieties, or the narratives within which they figure. Depending on the viewer or the reader, such representations engage particular admixtures of identification or dis-identification, projection or introjection. Given the mechanisms of sexual difference and how they are mobilized in cultural reception (and as Dumas himself appeared to recognize), we also need to acknowledge the unconscious mechanisms of sadism, however disavowed. For these and other factors, while male protagonists may be sorely tried and endure afflictions of one kind or another, the point to be made is that "torture the hero" is not an equivalent formulation.

In this respect, it is worth remarking that when newspaper photos illustrate wars and other disasters with an individual victim, often as not it is the grieving woman who performs this synechdochal function. Which is to say that the designated figure for collective affliction (mother of the slain, widow or mother of the dead, etc.) is a woman, because the public depiction of her sorrow is deemed somehow more natural, more fitting than would be the image of a sobbing man. There are, of course, subcategories within this trope: mother (from Mater Dolorosa to Mother Courage), widowed wife, lover, and so forth. And while classical and postclassical Western culture has its various male analogues to emblematic figures of loss and mourning, Laing is drawing on a quintessentially modern division of expressive labor, whereby the feminine is privileged as the incarnation of emotional affect and expressivity.

In her notes for this project, Laing remarked on one aspect of it that resonates with other of her works, namely the issue of mediation. Here, it is not the layers of technical, photomechanical, or electronic mediation that separate a given event or situation from its representations, as in *Natural Disasters*, but rather the symbolic articulations by which collective experience is visually embodied: "During the instigation of this project," she recalls, "I considered that we had been through an abrasive political period. Since then, things that were formerly impossible have happened (e.g. Sorry Day), or are back on the agenda (e.g. the Republic). For many, the symbolic gestures of these meaningful events represent an overwhelming experience—they are loaded arrivals after prolonged expectations ruined many times along the way. I think about the symbolic nature of organised events arranged to mark the national psyche. I also think about if these things can manifest practical change."[3] And, as she further remarks, "Somewhere between the spaces of privilege and numbness—there is inexplicable grief that finds form in us when we don't expect it. At times, in proximity to the tragedies of others, a grief that we don't own, elicits its effect upon us. Obtusely, we may feel better, or more in touch with the fact we feel as well as function. But, most likely we will fail to action anything worthily practical to the situation of our response and [its] configuration."[4]

Given the adjective "useless" employed in her title, given too the staged and choreographed aspect of the sequence, *grieving blondes* suggests that like the Greek chorus of classical tragedy, to which Laing has also referred in written notes, what happens in the tragedy can only be remarked and responded to, not materially affected. The surrogacy by which the mass media individualize the catastrophic or traumatic event achieves its effect through the rhetoric (visual or textual) of pathos, the appeal to the emotions that Aristotle, in his *Rhetoric*, distinguished from logos—reason and logic. Pathos also operates on the register of sensation: the spectator "feels" for the victim and is, as we say, "moved" by the representation. Similarly, the orchestration of public sentiment in the media, whether in the service of patriotism and nationalism or in the service of compassion and appeals for aid, attempts (and sometimes succeeds) to galvanize response through emotional appeal. These are what motivate viewers and readers to donate money after a devastating tsunami or to prompt their response to famine or other humanitarian crises.

As a general rule, such direct appeals to the emotions are not part of contemporary-art practice. This was, however, very much an artistic goal in much of the culture of Europe in the eighteenth and nineteenth centuries (think here of Richardson and Dickens in literature, Greuze in painting, and subsequently, countless Victorian depictions of waifs and orphans). This is now the domain of kitsch, and where the mobilizing of pathos has any currency, it is perhaps in the domain of documentary photography.[5] Here, however, it is the considerable professional skill of actresses, able to weep on demand, who mimic the real grief that is a staple of news photography or other "reality-based" representation. In deploying, therefore, the debased currency of sentiment in an artificial sequence of feminine suffering, Laing is aligning, as always, two very different registers of depictions: on one level, the indexical properties of the photographic image, for notwithstanding supplementary makeup, lighting effects, or production in a studio, the women were "really" posed before the camera, were "really" weeping; on another level, the iconic qualities of what these women represent in the cultural imaginary (e.g., "blonde-ness," "whiteness," feminine desirability, etc.). Furthermore, the series prompts questions about the nature of the symbols that figure in mediated depictions of actual grief and actual affliction, especially as the viewer's perception is shaped by his or her own situation, location, and identity. In this respect, one might remark that the spectacle of suffering is in the media subject to the same procedures of commodification that other human drives or emotions are. Last, but by no means least, they return to themes that figure in the collaborative series of 2003 made with Stephen Birch (*between heaven and belonging*, *between a rock and a place with no fish*, and *remembering Babylon #5, #6*, and *#7*) that pivot on what Laing herself describes as "failure," namely, a failure "to action anything worthily practical to the situation."[6] This failure of will or effort, individual or collective, is the designated lot of many progressive intellectuals in Western democracies, and although the tenor of Laing's work is not bleak or despairing, in its entirety, its implications are disturbing, perhaps especially when most visually electrifying.

Nowhere is this effect more gripping than in the photographs that make up the 2006 series *weather*. In this project, Laing returns to her revisionary works on landscape imagery, which are integrated into another set of images made, like *grieving blondes*, in the studio. With respect to the landscape imagery, Laing's journeys for this series included the farming region of the Darling Downs in southeast Queensland and the small fishing town of Eden on the southern coast of New South Wales.[7] In these travels for the project, Laing observed comparable economic as well environmental circumstances in both regions. Respectively, these included the loss of family farms unable to compete with the pressures of corporate agriculture and long-term drought. On the coast, equivalent difficulties were experienced by local fishermen, affected by industrial fishing and diminished fish stocks.

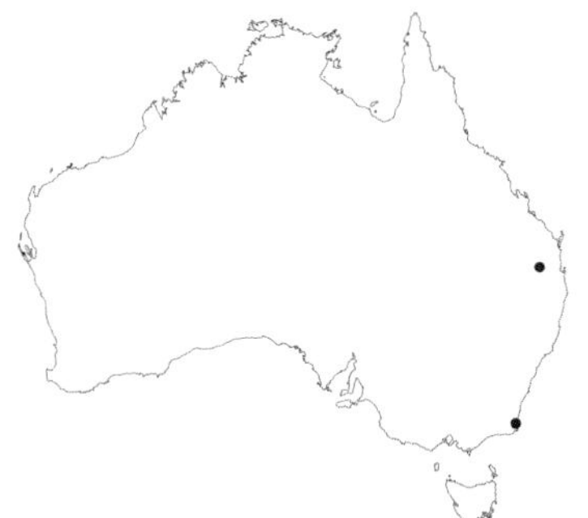

weather (Eden) #1 and *#2*, with their subdued lighting, dominant grays and browns, flattened branches, and dense surface incident, far from inviting imaginative entry to the viewer, induce claustrophobia. The blur of branches, in the dead center of the upper frame and at the far left of *#1*, is the optical sign of wind—indeed of weather. In fact, this landscape and atmosphere are typical of the region's geography and climate, melaleuca-clad headlands shaped by the lashing violent coastal storms leaving in their wake crashed and flattened trunks and branches. The horizontal rhythms produced within their composition move the eye across their surface, but they nevertheless obstruct the fictive entry into the landscape that classical landscape forms invite. But the vivid carmine shape in *#1* that leaps from the surface (a fishing net) links it symbolically to the fishing communities that are part of the larger regional economy. In his discussion of *weather (Eden) #1* and *#2*, Wayne Tunnicliffe indicates some of the site's particularities: "Eden was one of the most important whaling centres in NSW, one in which a truly edenic landscape was the site of belching whale blubber and meat processing works, and the bay would be rinsed red with blood during a kill. After dispossession, the local Thawa Aboriginal people were primarily employed in the whaling industry.... Eden is a beautiful, decaying and scarred location (which has echoes in many places around the world), haunted by this past and trying to find an economic future through a now unsustainable fishing industry."[8]

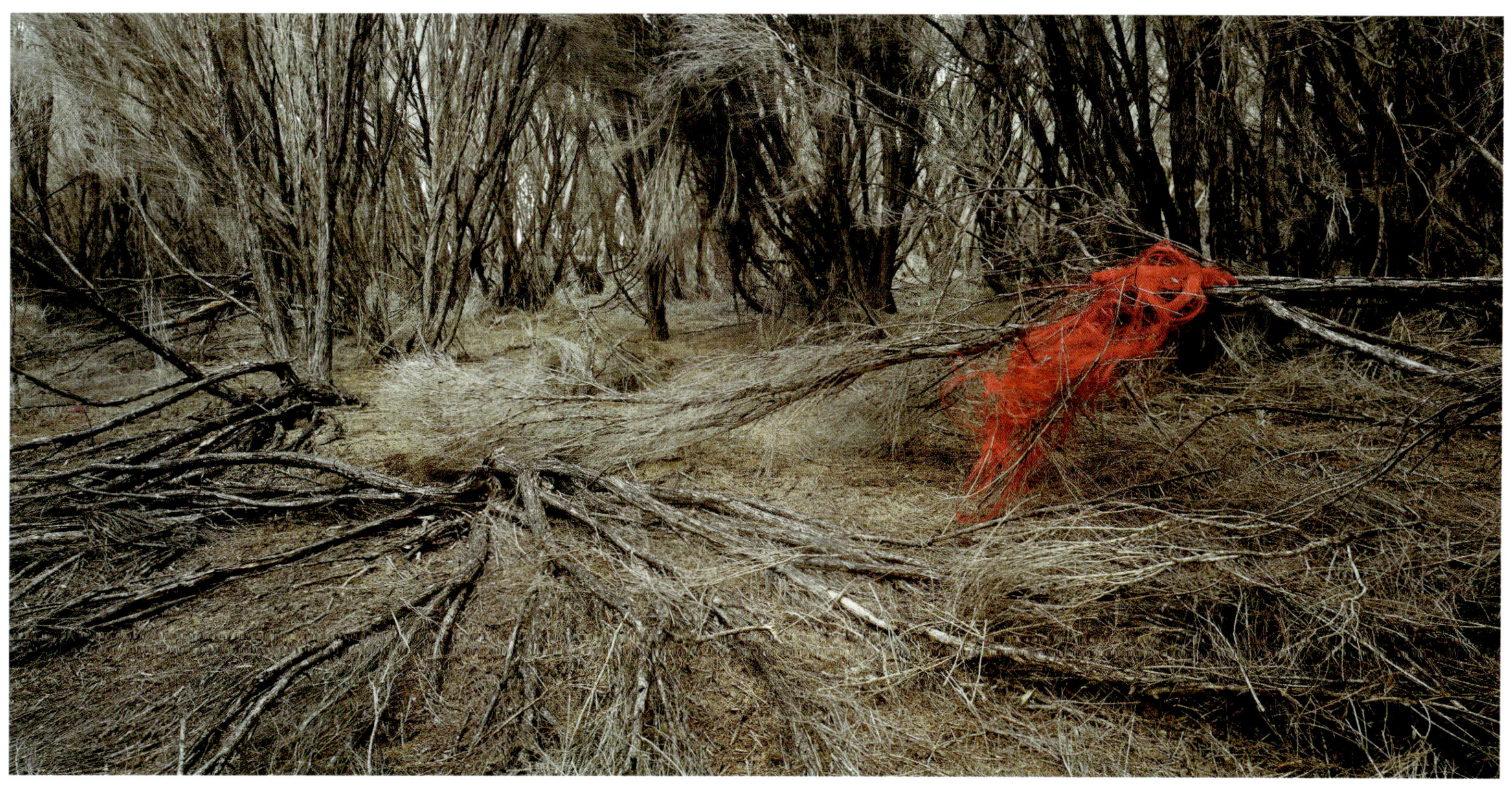

weather (Eden) #1, 2006 (page 142)

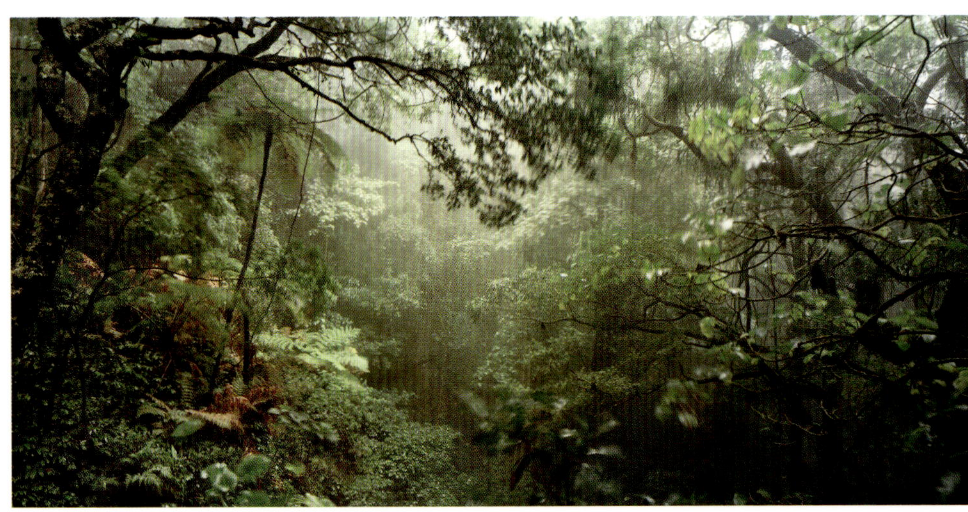

weather (Paradise falls) #14, 2006–07 (page 152)

It is only in *weather (Paradise falls) #14*, made in the Bunya Mountains on the northern boundary of the Darling Downs, where the composition of the forest space approaches—barely—the conventions of landscape. But even as it registers the living green of foliage (interrupted on the left with a reddish brown of dead leaves), the view is muted by a scrim of drenching rain. Framed left and right by the diagonals of arching branches, the composition positions the viewer above the ground, below the treetops, but in an uncertain relation to the depicted forest, spatially ungrounded, with only a shallow space with which to penetrate the lateral expanse. The Bunya Mountains still retain a vestige of this depicted dense subtropical vegetation.

Belying their place names, three pictures in the series, *weather (Eden) #1* and *#2*, and *weather (Paradise falls) #14*, are not particularly Edenic. Laing's titles were suggested not only by the actual name of the places Eden and Paradise Falls, but also for their allusion to her own earlier *from Paradise work* (1990–92).

Where "weather" in these photographs is given visual form in its empirical and atmospheric senses, it is in the studio photographs that it is given metaphoric expression. Violently tossed in a confetti-like blizzard of multicolored paper scraps, a generic female figure (again the stuntwoman Gillian Statham) tumbles helplessly against an undifferentiated gray background. Dressed in a shift-like garment, nonspecific to time or place, she is hurled or propelled in various directions. In maelstrom-like gusts of paper flutter, she tumbles sideways, upside down, and—in one strikingly surreal image—is suspended vertically in empty space, facing away from the viewer, like a limp rag doll, weightless in a void.

In her notes on the project, Laing emphasizes that neither the weather of the landscapes nor that of the simulated cyclone in the studio are limited to metaphors of climate change or particular weather events. "It isn't really about literal weather. This weather doesn't speak simplistically to an outcome of natural weather systems; we create 'weather' that was once the uncontrollable external force (of say, my 1988 series *Natural Disasters*). It is this other weather that significantly now affects our daily cultural lives."[9] The "other" weather we create, as Laing indicates, is thus not only the result of fossil fuels, pollution, global warming, and their various destructive effects, but closer to what is meant when we refer to political and social climates, such as those that prevent the implementation of, for example, the Kyoto Accords, the internment of refugees, the abandonment of ideals of social justice, or more broadly still, the

"globalization" whose fallout on lives and lands is as evident in the economy of a
coastal fishing village in New South Wales, as it is say, in a family farm in Queensland.
It is the "weather" that may, in its most hopeful incarnations, facilitate the processes
by which the historical past is directly and however painfully acknowledged and
confronted, and that makes possible the projects of reconciliation, restitution, and
renewal. This "weather" seems progressively infrequent, whether we consider it in
its Australian manifestations or elsewhere, for example in the United States. It is this
far less propitious weather, within which the individual is buffeted by gales without
identifiable origin, in a blitz of synthetic stuff, unmoored, unanchored, ungrounded,
which Laing excels in representing.

If one of the purposes of the Western landscape tradition in its several centuries
of development was to affirm reassuringly the viewer's secure grounding in the world
(the depiction of which reconciles the contradictions of the real), then it seems right
to say that Laing's is a project that rejects or undoes these compensatory projections.
Insofar as she engages with real places on the Australian continent, it is not in the
guise of artist-as-nomad, for whom, as art historian Miwon Kwon has observed, a site
is simply "one place after another." On the contrary, the places that Laing has used for
her own "site-specific" production are those that pertain to the dilemmas of national
and cultural identity beyond the singularity of the individual subject in his or her
location and situation. These are collective dilemmas, and thus most appropriately
the overarching subject for critical—indeed political—art making. In her eponymous
book, Kwon raises these very questions about the imbrication of place, location, and
situation in the making of art. "What would it mean now," she asks, "to sustain the

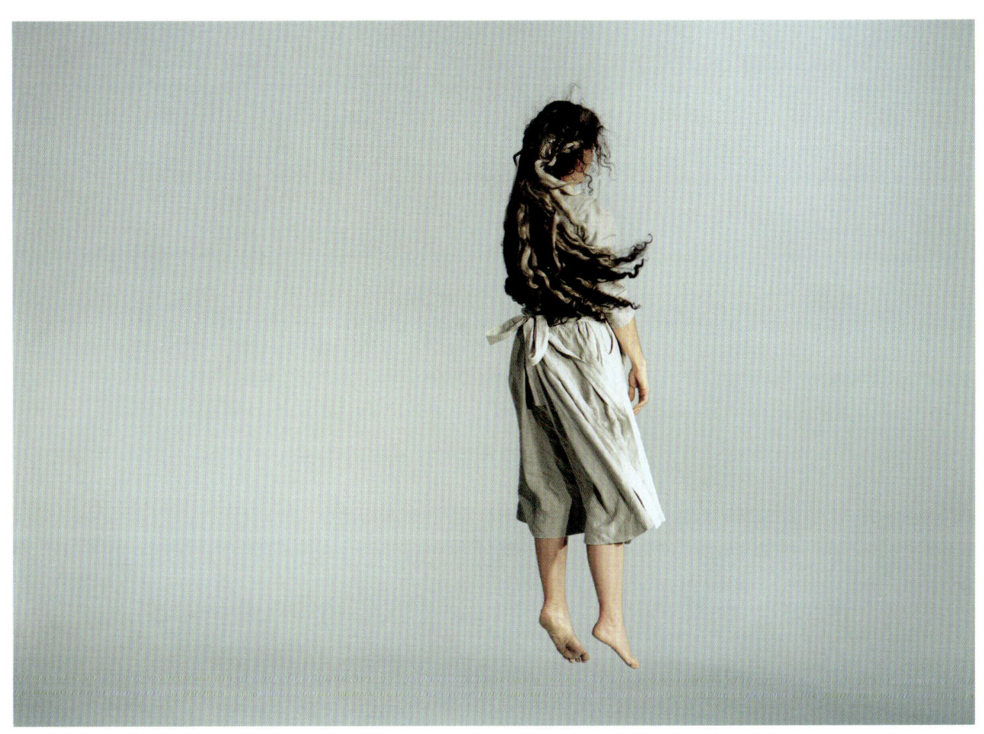

weather #5, 2006 (page 145)

cultural and historical specificity of a place (and self) that is neither a simulacral
pacifier nor a willful invention?"[10] Laing's career-long investigation of the possibilities
of a re-invented landscape photography and its thematic integration with studio-based
photography provides us with an extraordinary body of work that might well be said to
demonstrate what this can be.

Notes

chapter 1

1. Graham Forsyth, "*flight research, spin*," in *Rosemary Laing: A Survey, 1995–2002*, exh. cat. (Brisbane: Brisbane City Art Gallery, 2003), 29.

2. Ibid.

3. Since 1990, all Laing's titles are given in lower case, with the exception of proper names. This decision, like many others that underpin her works, has a feminist, and indeed an ethical, resonance. It rejects the implicit hierarchy of capitalization (where the title dominates the work itself, and declares its relative importance) and suggests a certain humility in how she artistically confronts what are important and historically weighty issues.

4. See the excellent essays on this work by Tanya Peterson, "Hallucinations," in *Rosemary Laing: to walk on a sea of salt*, exh. cat. (Adelaide: Contemporary Art Centre of South Australia, 2008) and Wayne Tunnicliffe, "Rosemary Laing: You can not get past the fence," in Robert Storr, *Think with the Senses, Feel with the Mind*, vol. 3, *Pages in the Wind: A Reader; Texts Chosen by the Artists of the 52nd International Art Exhibition* (Marsilio: La Biennale di Venezia, 2007).

5. See "Parliament of Australia: Senate: Committee: Inquiry into the Migration Act 1958—Report," http://www.aph.gov.au/Senate/committee/legcon_ctte/completed_inquiries/2004-07/Migration/report/d01.htm.

6. Tunnicliffe, "Rosemary Laing," 54.

7. Peterson, "Hallucinations," n.p.

8. Among recent texts on contemporary Aboriginal art, see Michele Grossman, coordinating ed., *Blacklines: Contemporary Critical Writing by Indigenous Australians* (Carlton, Victoria: Melbourne University Press, 2003); see esp. Part II, "Imaging Indigeneity: Art, Aesthetics, Representations," 82–126. Less politically nuanced surveys include Wally Caruana, *Aboriginal Art* (London: Thames & Hudson, 2003) and Susan McCulloch, *McCulloch's Contemporary Aboriginal Art: The Complete Guide* (Carlton, Victoria: McCulloch & McCulloch, 2008).

9. George Alexander, "Rosemary Laing," in *Face Up*, exh. cat. (Berlin: Nationalgalerie im Hamburger Bahnhof, 2003), 103.

10. Paul Virilio, *The Aesthetics of Disappearance*, trans. Philip Beitchman (New York: Semiotext(e), 1991), 81.

11. Australia's history of colonization, settlement, and immigration from the 1780s onward is complex, involving successively (and simultaneously) changing populations arriving from Europe, the Torres Strait and Pacific Islands, Asia, etc., and changing government policies (pre- and post-Federation), including such notorious policies as those associated with the White Australia movement at the time of Federation (1901). In the past decade there have been major controversies around the status of asylum seekers and refugees. See, for example, Mingo MacCallum, "Girt by Sea: Australia, the Refugees, and the Politics of Fear," *Quarterly Essay*, no. 5 (2002). Which is merely to say that issues to do with the politics of demography, origin, race, and ethnicity vastly exceed a simple opposition of White/Aboriginal.

12. The legalization of the doctrine by governmental proclamation occurred in 1835. It held that indigenous Australians had no right to sell or assign land, which could be acquired only by royal distribution. (This decision, however, did not invoke the literal term *terra nullius*.) The Australian High Court's overturning of the doctrine in the epochal 1992 *Mabo* case has not, however, resolved the omnipresent conflicts around titles, land ownership, and land use.

13. Helen Ennis, "Other Histories: Photography and Australia," in *Journal of Art Historiography*, no. 4 (June 2011). See as well her book *Photography and Australia* (London: Reaktion Books, 2007). Historical accounts include Jack Cato, *The Story of the Camera in Australia* (Melbourne: Georgian House, 1955); Gael Newton, *Shades of Light: Photography and Australia 1839–1988* (Canberra: Australian National Gallery and Collins Australia, 1988); Anne-Marie Willis, *Picturing Australia: A History of Photography* (Sydney: Angus & Robertson, 1988).

14. Abigail Solomon-Godeau, "Photography after Art Photography" and "Sexual Difference: Both Sides of the Camera," in Solomon-Godeau, *Photography at the Dock: Essays in Photographic History, Institutions, and Practices* (Minneapolis: University of Minnesota Press, 1992). A very useful summary of the impact of feminism on Australian artists and women artists' embrace of the photographic medium may be found in Bernice Murphy, "Contemporary Photographic Art from Australia," in *Zeitgenössische Fotokunst aus Australien*, exh. cat. (Berlin: NBK, 2000).

15. Vivienne Webb, "Exploring Place," in *The Unquiet Landscapes of Rosemary Laing*, exh. cat. (Sydney: Museum of Contemporary Art, 2005), 7.

chapter 2

1. Ross Gibson, "Camera Natura: Landscape in Australian Feature Films," in *Southern Crossings: Empty Land in the Australian Image* (London: Camerawork, 1992), 33. Cited in Judy Annear, *Photography & Place: Australian Landscape Photography 1970s Until Now*, exh. cat. (Sydney: Art Gallery of New South Wales, 2011), 2.

2. The title of this chapter echoes themes that may be identified in contemporary work by South African artists. See Tamar Garb, Okwui Enwezor, and Ivan Vladislavic, *Home Lands—Land Marks: Contemporary Art from South Africa* (London: Haunch of Venison, 2008). This in turn suggests histories of former colonial nations, especially those involving racial conquest and domination, and reveals parallelisms notwithstanding all the features particular to each history.

3. Ross Gibson, *Seven Versions of an Australian Badland* (Queensland: University of Queensland Press, 2002), 166.

4. One of the most incisive discussions of this art-historical process of "spectacularization" (although it deals exclusively with French landscape art) is Nicholas Green, *The Spectacle of Nature: Landscape and Bourgeois Culture*

in Nineteenth-Century France (Manchester: University of Manchester Press, 1990).

5. As Marcia Langton has observed, the discursive meanings of "wilderness" are themselves part of the colonial project of appropriation and expropriation: "The popular definition of 'wilderness' excludes all human interaction within the allegedly pristine areas, even though they are and have been inhabited and used by indigenous people for thousands of years. Like the legal fiction of *terra nullius* which imagined us [Aboriginal people] out of existence until the High Court decision in the Mabo case, popular culture imagines us out of existence." Even more forcefully, and with respect to current legal battles pitting national-park authorities against Aboriginal claims, she further notes that in at least one legal decision "the Australian use of the term 'wilderness' was a mystification of genocide. Where Aboriginal people had been brought to the brink of annihilation, their former territories were recast as 'wilderness.'" Marcia Langton, "What Do We Mean by 'Wilderness'? Wilderness and Terra Nullius in Australian Art," *The Sydney Papers* 8, no. 1 (1996): 20.

6. See in this respect Elizabeth Johns, ed., *New World Landscapes from Old*, exh. cat. (Canberra: National Gallery of Canberra, 1998).

7. See Vivienne Webb's excellent discussion of Heysen and Cazneaux's iconic images and Laing's revisionary uses of them in Webb, "Exploring Place," in *The Unquiet Landscapes of Rosemary Laing*, exh. cat. (Sydney: Museum of Contemporary Art, 2003).

8. Helen Ennis, *Photography and Australia* (London: Reaktion Books, 2007), 54.

9. Ibid.

10. Rosemary Laing, unpublished studio notes: *greenwork*, c. 1995–96.

11. Ibid.

12. Ibid.

13. See: "Sydney Water," http://www.sydneywater. com.au/Sustainability/OurHeritageAssets/_ item_view.cfm?hi=4572730.

14. See "Shipwrecks NSW," http://www.abc.net. au/backyard/shipwrecks/nsw/default.htm. Wreck Bay, just south of Kiama, received its name in the nineteenth century because of the many shipwrecks that occurred at the site. "So treacherous was this part of the coast that Welbank's *Nautical Almanac* earnestly warned masters of sailing vessels in time of fog or thick weather to keep a good distance off the coast."

15. "The issue which gives immense urgency to our concerns about the future of our ecosystems is the egocentric quality of standard European and American-derived concepts of wilderness. *They all involve the peculiar notion that if one cannot see traces or signs of one's own culture in the land, then the land must be 'natural' or empty of culture. In the context of Australian settlement by Europeans, it does not require a great leap of imagination to realise that the concept of terra nullius (land that was not owned) depended on precisely this egocentric view of landscape.* Not seeing the signs of ownership and property to which they were accustomed, many settlers assumed that there was no ownership and property, and that the landscapes were natural."

Deborah Bird Rose, *Nourishing Terrains: Australian Aboriginal Views of Landscape and Wilderness* (Australian Heritage Commission, 2001), 17 (emphasis added).

16. George Alexander, "*groundspeed*," in *Rosemary Laing: A Survey, 1995–2002*, exh. cat. (Brisbane: Brisbane City Gallery, 2003), 39.

17. Judy Annear's excellent essay on Australian landscape photography parallels much of my own discussion. Her essay also discusses twenty other contemporary artists for whom place functions as a central motif. See Annear, *Photography & Place*.

18. Rosemary Laing, personal communication with the author.

19. From the Cultural Survival website, http:// www.culturalsurvival.org/australia?gclid=CL6_ kf-grqwCFQULfAod6zcMHg). "Under several federal and state programs that continued into the 1970s, the government forcibly removed Aboriginal children from their families and sent them to white families and church-run institutions for cultural reprogramming. A recent national report on the policies found that there was not a single Indigenous family that did not have at least one child taken away…. The new administration [the Labor government elected in 2008] also reversed the country's opposition to the UN Declaration on the Rights of Indigenous People."

20. George Alexander, "Post Natural Nature: Rosemary Laing," *Artlink* 21, no. 4 (2001): 23.

21. See the series *one dozen unnatural disasters in the Australian landscape* (2003) and the individual works *between a rock and a place with no fish*, a collaboration with Stephen Birch (2003) and *remembering Babylon #5, a collaboration with Stephen Birch* (2003), respectively. See also Wayne Tunnicliffe, *one dozen unnatural disasters: a collaboration with Stephen Birch*, exh. cat. (Sydney: Grant Pirrie Gallery, 2005).

22. In late October 2011, Queen Elizabeth II of England traveled to Australia for an eleven-day tour. In news media much was made of the fact that the Australian Prime Minister, Julia Gillard, bowed and shook the Queen's hand upon meeting her, instead of performing the traditional curtsey. See, for example, Megan Levy, "No Backing Down for Gillard in Royal Bow Row," *Sydney Morning Herald online*, http://www.smh.com.au/national/no-backing-down-for-gillard-in-royal-bow-row-20111020-1m90i.html#ixzz1dwhU93IA.

23. Rosemary Laing, unpublished studio notes: *flight research*, c. 2001–02.

24. Rosemary Laing, unpublished studio notes: *leak*, c. 2010–11.

25. Europeans began settlements in this area in the 1820s; within twenty years there were 2,000 people, 500,000 sheep, and 50,000 cattle.

26. Samantha Littley, "Rosemary Laing: The Moving Image," in *New Volume 2: Selected Recent Acquisitions 2009–2011* (Brisbane: University of Queensland Art Museum), 2012.

27. Ibid., unpag. at the time of this writing.

28. Robert Nelson, "World Turned Upside Down," *The Age*, March 2, 2011, 21.

29. Ibid.

chapter 3

1. David Malouf, *Remembering Babylon* (London: Vintage, 1994), 8.
2. Rosemary Laing, personal communication with the author.
3. "Cyclone Tracy struck the city of Darwin in the Northern Territory. One hundred and ninety-five millimetres of rain fell in less than nine hours, and winds of around 250 km per hour flattened the city. In terms of damage to a community, Cyclone Tracy remains Australia's most destructive for property damage. 71 people were killed and many thousands injured. Of a population of 43,000, 25,000 were left homeless." http://australia.gov.au/about-australia/australian-story/natural-disasters.
4. Balgo Hills (Wirrimanu) Art and Community Online, http://www.aboriginalartonline.com/regions/balgo.php.
5. *A Piece of the Story: National Directory of Records of Catholic Organisations Caring for Children Separated from Families* (Curtin, Australian Capital Territory: Australian Catholic Social Welfare Commission, 1999), 126.
6. Rosemary Laing, unpublished studio notes: *one dozen unnatural disasters in the Australian landscape*, c. 2003–04.
7. George Alexander, "Rosemary Laing," in ed. Penelope Curtin, *2004 Adelaide Biennial of Australian Art: Contemporary Photomedia*, exh. cat. (Adelaide: Art Gallery of South Australia, 2004), 22.
8. Ibid.

chapter 4

1. Gibson, *Seven Versions of an Australian Badland*, 158.
2. Anna Sansom, "Rosemary Laing: a dozen useless actions for grieving blondes," *Eyemazing*, no. 3 (2009): 20.
3. Rosemary Laing, unpublished studio notes: *a dozen useless actions for grieving blondes*, c. 2008.
4. Ibid.
5. This is something of an oversimplification, and there is, in fact, a body of serious art criticism that argues for the uses of empathic identification in artistic production, primarily with respect to the representation of historical trauma. This turns less on the rhetoric of pathos, and more on the mechanisms of visceral and affective identification and response. Such arguments inform Jill Bennett's thoughtful study *Empathic Vision: Affect, Trauma, and Contemporary Art* (Stanford: Stanford University Press, 2005).
6. Laing, unpublished studio notes: *a dozen useless actions for grieving blondes*, c. 2008.
7. The lands of Darling Downs were seized from the Barunggam, Jarowair, Giabal, and Kienjan Aboriginal peoples during the nineteenth century. The area is of personal significance to Laing, as her family and their descendants have lived and farmed there since the 1850s. See Wayne Tunnicliffe, unpublished text for *weather*, 2006. Certain aspects of the history of the Darling Downs feature in Andrew McGahan, *The White Earth* (New York: Soho Books, 2006).
8. Tunnicliffe, unpublished text for *weather*.
9. Rosemary Laing, unpublished studio notes: *weather*, c. 2005–06.
10. Miwon Kwon, "One Place after Another: Notes on Site Specificity," *October*, no. 80 (Spring 1997): 109.

plates

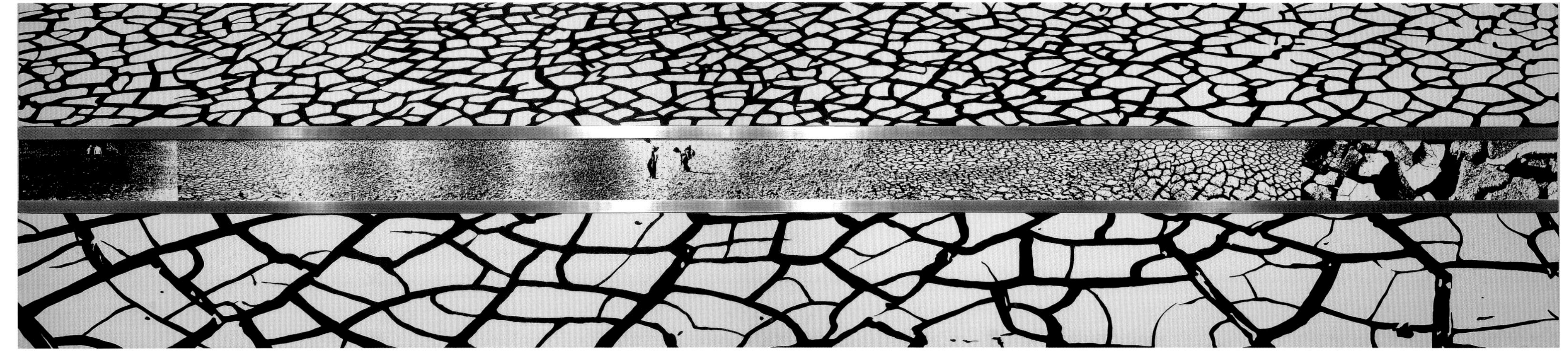

Still glides the stream and shall forever glide (droughts), 1988
Black-and-white photograph, stainless steel, wood, gesso, and acrylic
22 x 102⅜ x 1⅝ in. (56 x 260 x 4 cm)

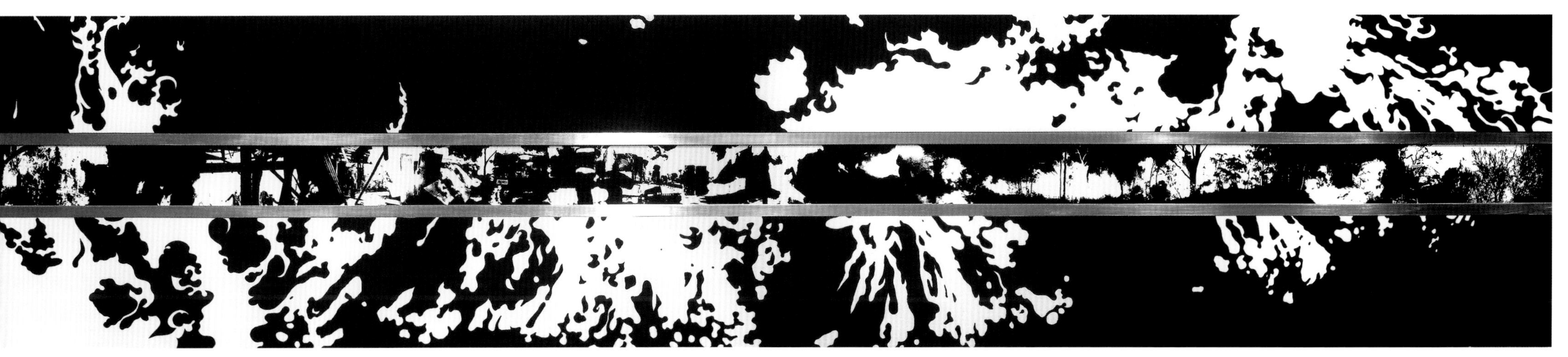

How we lost poor Flossie (fires), 1988
Black-and-white photograph, stainless steel, wood, gesso, and acrylic
22 x 107⅛ x 1⅝ in. (56 x 272 x 4 cm)

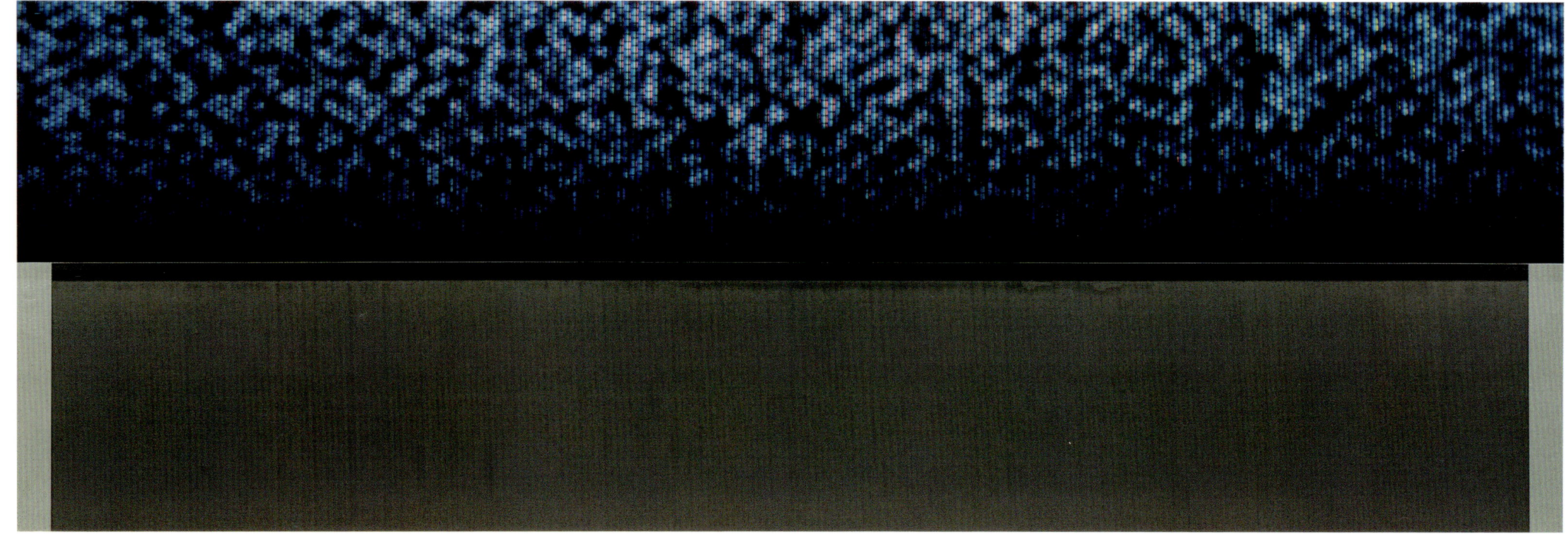

from Paradise work #5, 1991
Fujichrome, clear and tinted Shinkolite
31½ x 94½ x 3⅞ in. (80 x 240 x 10 cm)

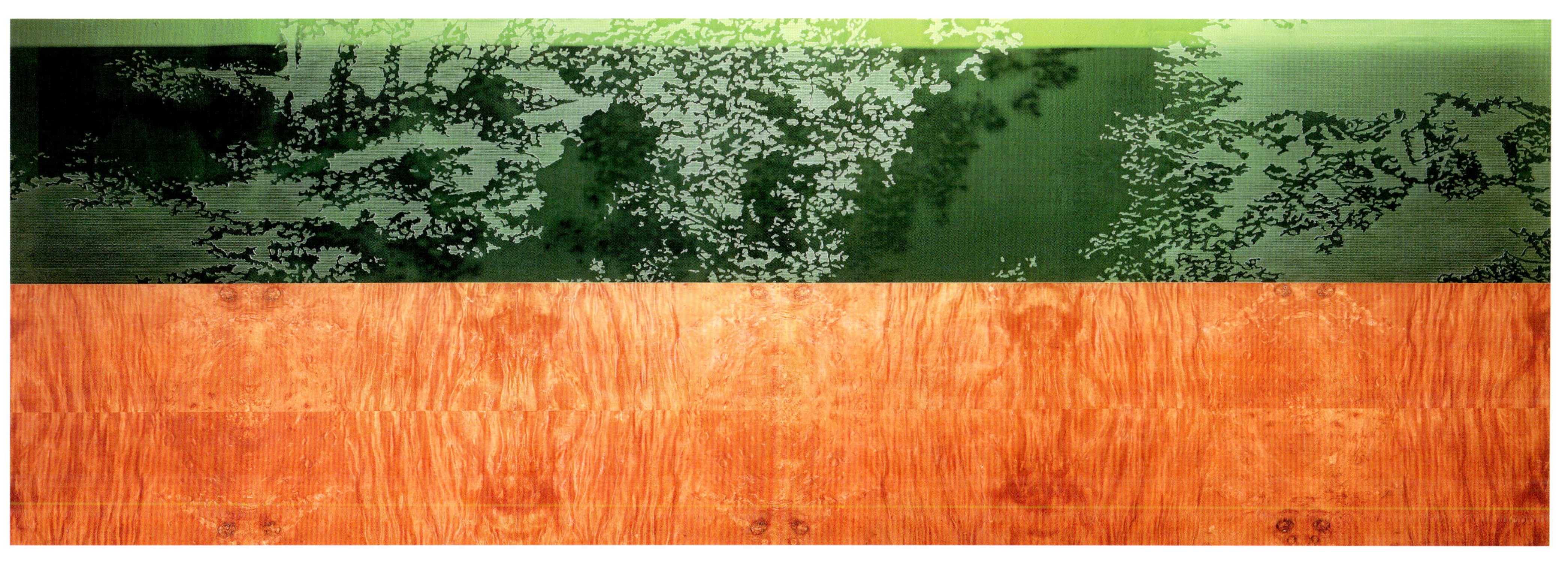

from Paradise work #4, 1991
Laser-etched Diaglas and wood veneer
31½ x 94½ x 3⅞ in. (80 x 240 x 10 cm)

Untitled

Untitled, 1992
Cibachromes, Perspex, and machined steel
7⅛ x 210¼ x 3⅞ in. (18 x 534 x 10 cm)

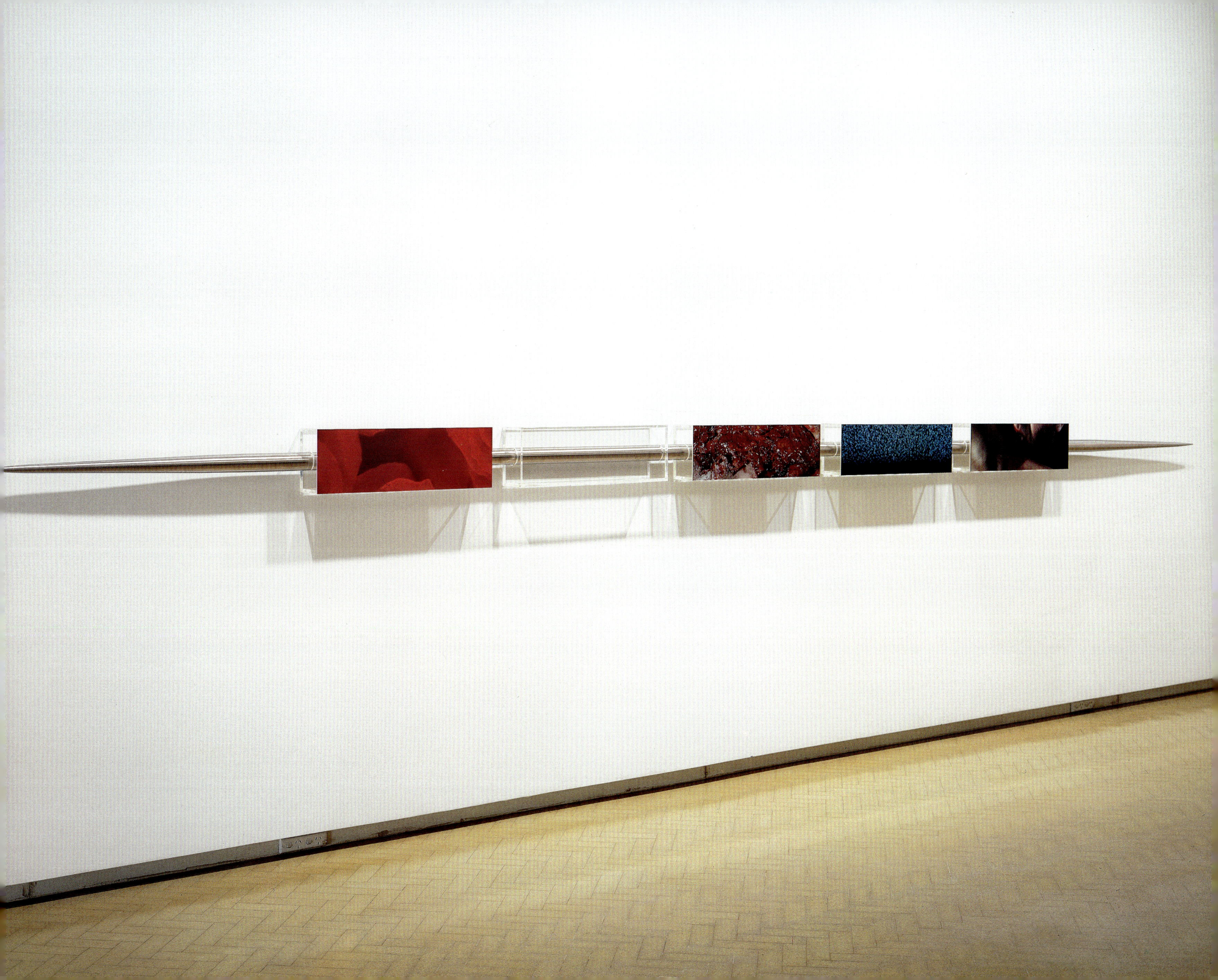

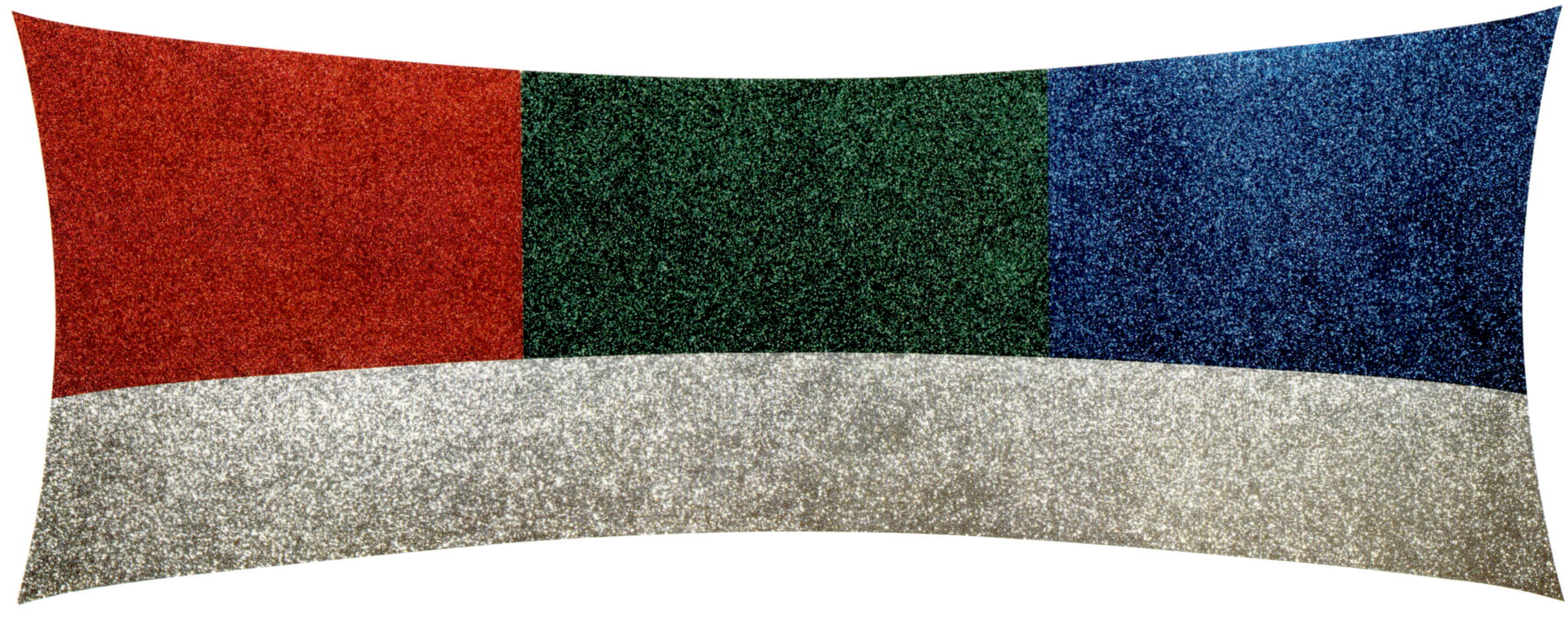

blow-out, 1993
Polyester particles in baked polyurethane, aluminum
37⅜ x 100⅜ x 2 in. (95 x 255 x 5 cm)

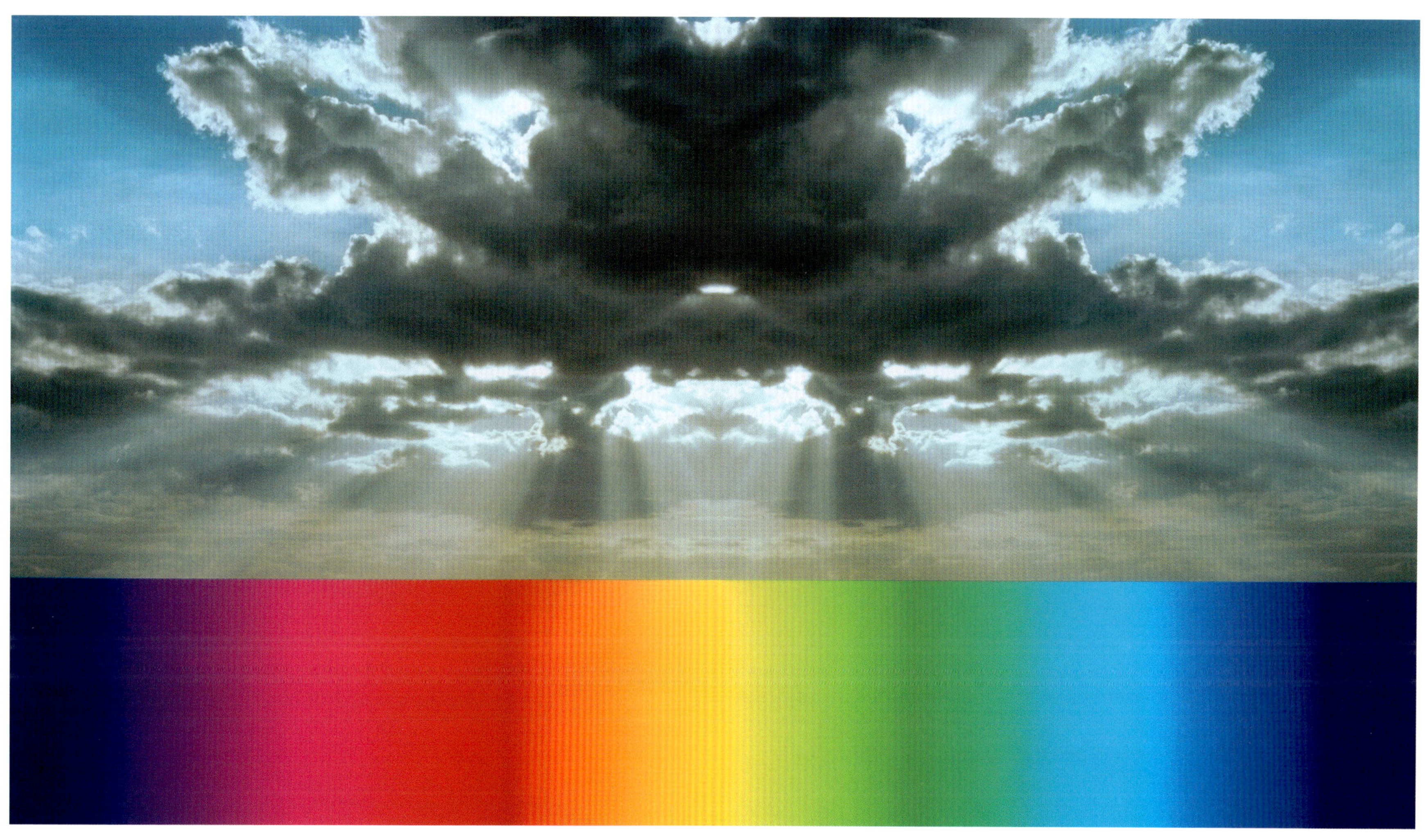

appearance, 1993
Ilfachrome, light box installed inside wall
44⅛ x 78¾ in. (112 x 200 cm)

greenwork, *aerial wall*, 1995
Digital vinyl print
77½ x 116½ in. (197 x 296 cm)

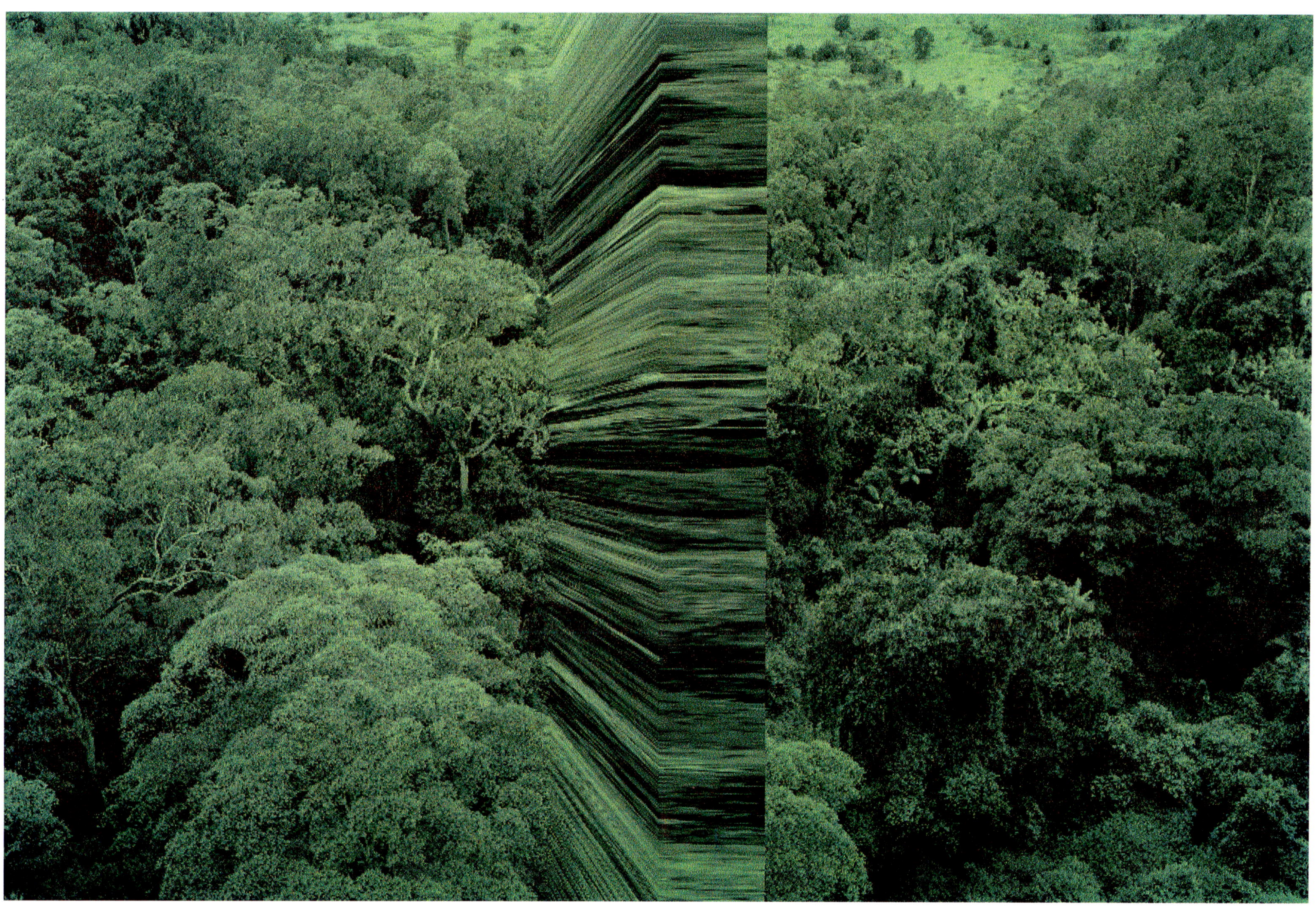

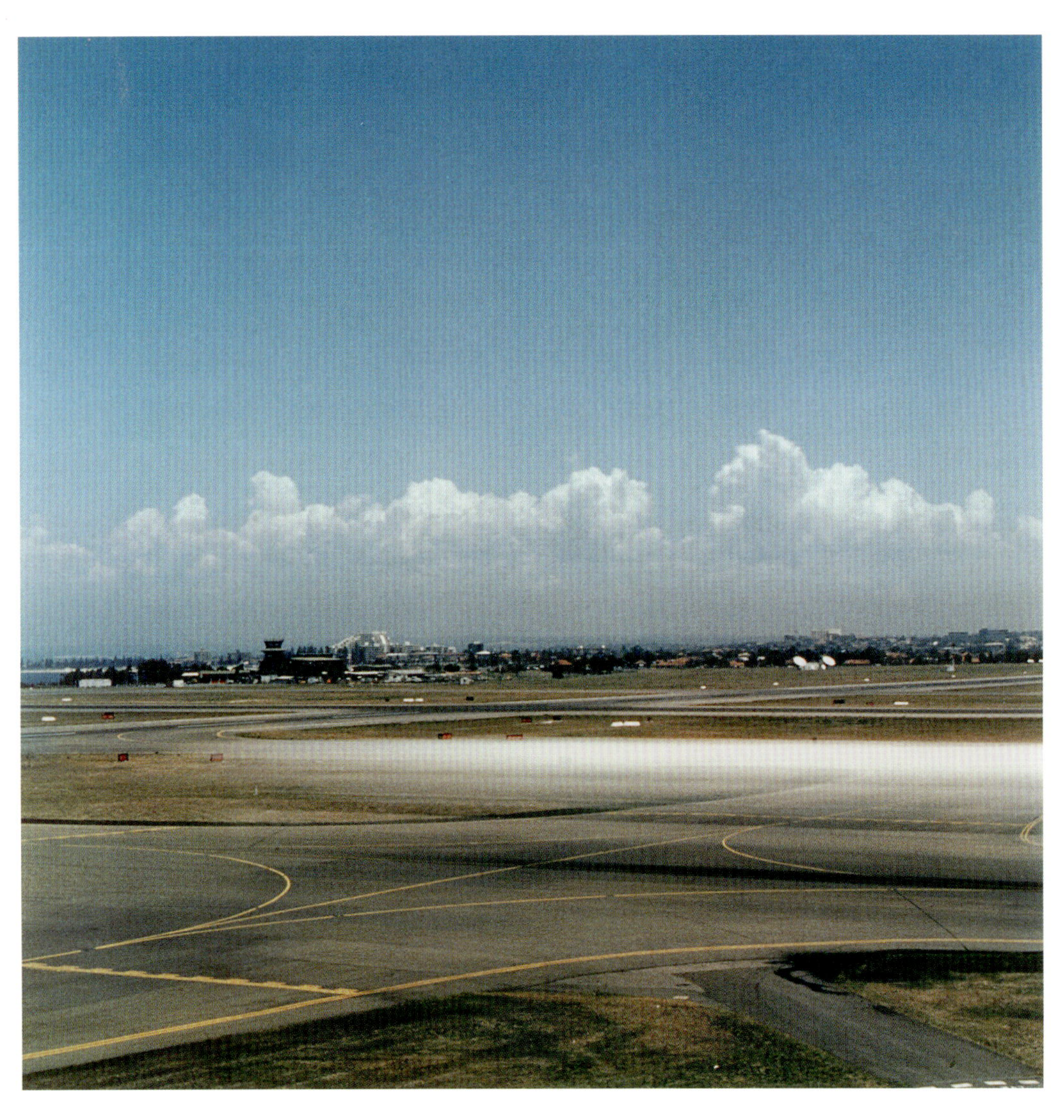

greenwork, TL #2, 1995
39⅜ x 39⅜ in. (100 x 100 cm)

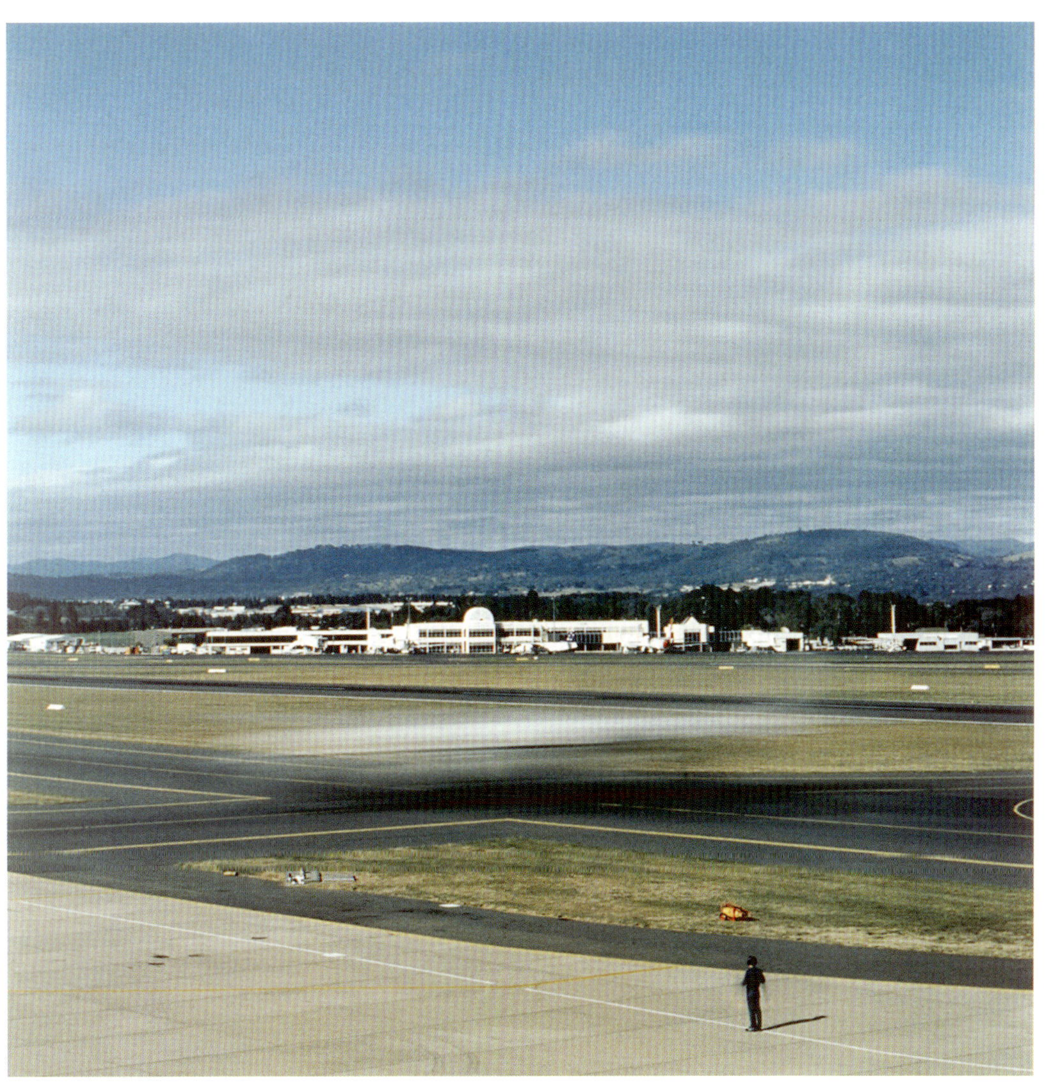

greenwork, TL #3, 1995
39³⁄₈ x 39³⁄₈ in. (100 x 100 cm)

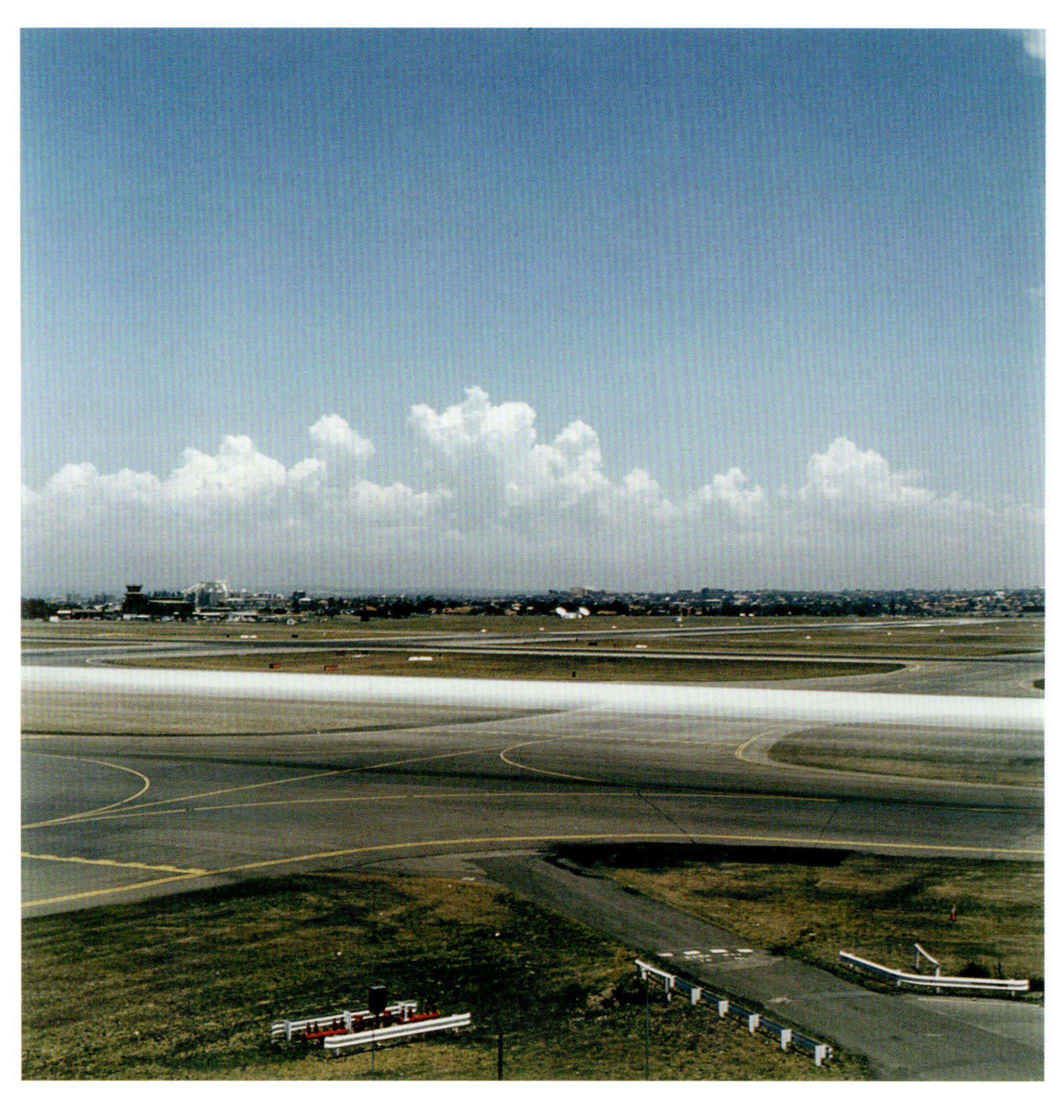

greenwork, TL #5, 1995
39⅜ x 39⅜ in. (100 x 100 cm)

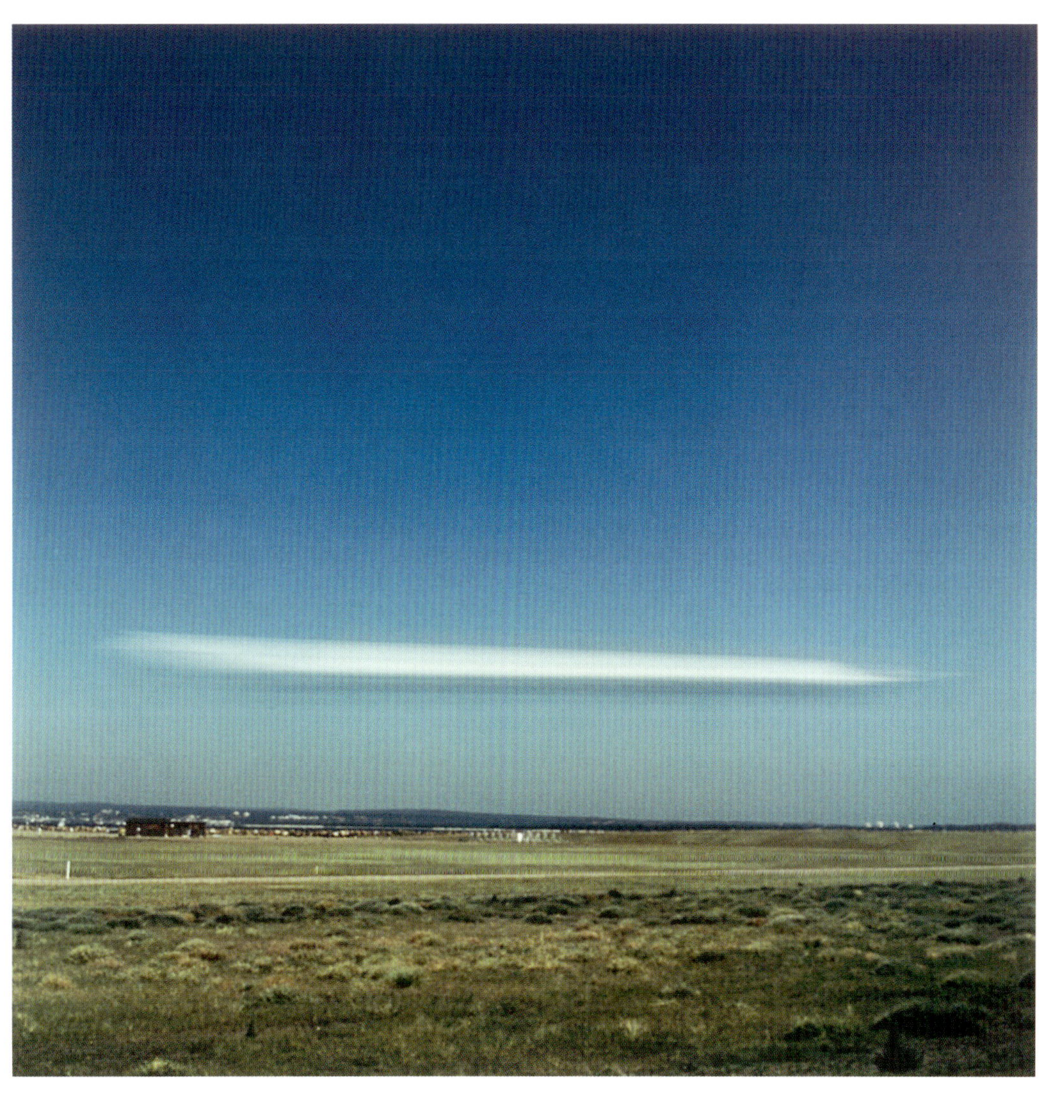

greenwork, TL #8, 1995
39³⁄₈ x 39³⁄₈ in. (100 x 100 cm)

brownwork #1, 1996
Duraflex photograph
47¼ x 96½ in. (120 x 245 cm)

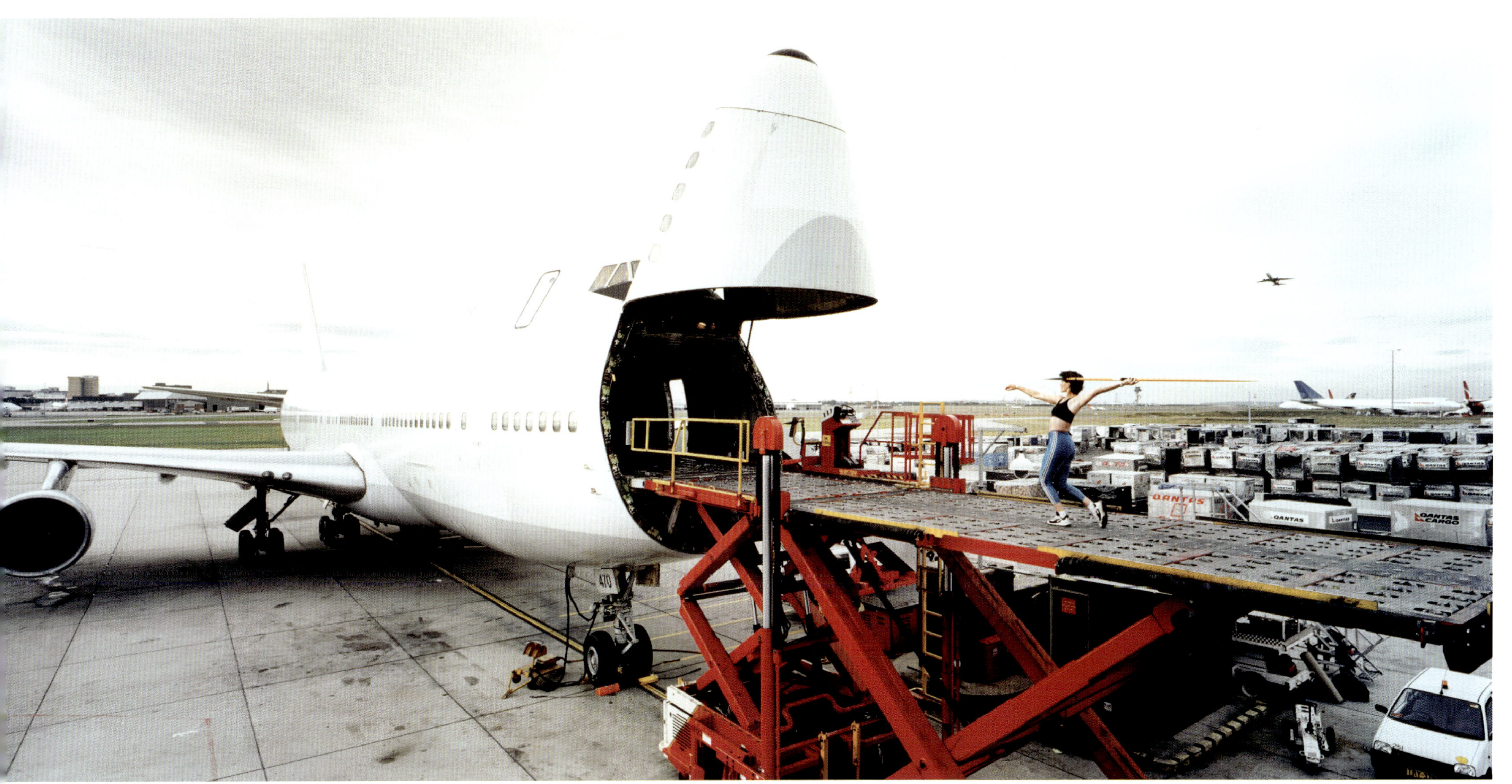

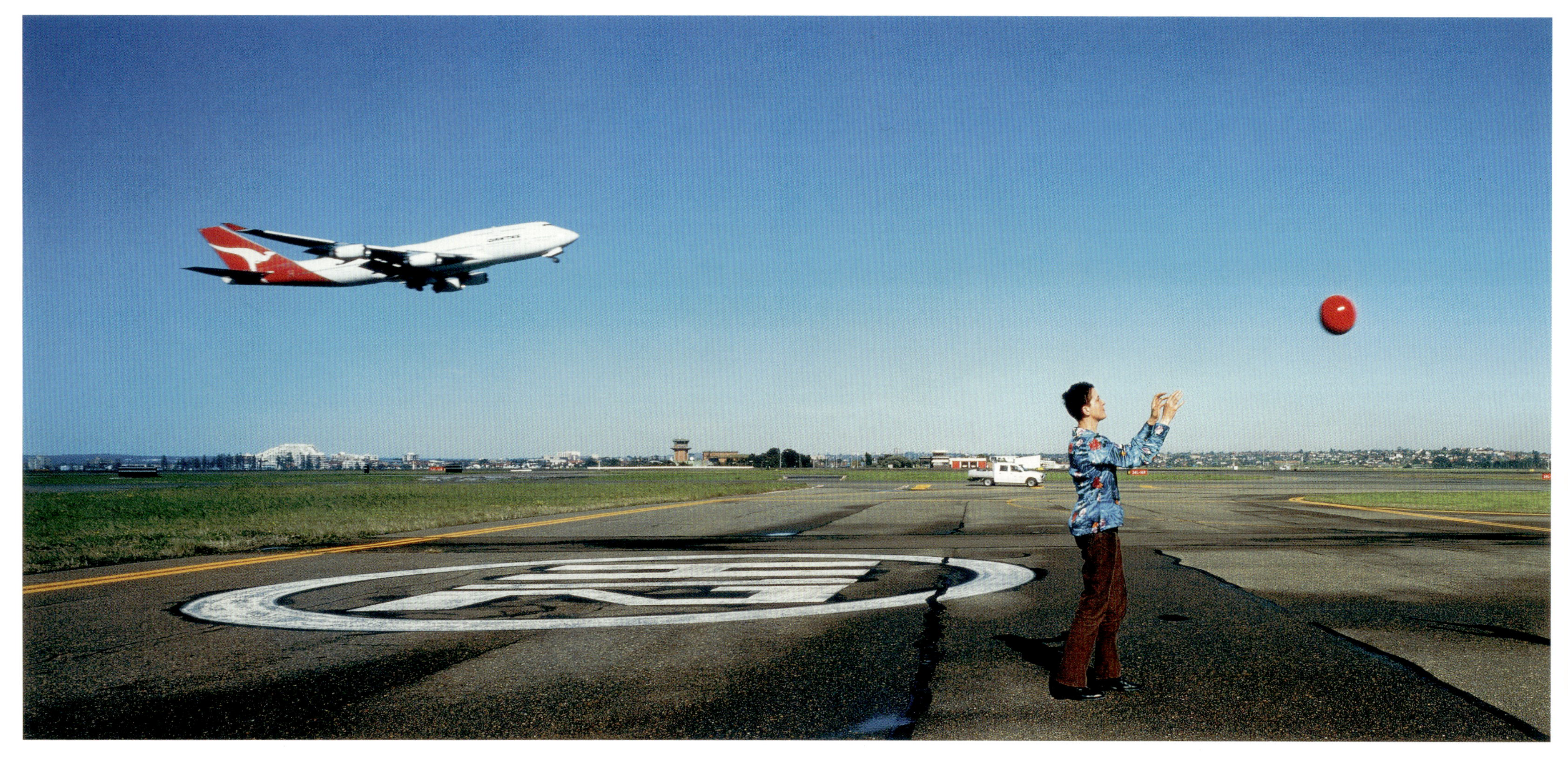

airport #2, 1997
46½ x 102 in. (118 x 259 cm)

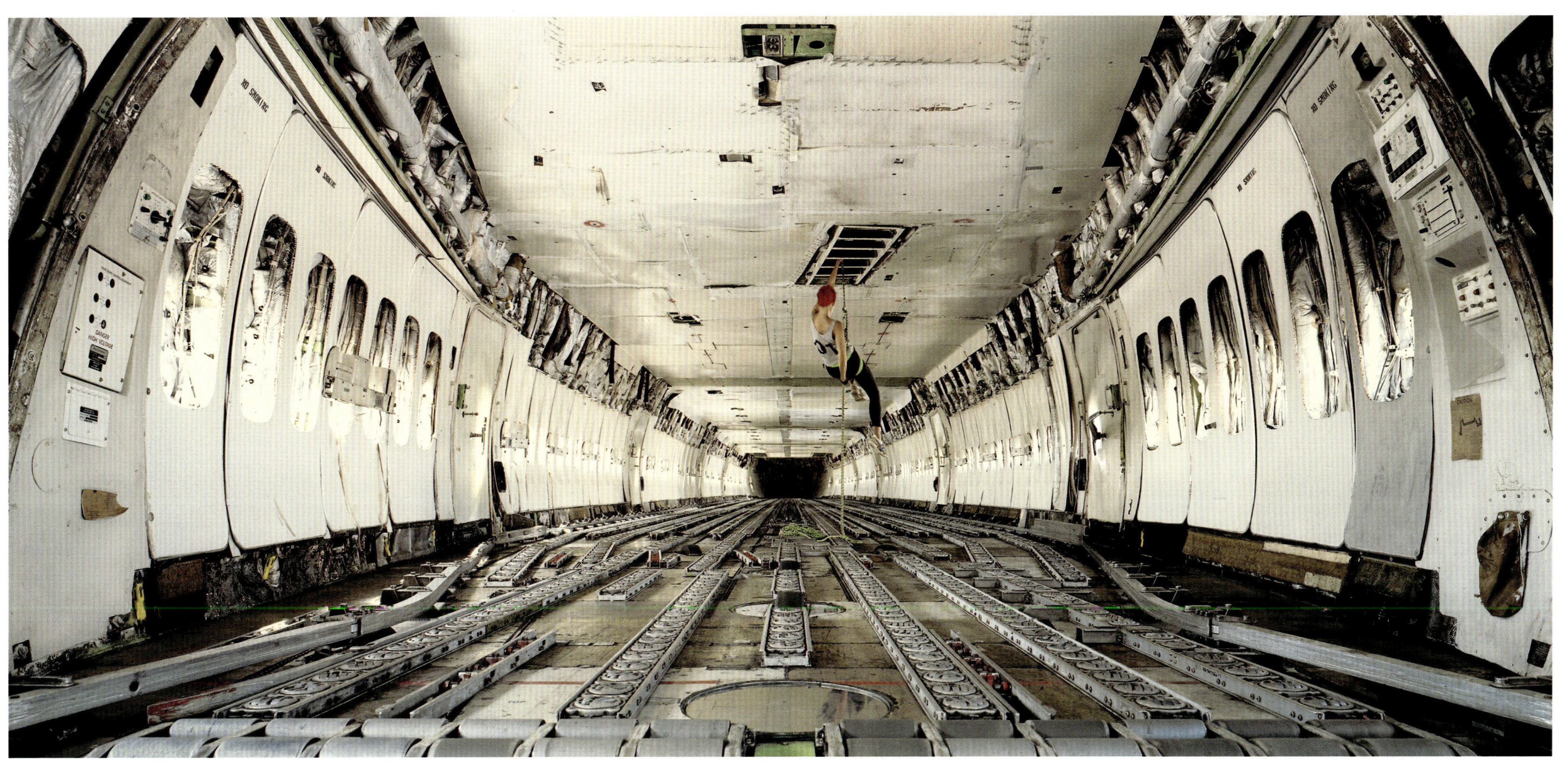

brownwork #9, 1997
46½ x 100 in. (118 x 254 cm)

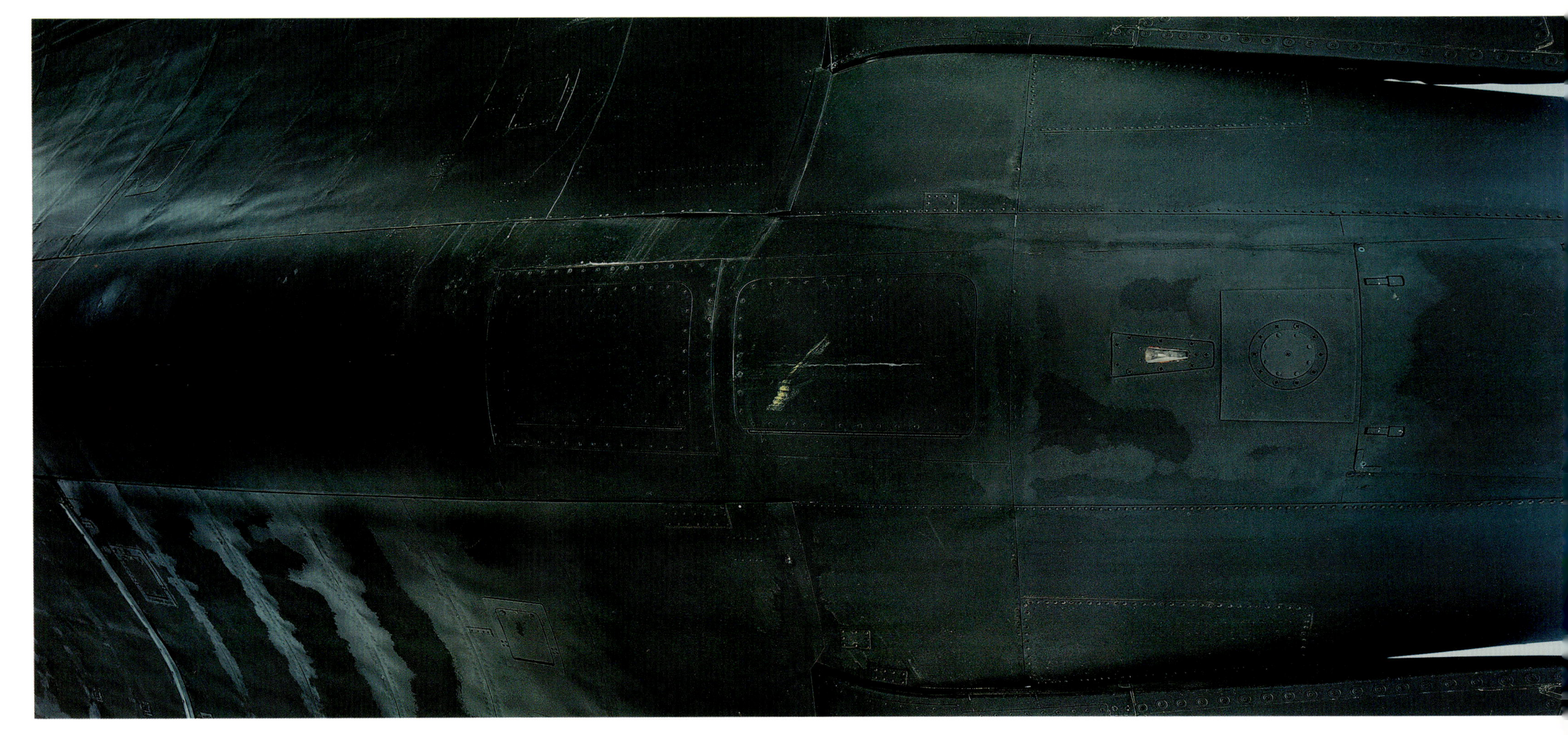

SKUNKWORKS — *Lockheed SR-71 Blackbird*, 1998–9
46½ x 102¾ in. (118 x 261 cr

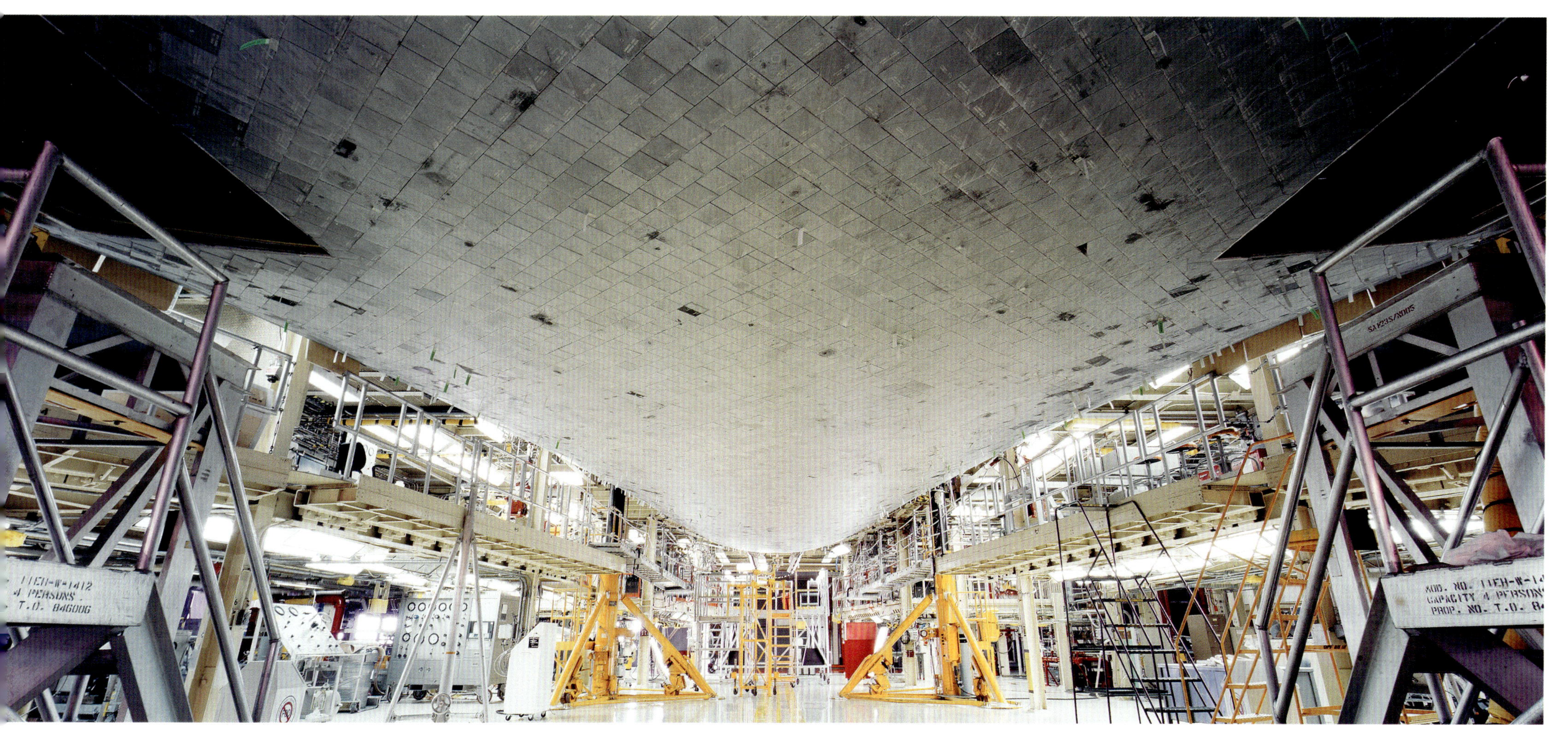

NASA — Kennedy Space Center #1, 1998–99
46½ x 104¾ in. (118 x 266 cm)

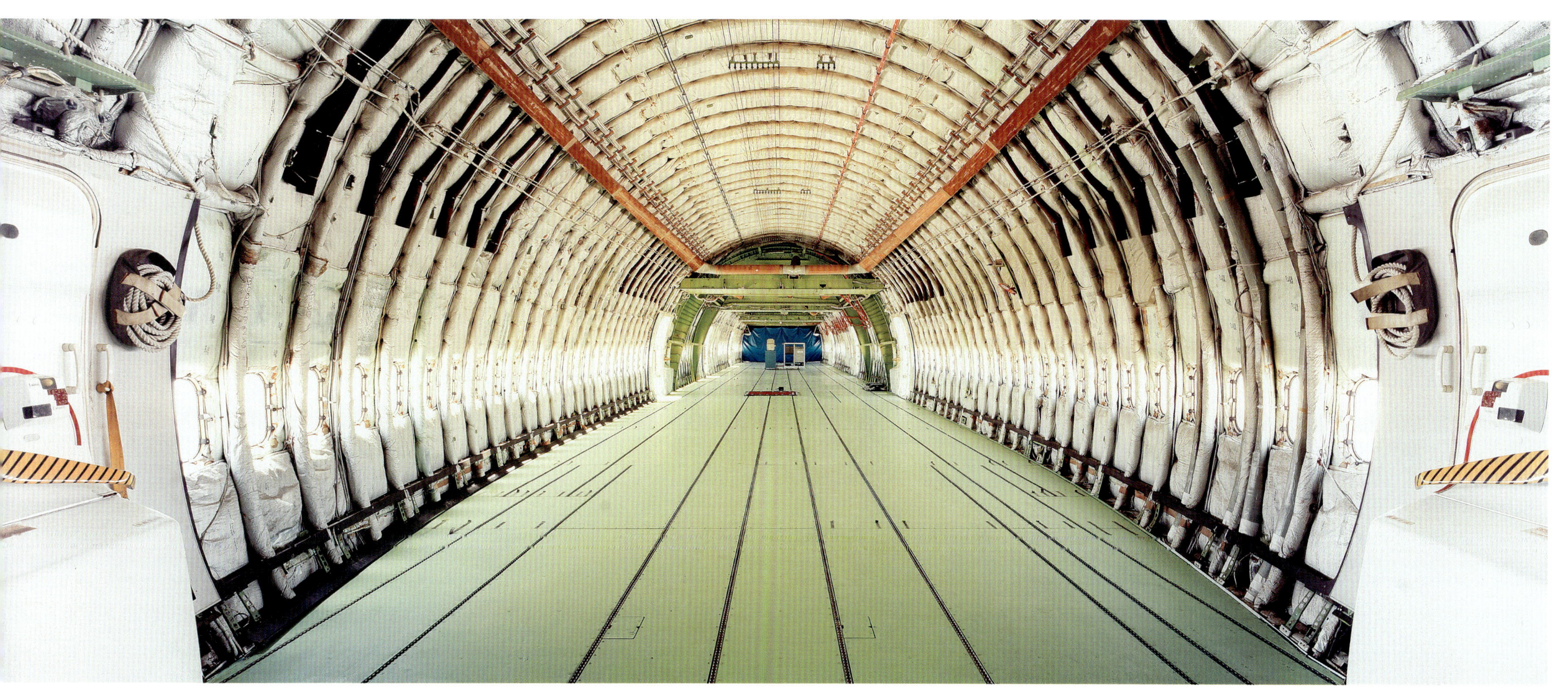

flight research #1, 1998
46½ x 103⅛ in. (118 x 262 cm)

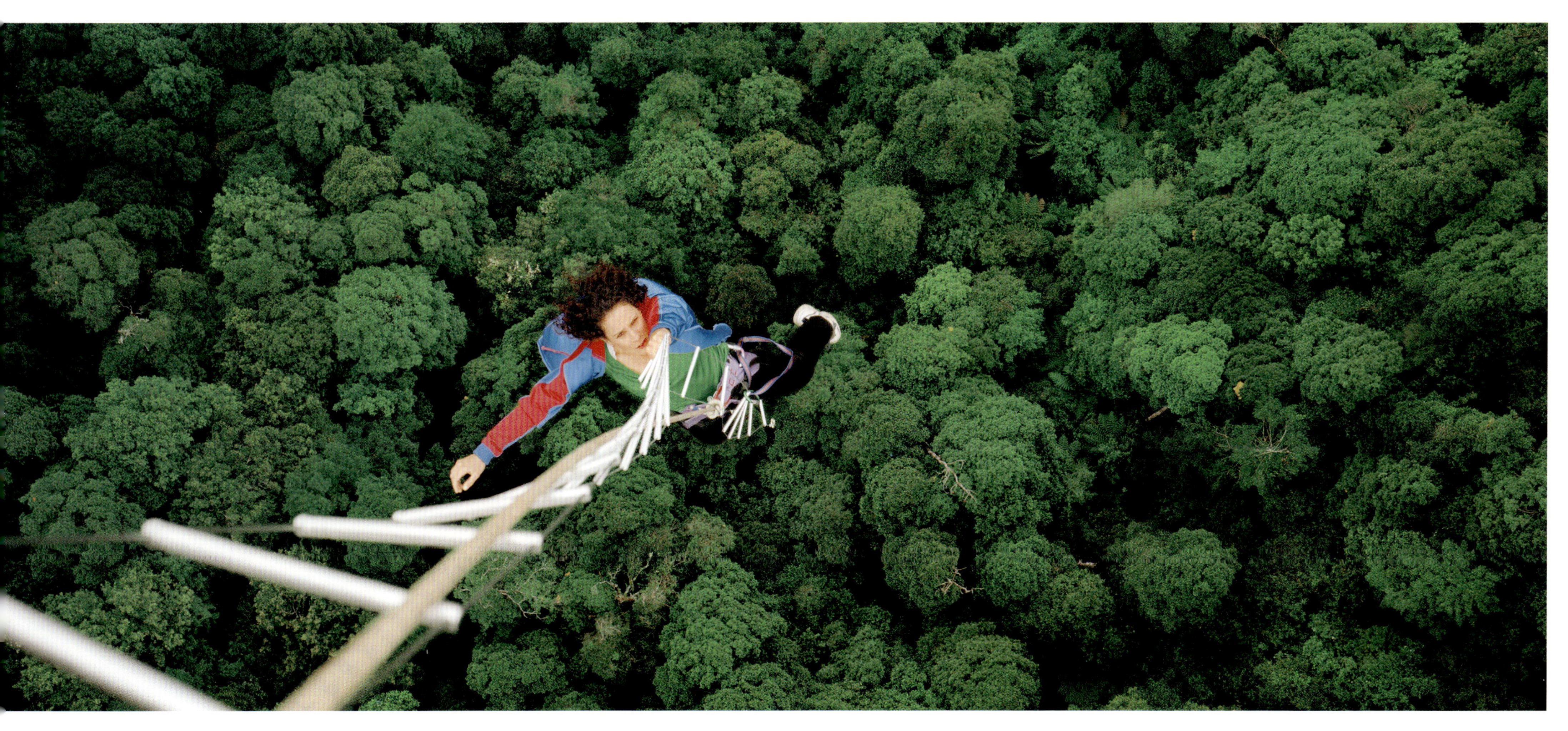

flight research #5, 1999
42⅛ x 94½ in. (107 x 240 cm)

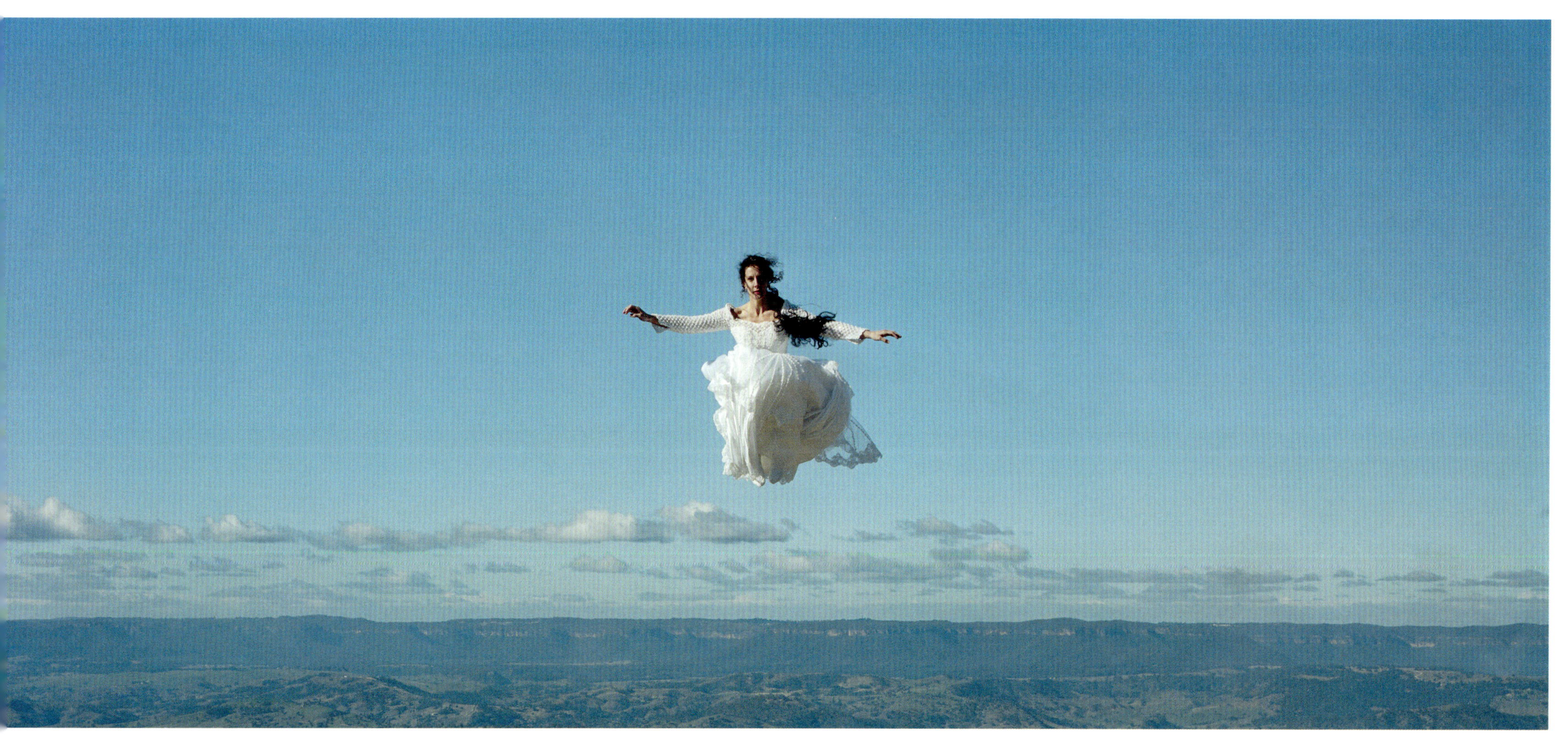

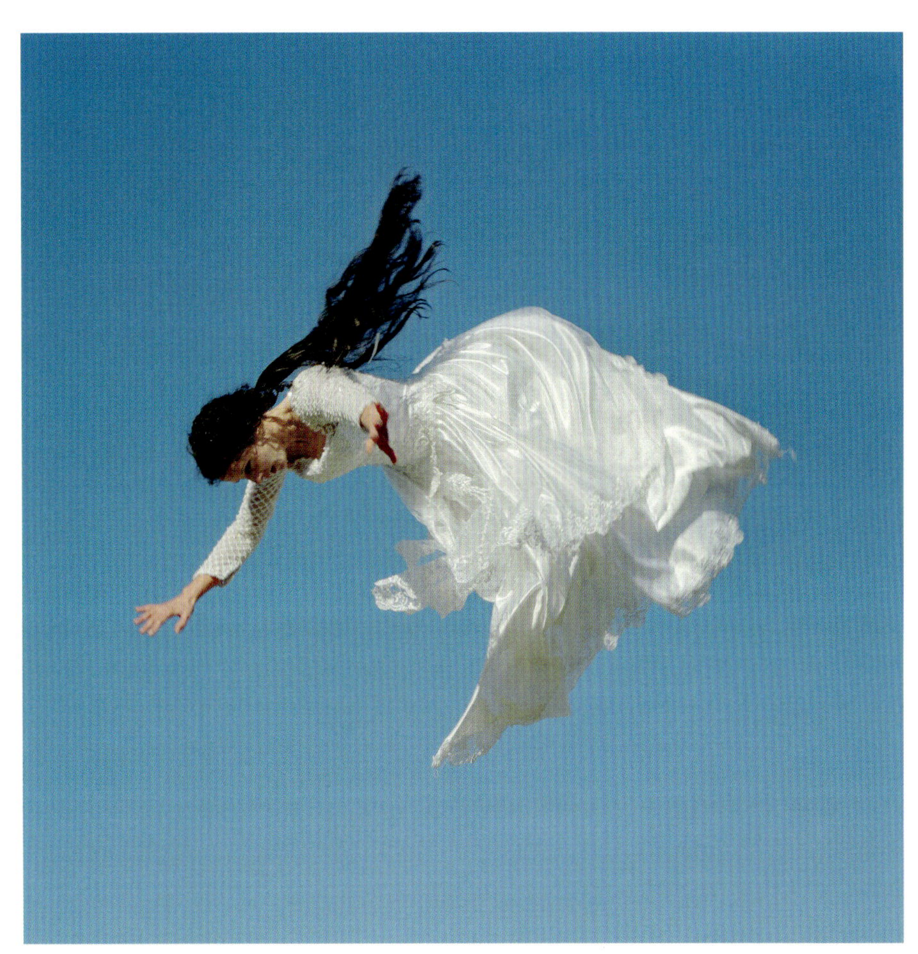

flight research #2b, 1999
31½ x 31½ in. (80 x 80 cm)

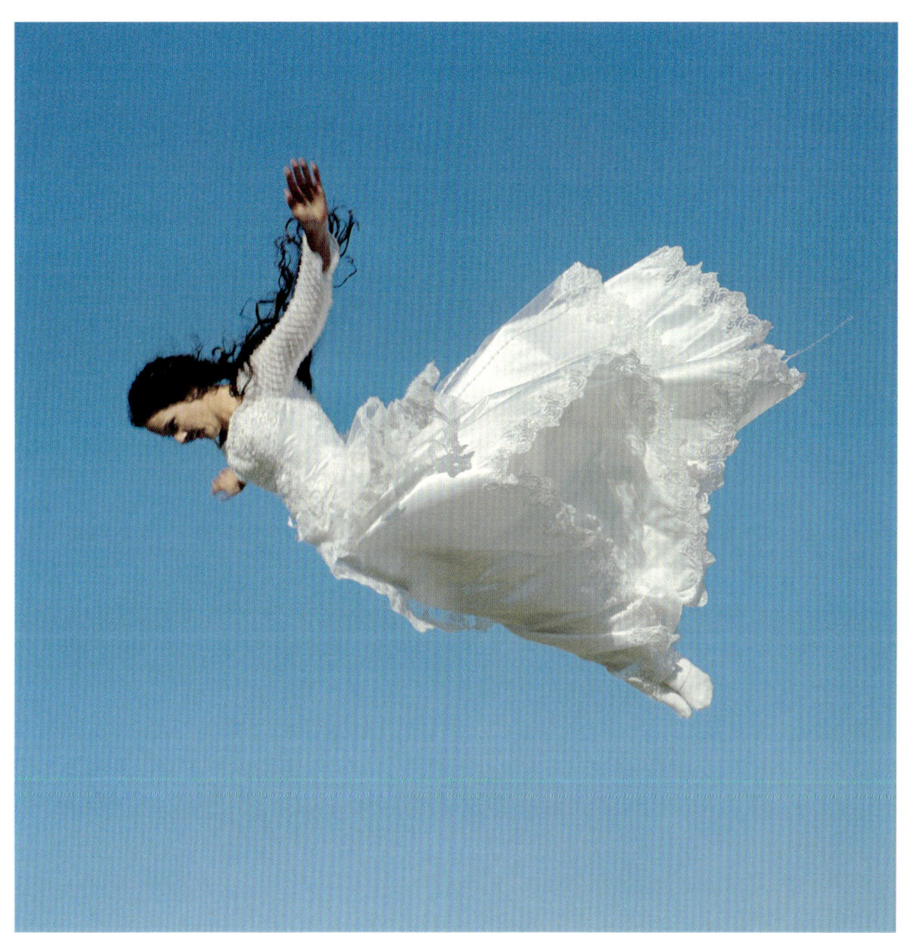

flight research #2a, 1999
31½ x 31½ in. (80 x 80 cm)

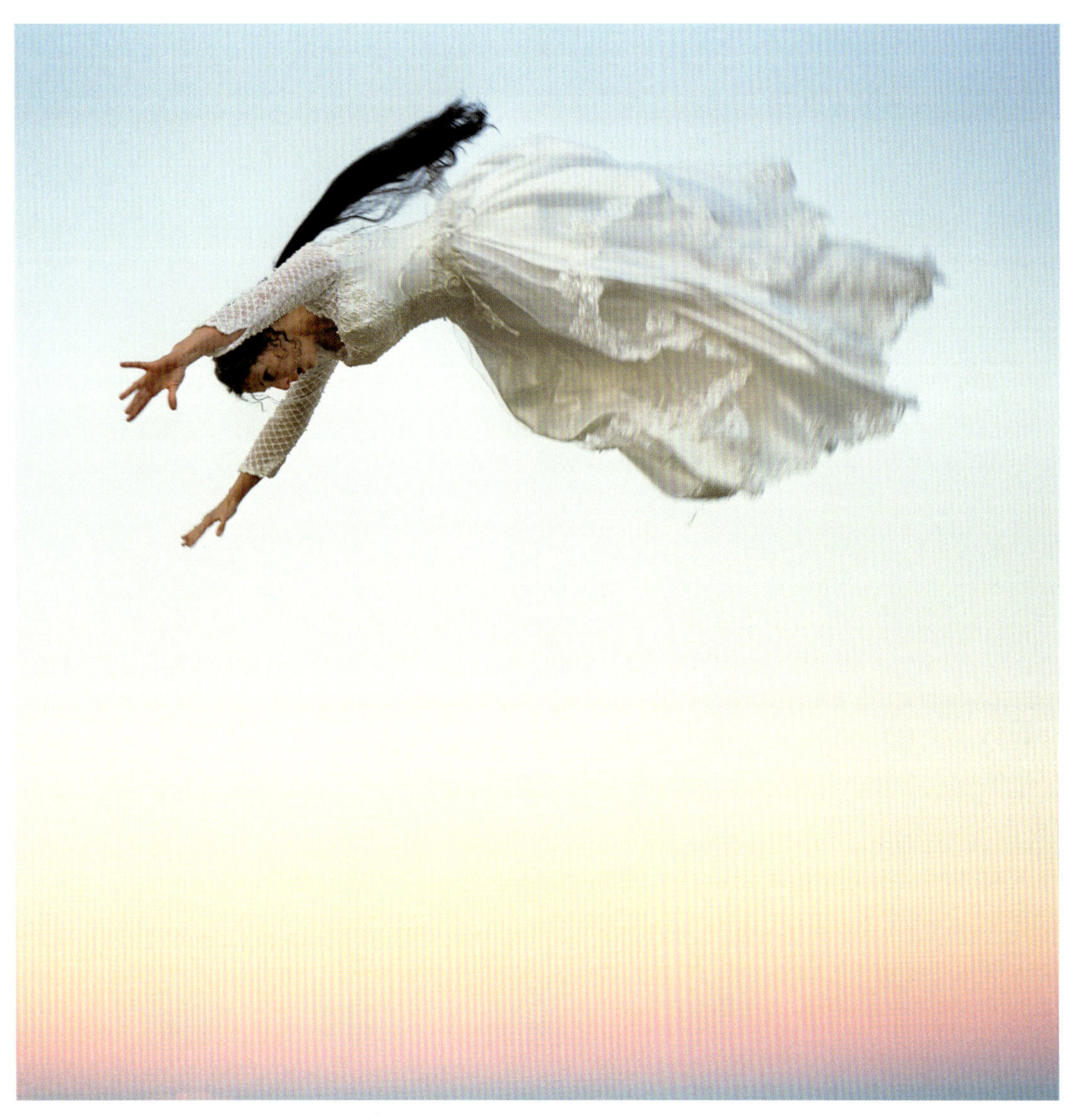

flight research #3, 1999
35⅜ x 35⅜ in. (90 x 90 cm)

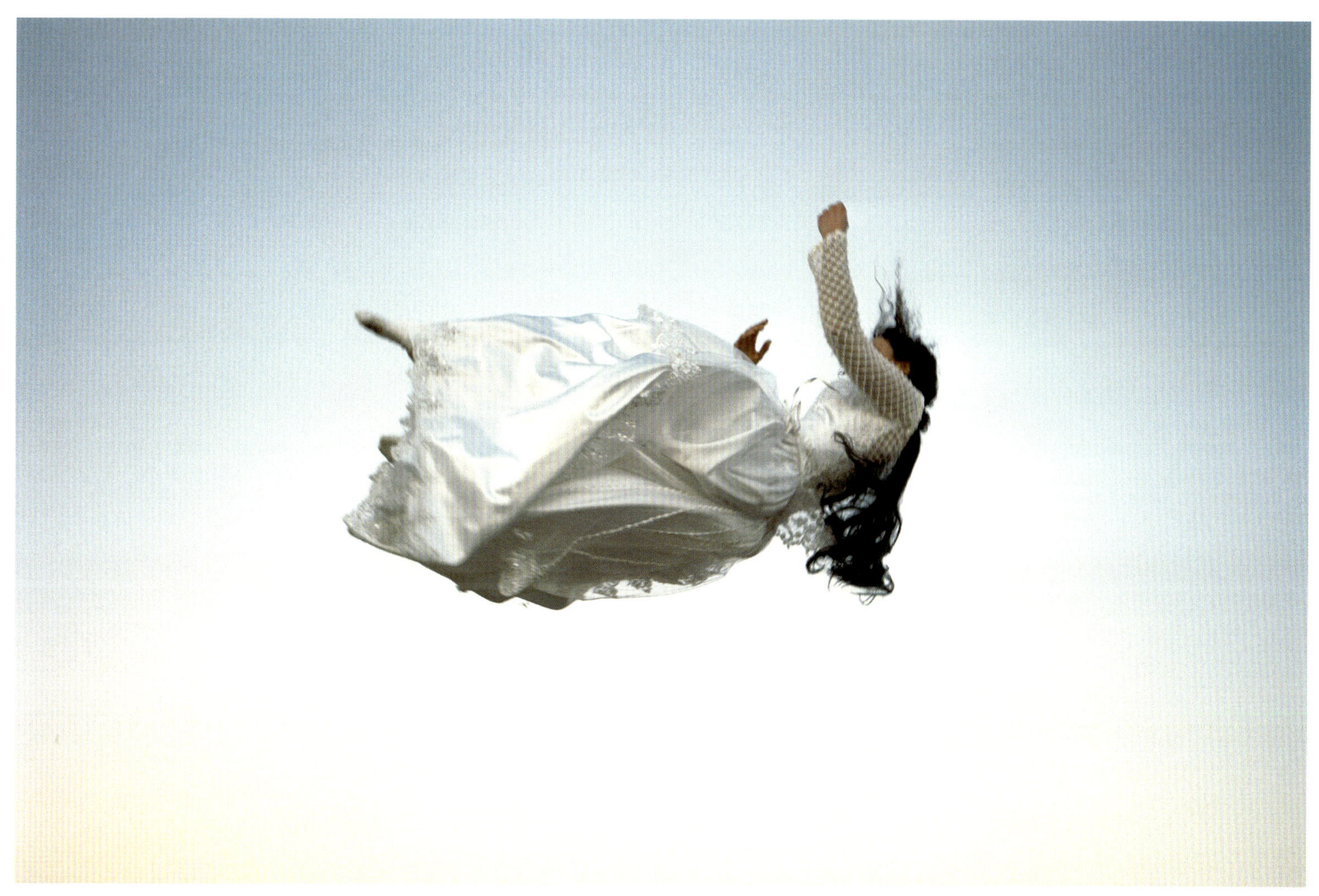

flight research #4, 1999
31½ x 48⅜ in. (80 x 123 cm)

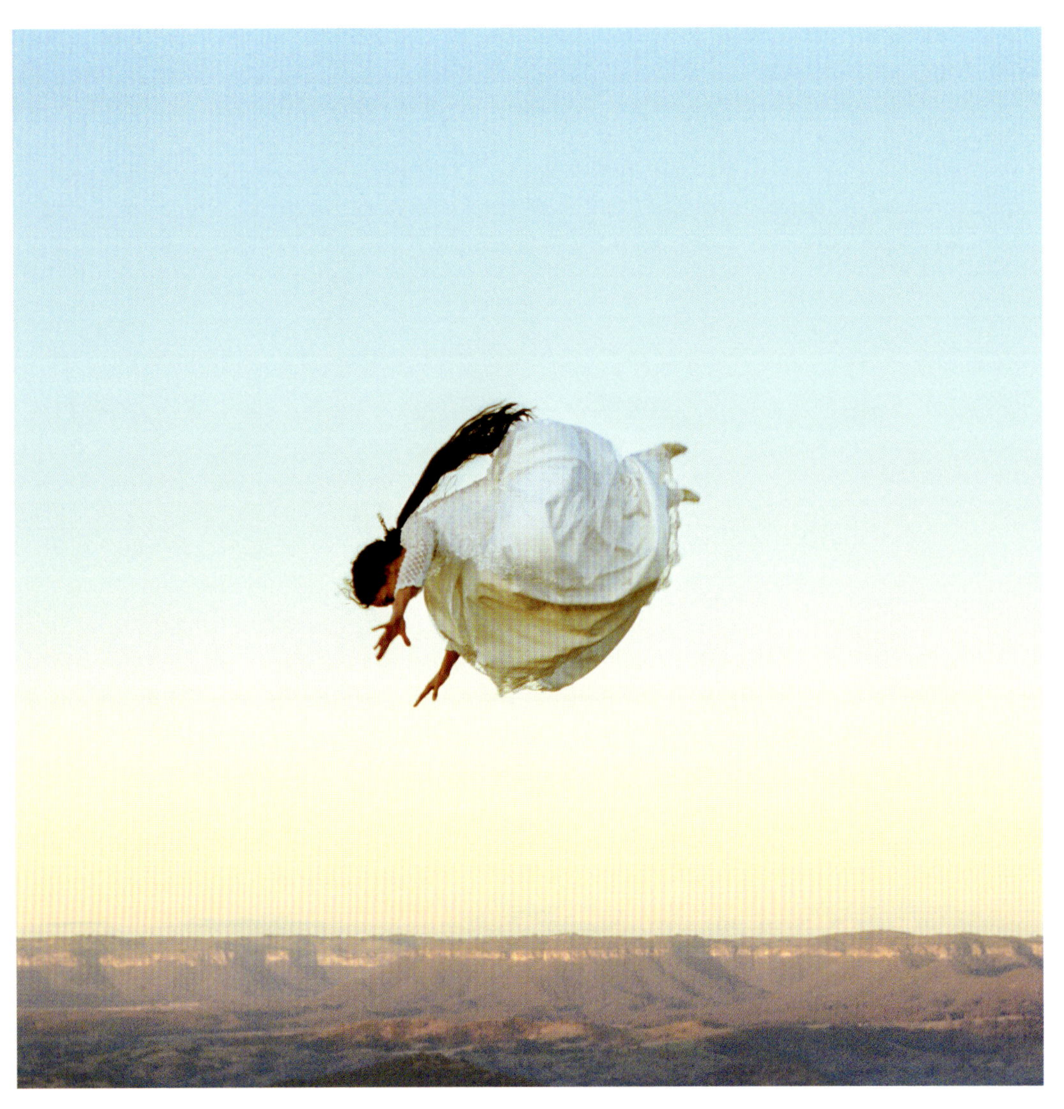

flight research #9, 1999–2000
23⅝ x 23⅝ in. (60 x 60 cm)

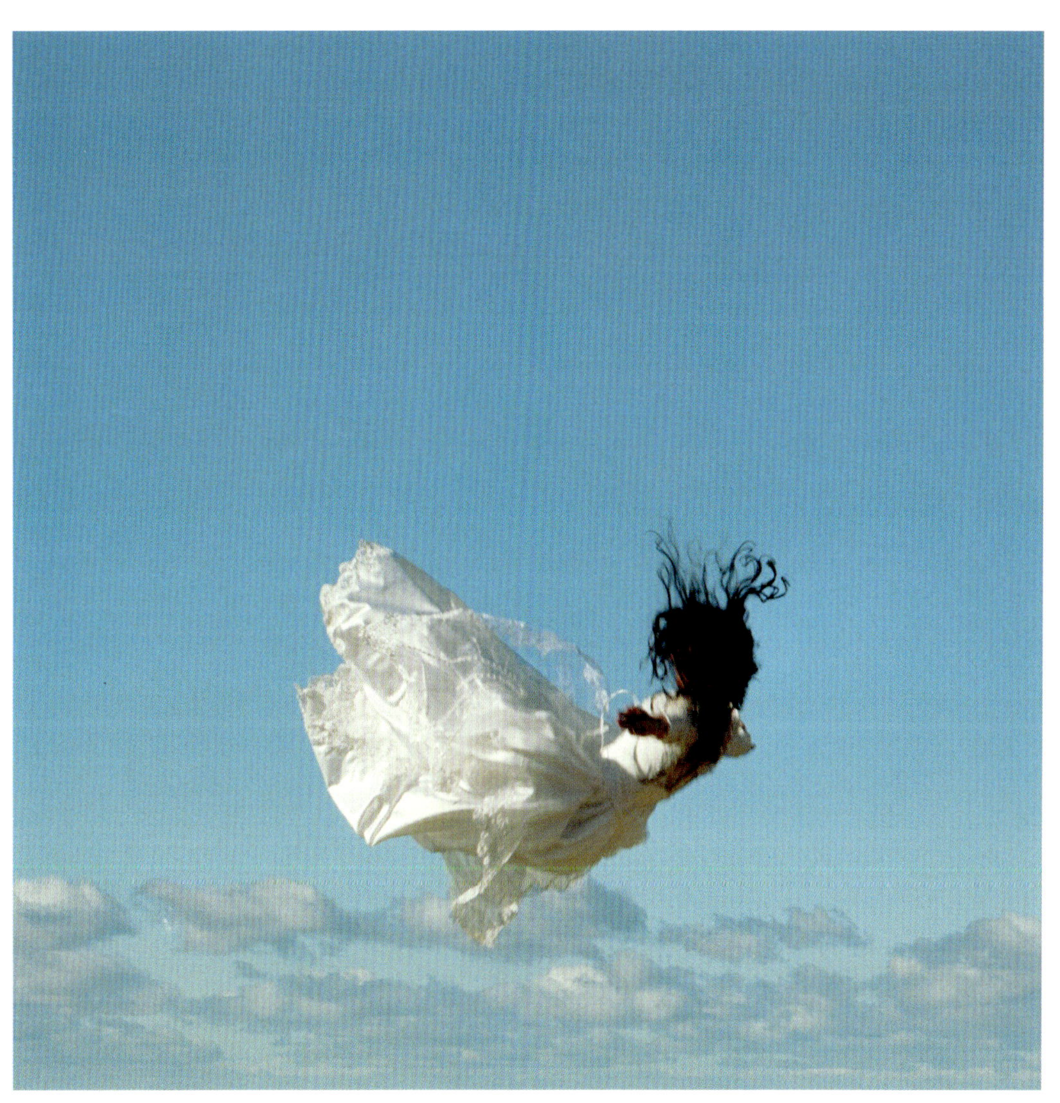

flight research #8, 1999–2000
23⁵⁄₈ x 23⁵⁄₈ in. (60 x 60 cm)

flight research #6, 1999–2000
27½ x 55½ in. (70 x 141 cm)

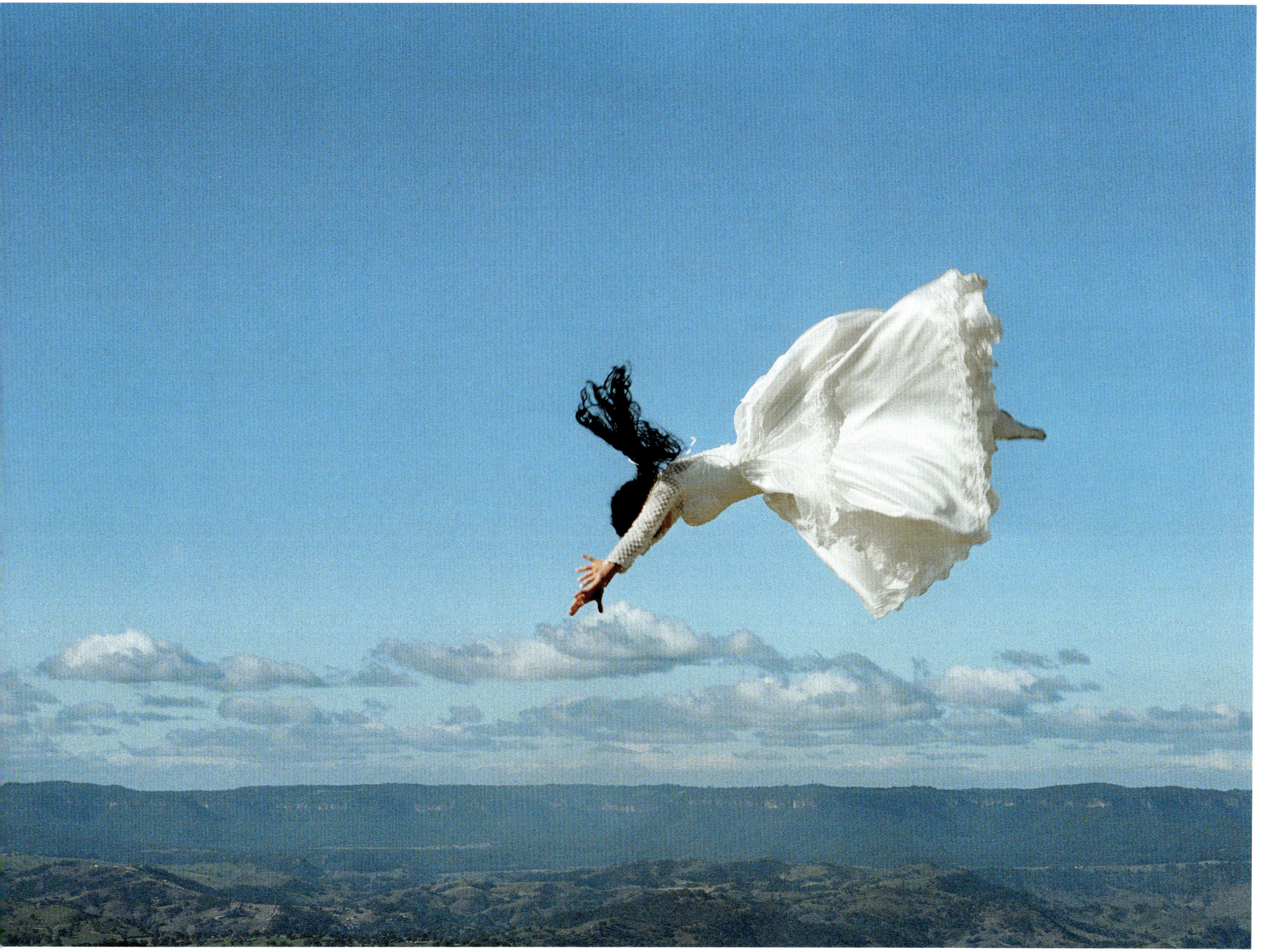

groundspeed #1, 2001
43¼ x 88⅝ in. (110 x 225.2 cm)

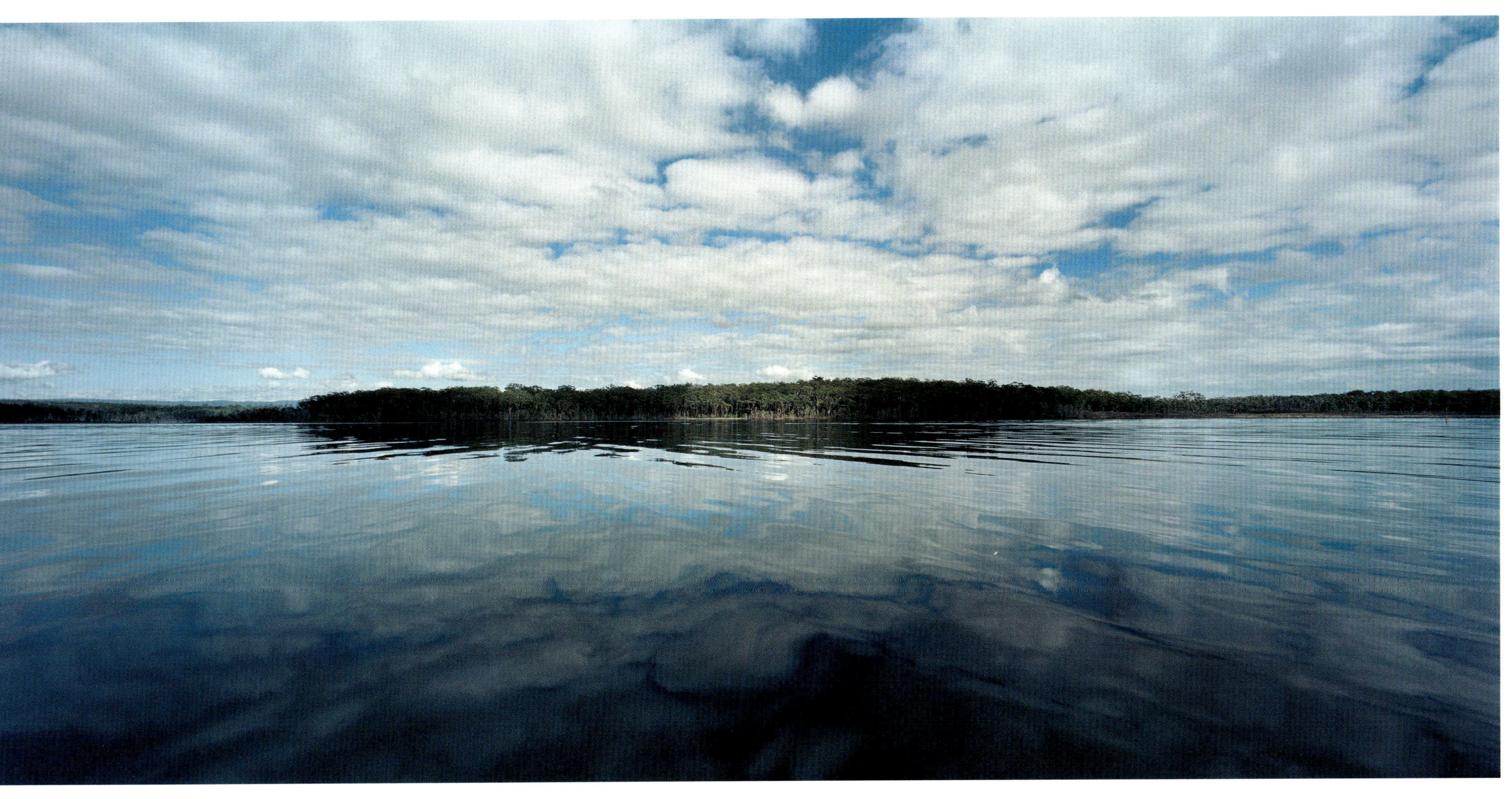

groundspeed (Harrogate Flower) #10, 2001
43¼ x 86 in. (110 x 218.5 cm)

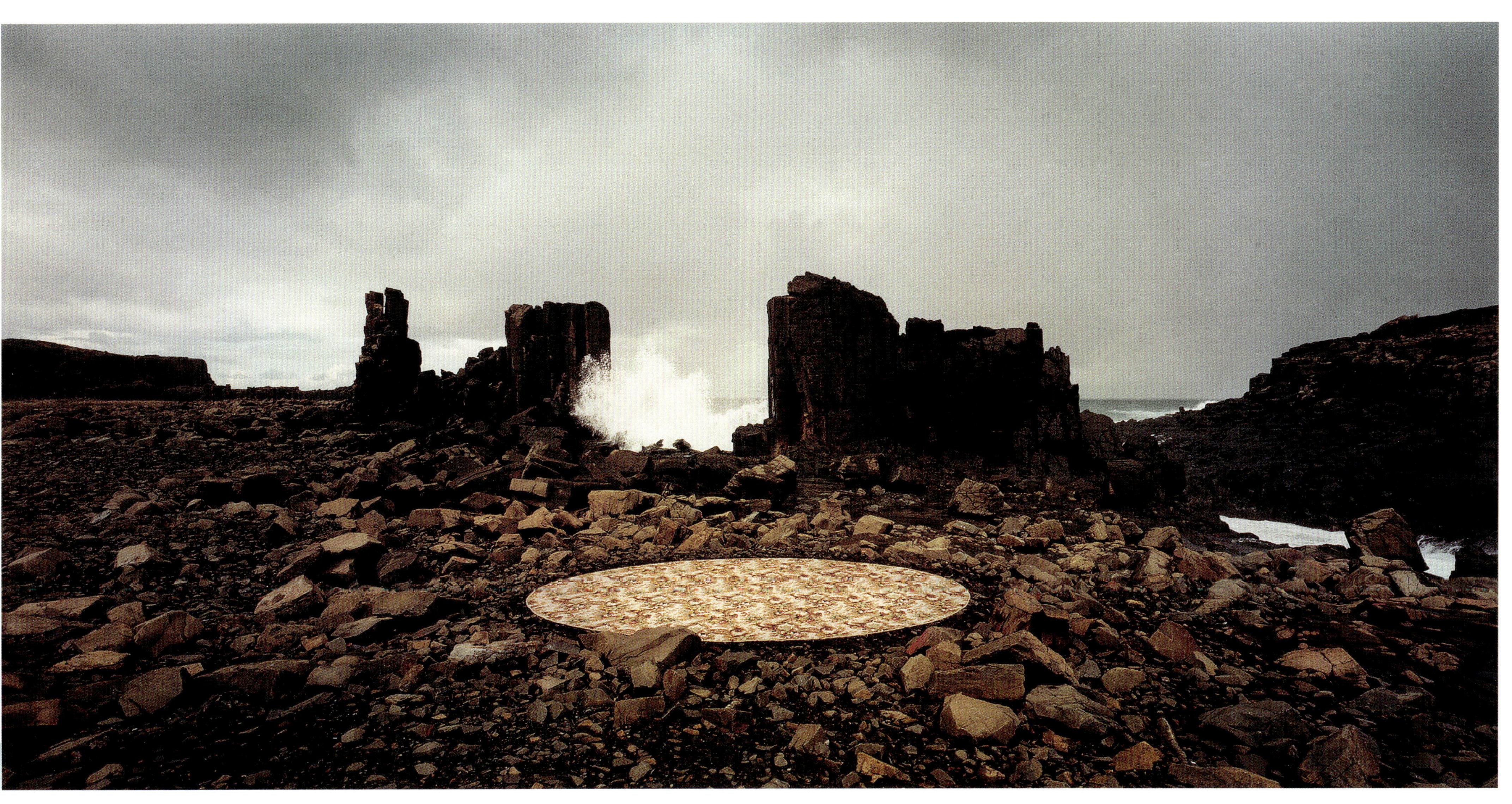

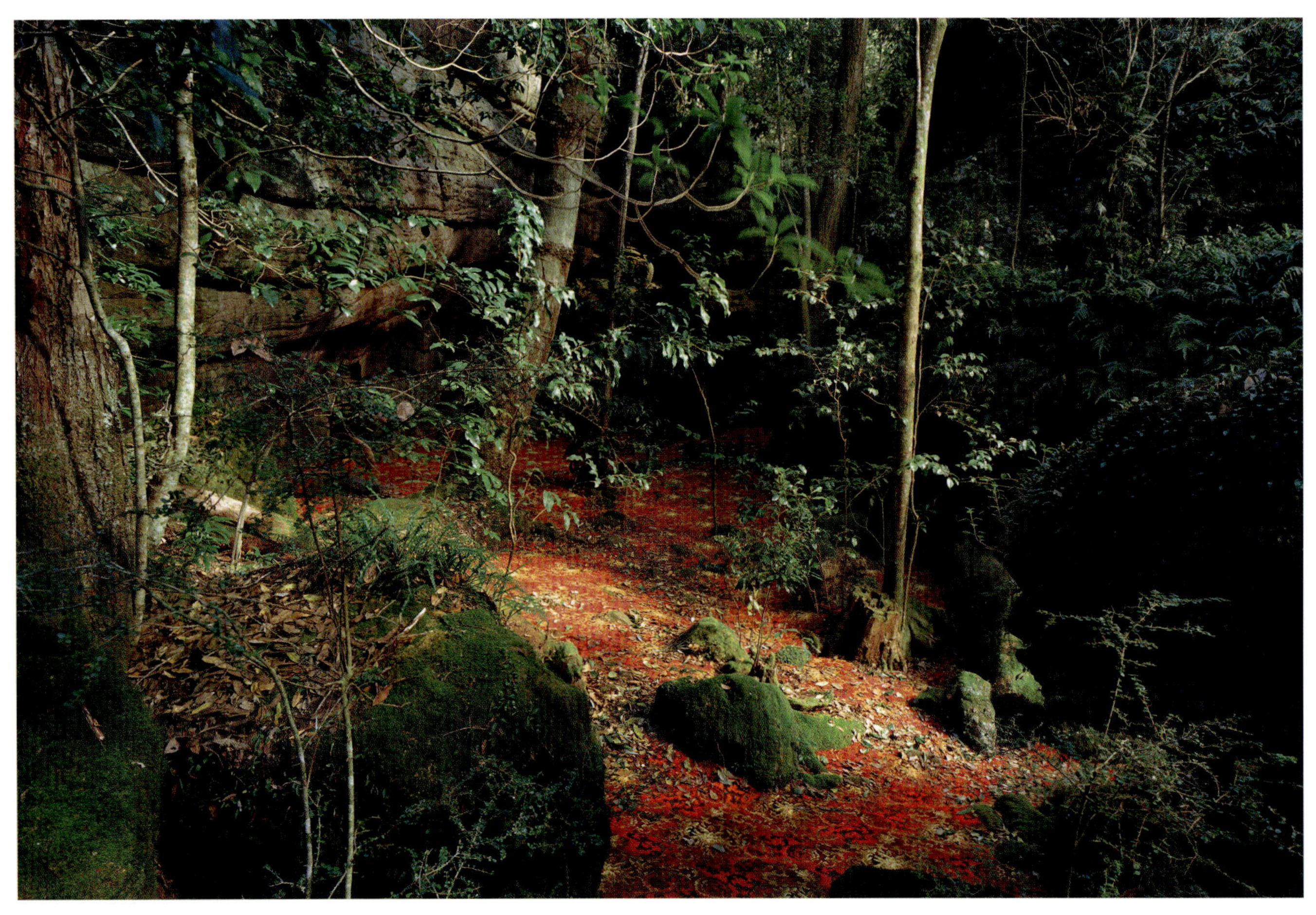

groundspeed (Red Piazza) #3, 2001
33½ x 50⅜ in. (85 x 128 cm)

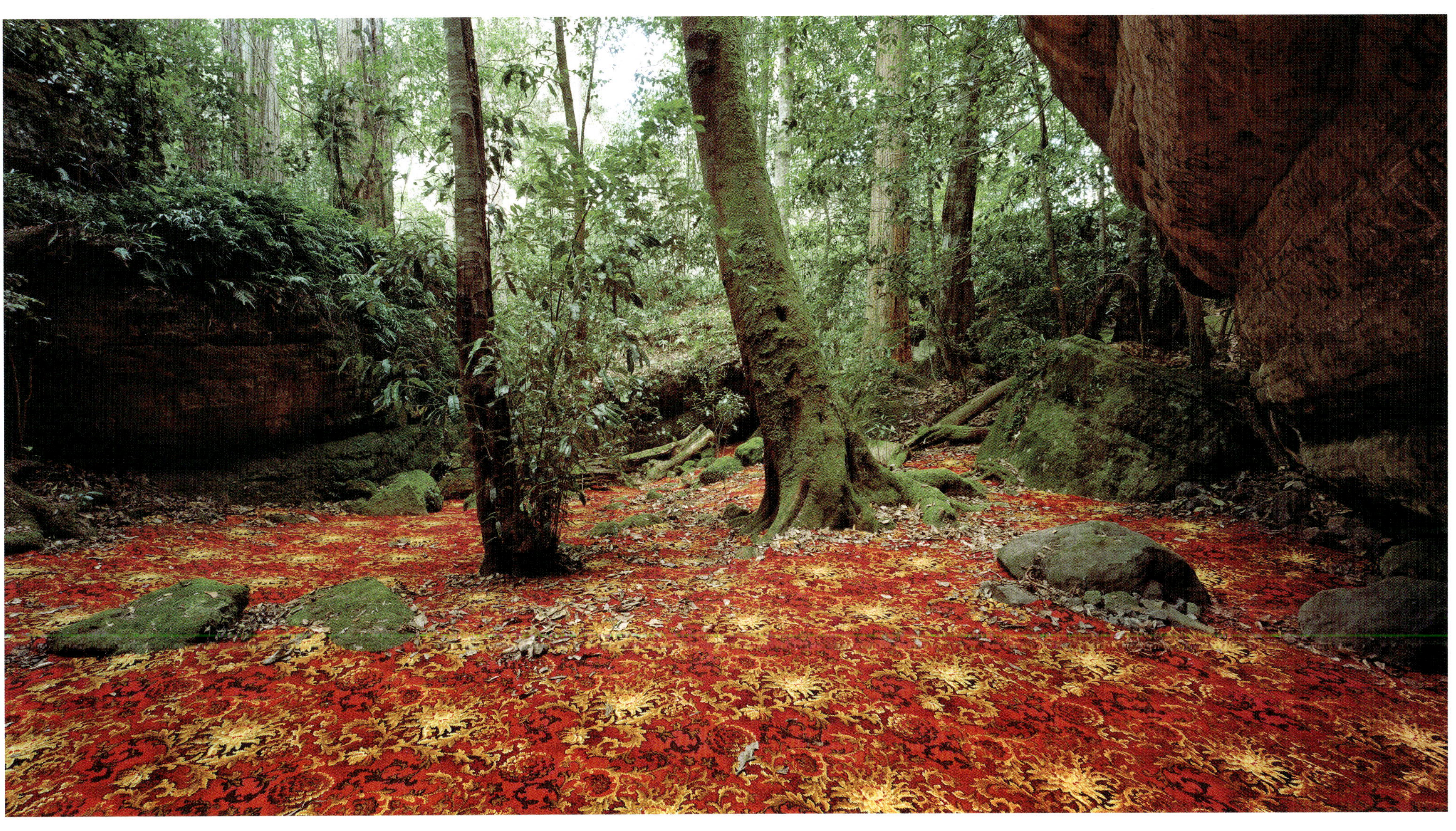

groundspeed (Red Piazza) #2, 2001
43¼ x 80¾ in. (110 x 205 cm)

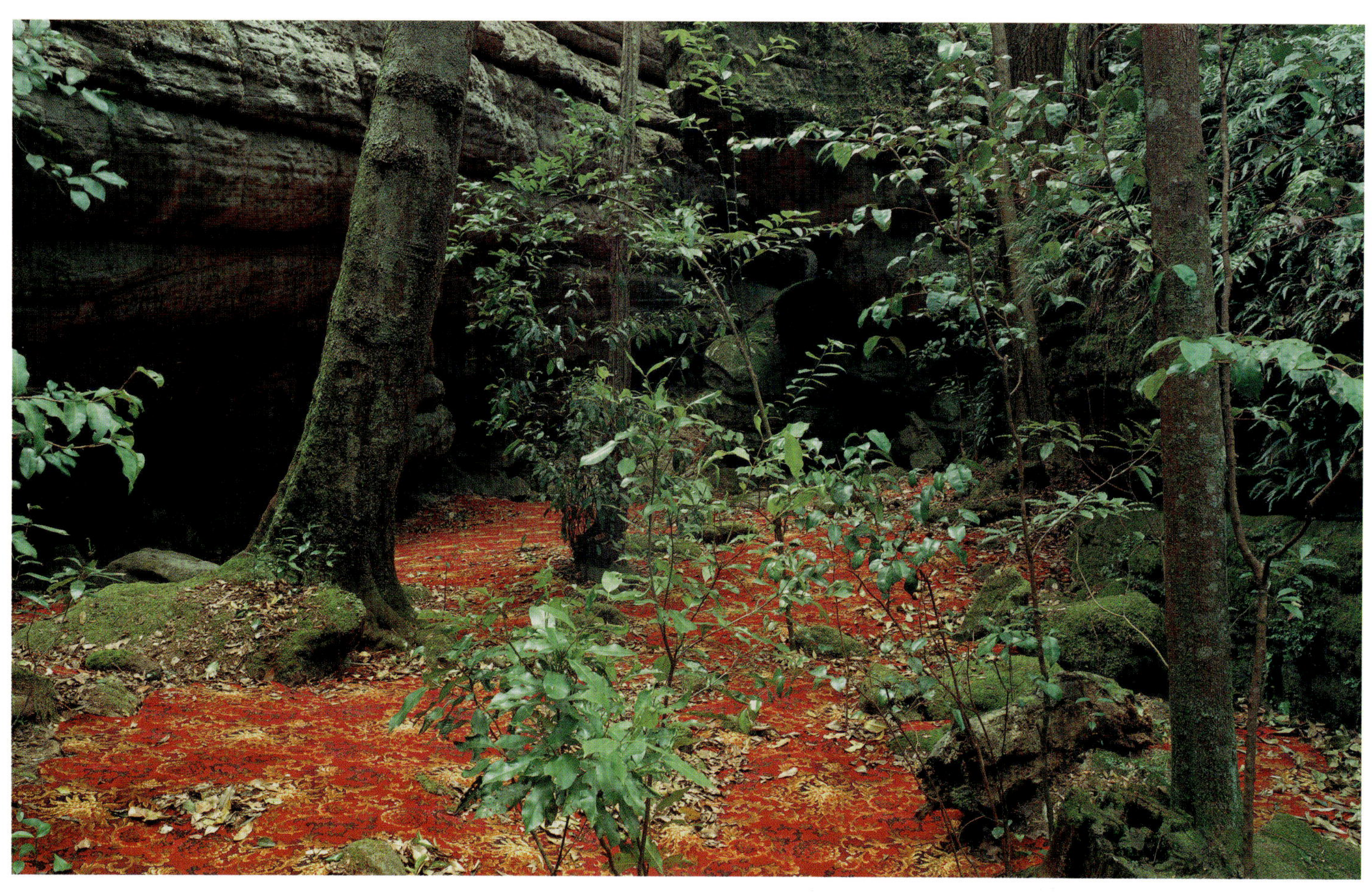

groundspeed (Red Piazza) #5, 2001
27½ x 44⅞ in. (70 x 114 cm)

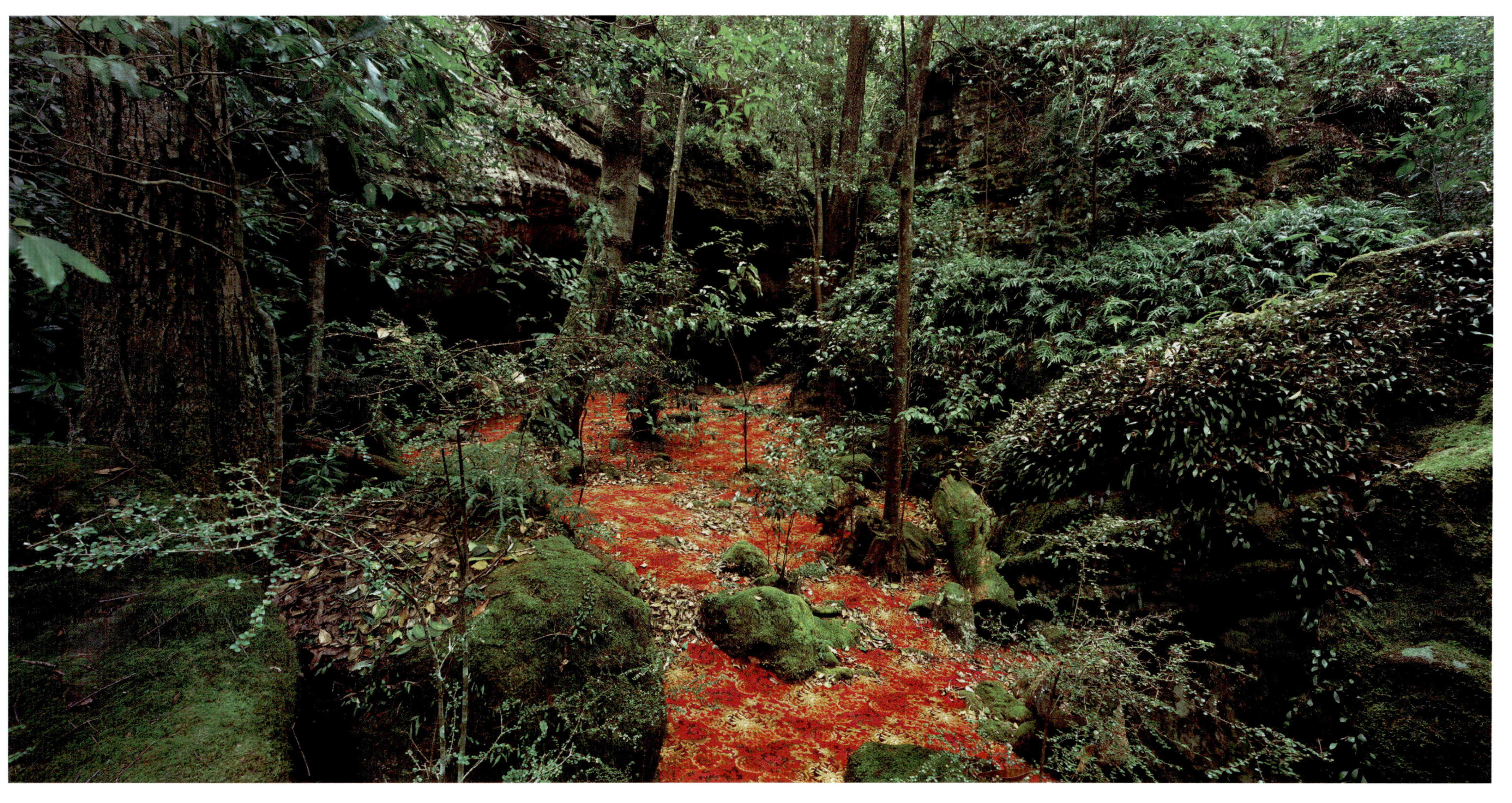

groundspeed (Red Piazza) #4, 2001
43¼ x 86¼ in. (110 x 219 cm)

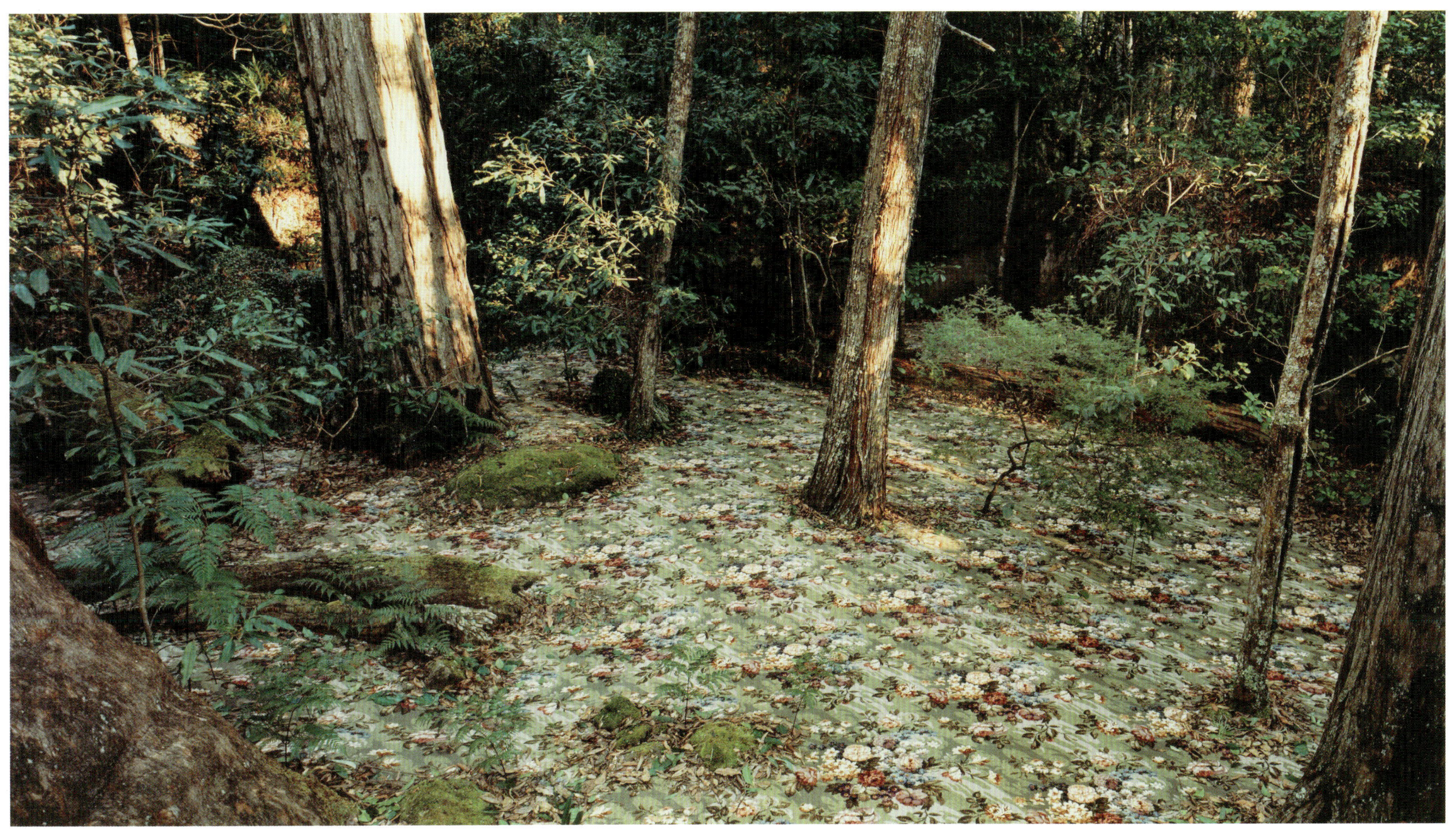

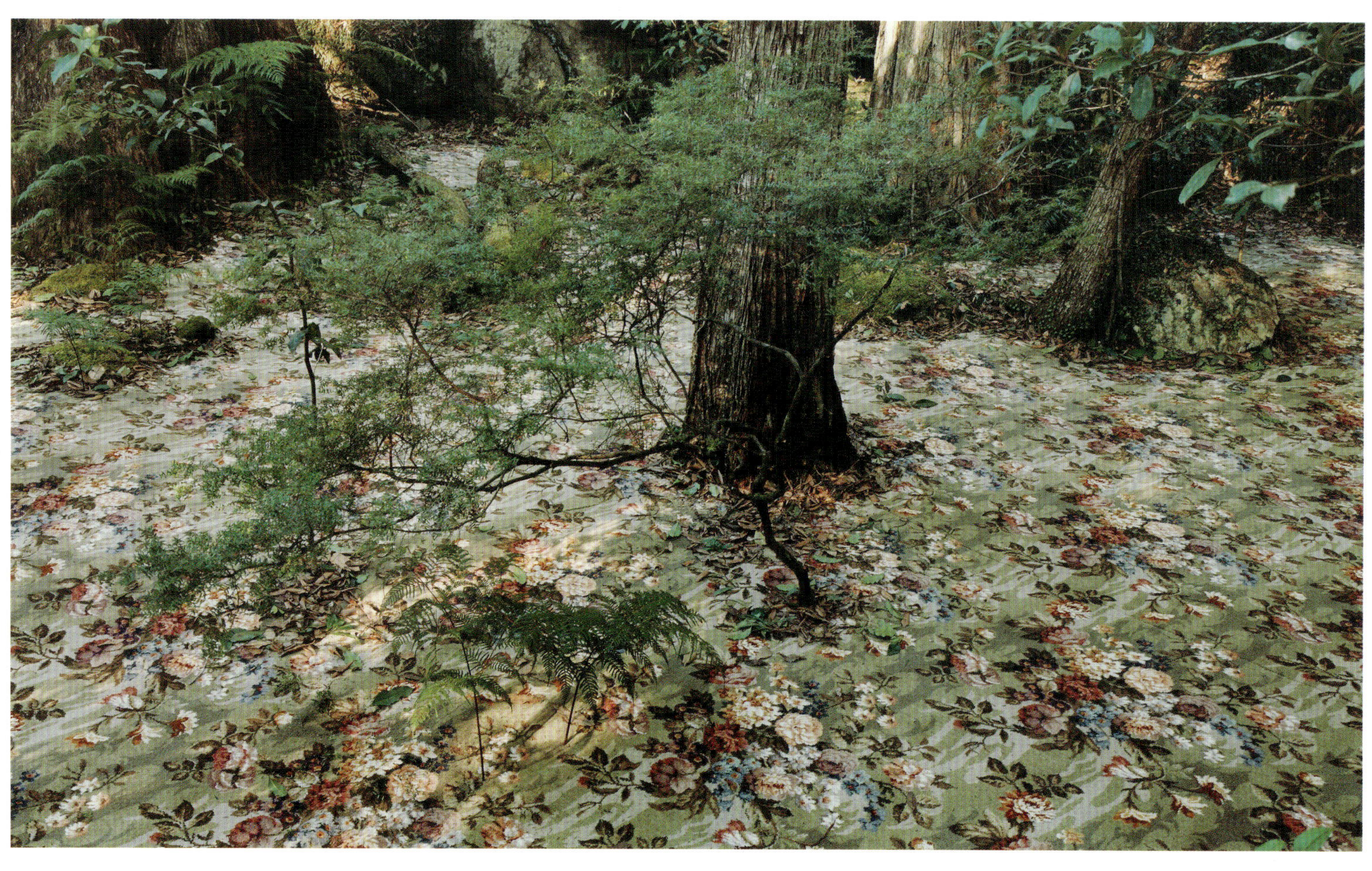

groundspeed (Rose Petal) #16, 2001
33½ x 56⅝ in. (85 x 144 cm)

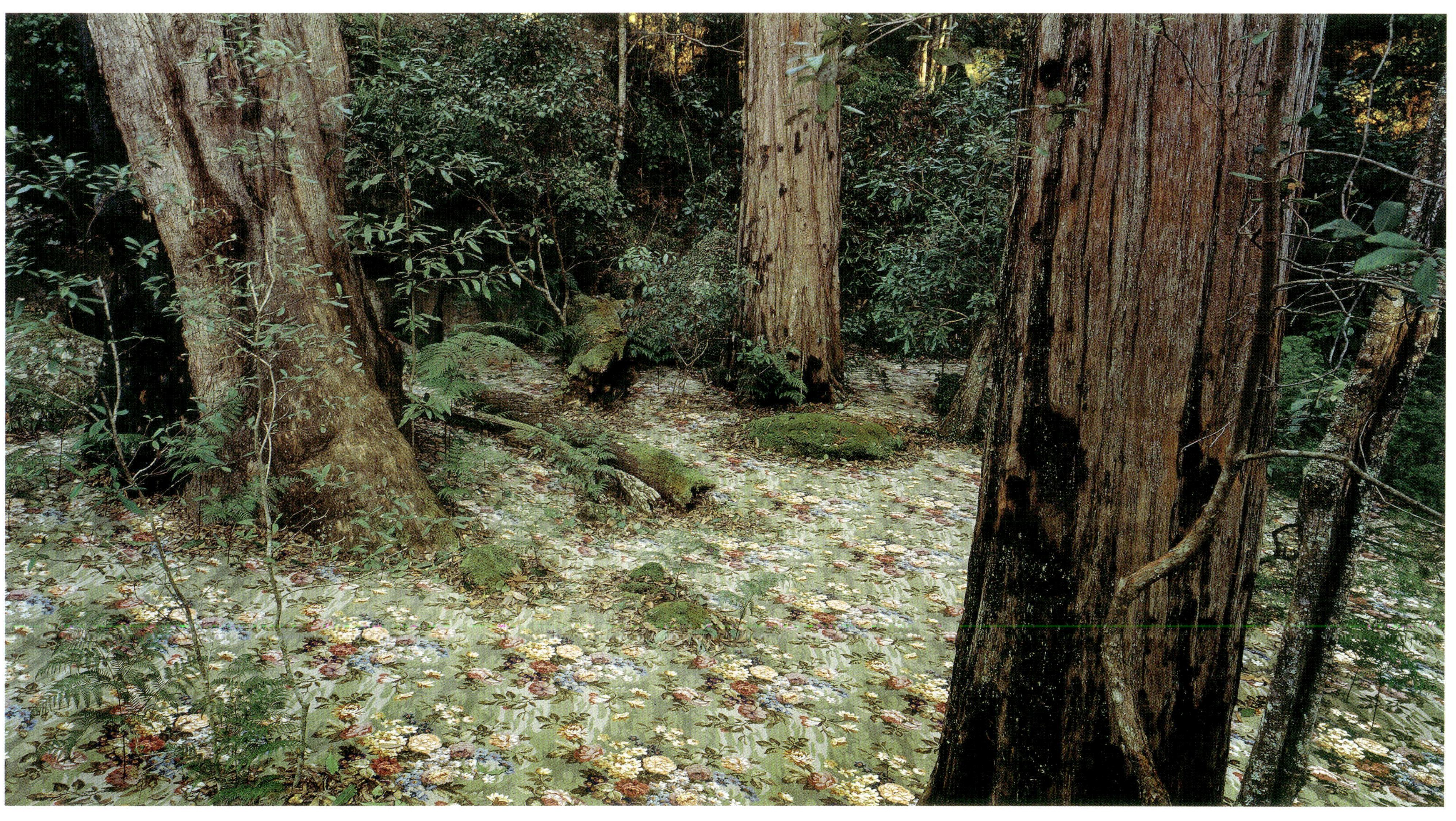

groundspeed (Rose Petal) #15, 2001
43¼ x 83⅛ in. (110 x 211 cm)

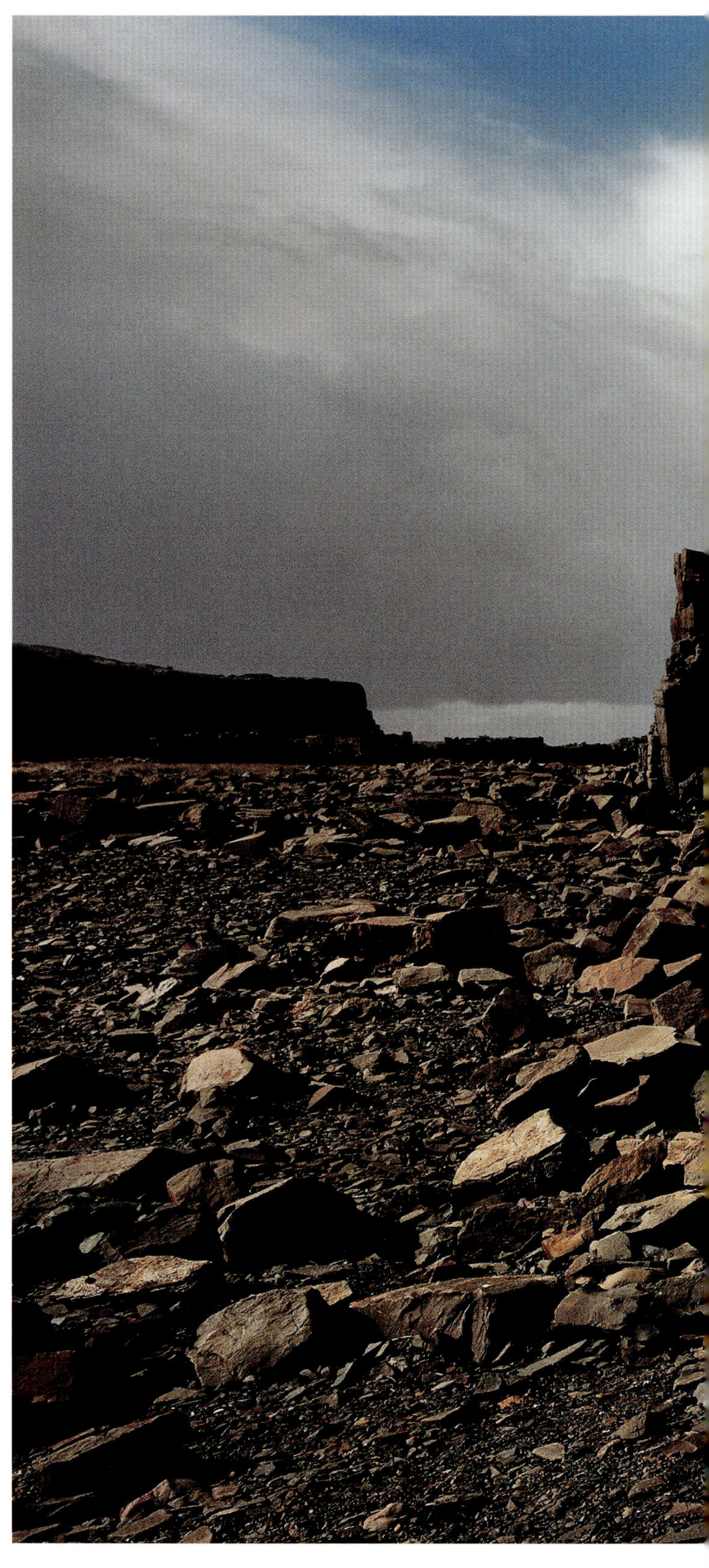

groundspeed (Harrogate Flower) #9, 2001
43¼ x 85⅞ in. (110 x 218 cm)

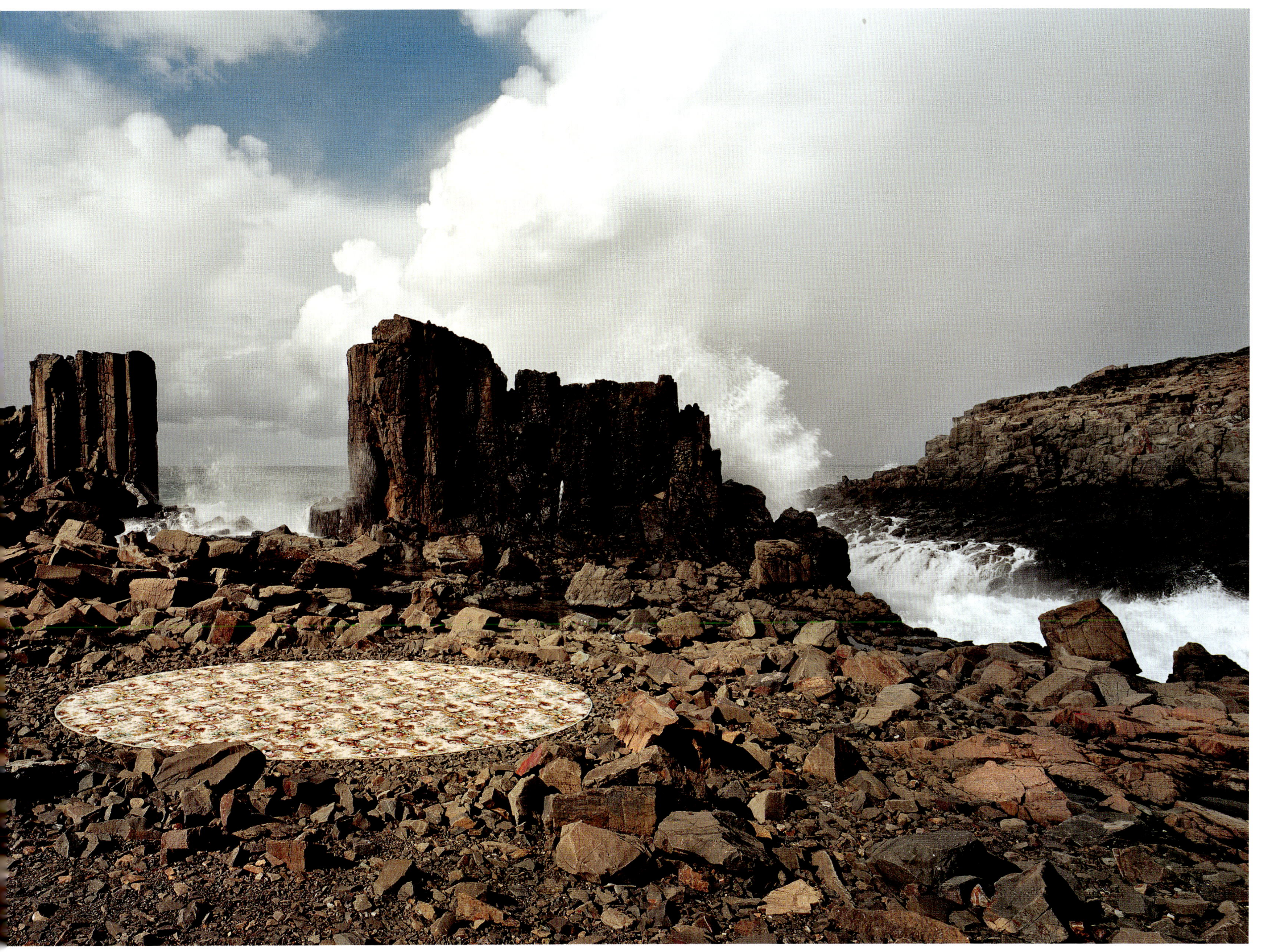

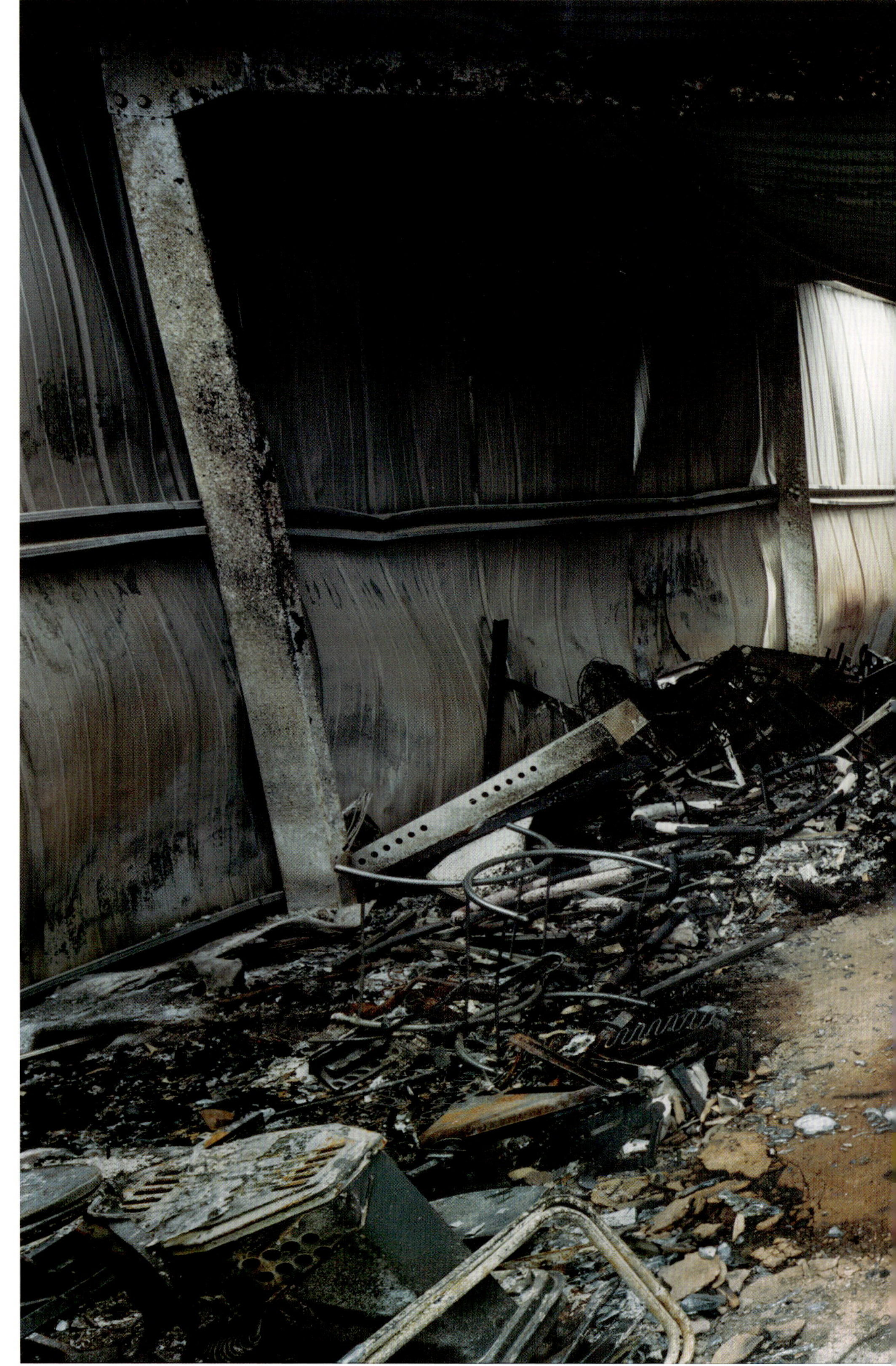

swanfires, *Chris's shed*, 2002–04
43¼ x 92¾ in. (110 x 235.5 cm)

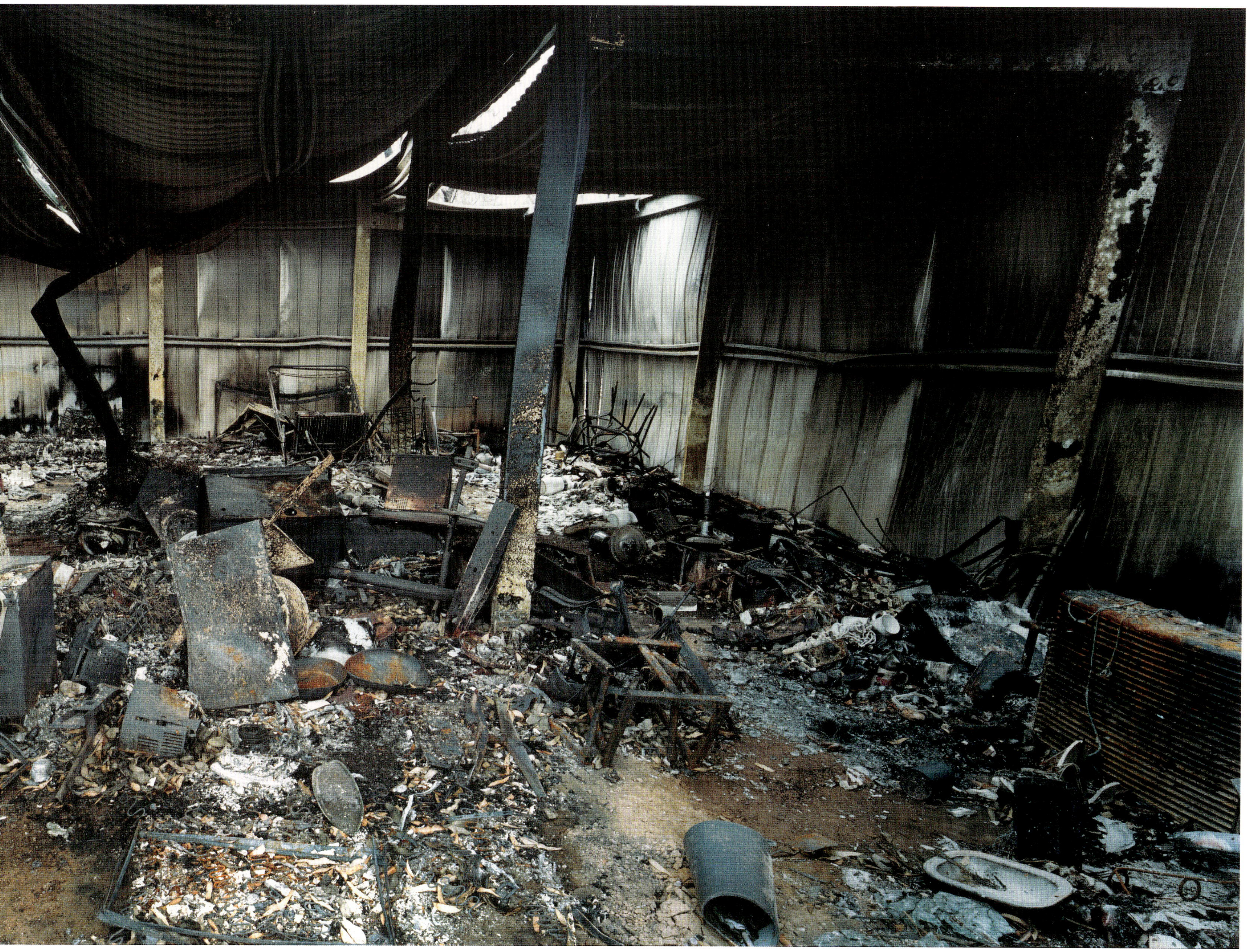

bulletproofglass #3, 2002
Type-C metallic photographic paper
47¼ x 76 in. (120 x 193 cm)

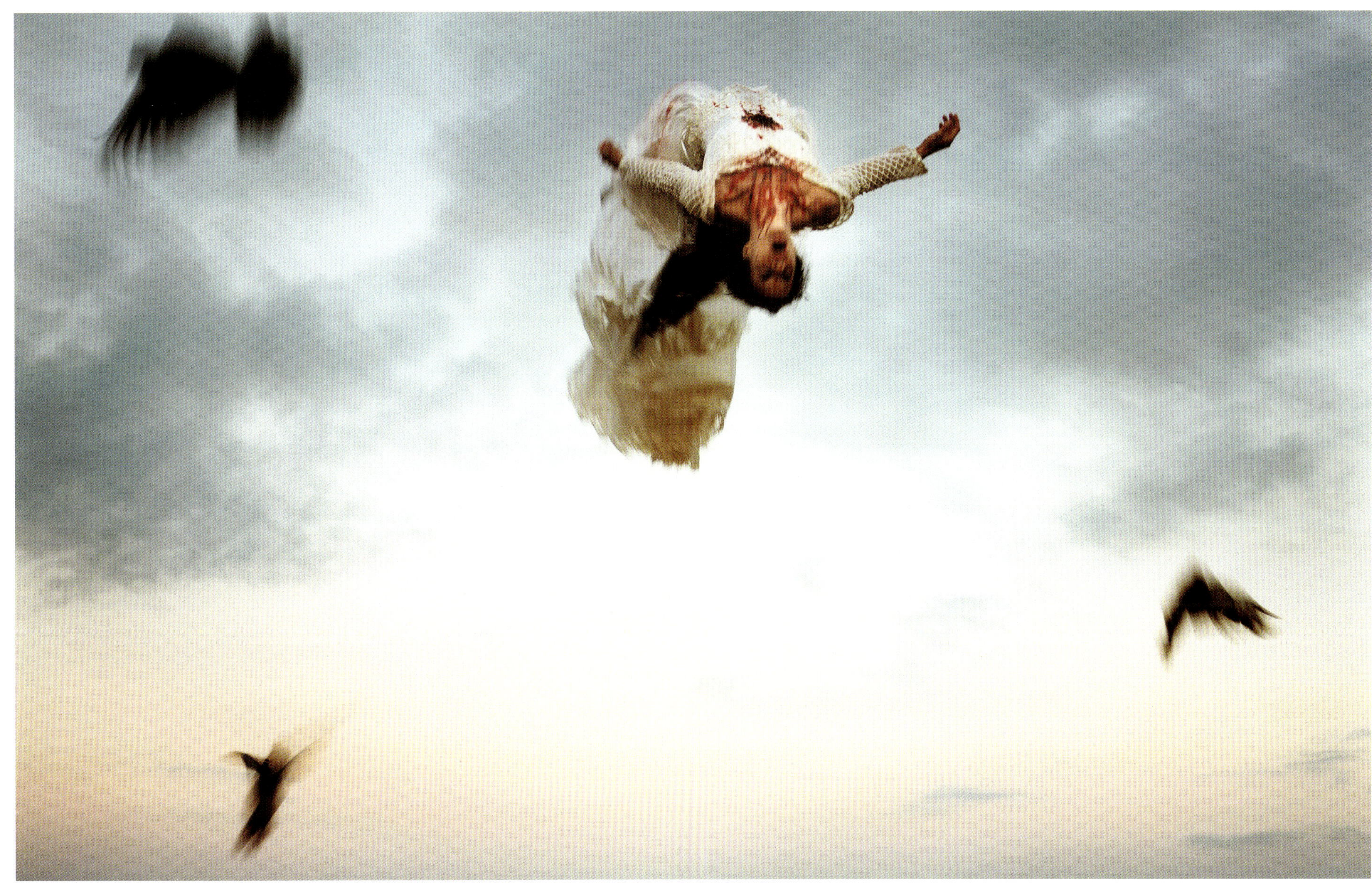

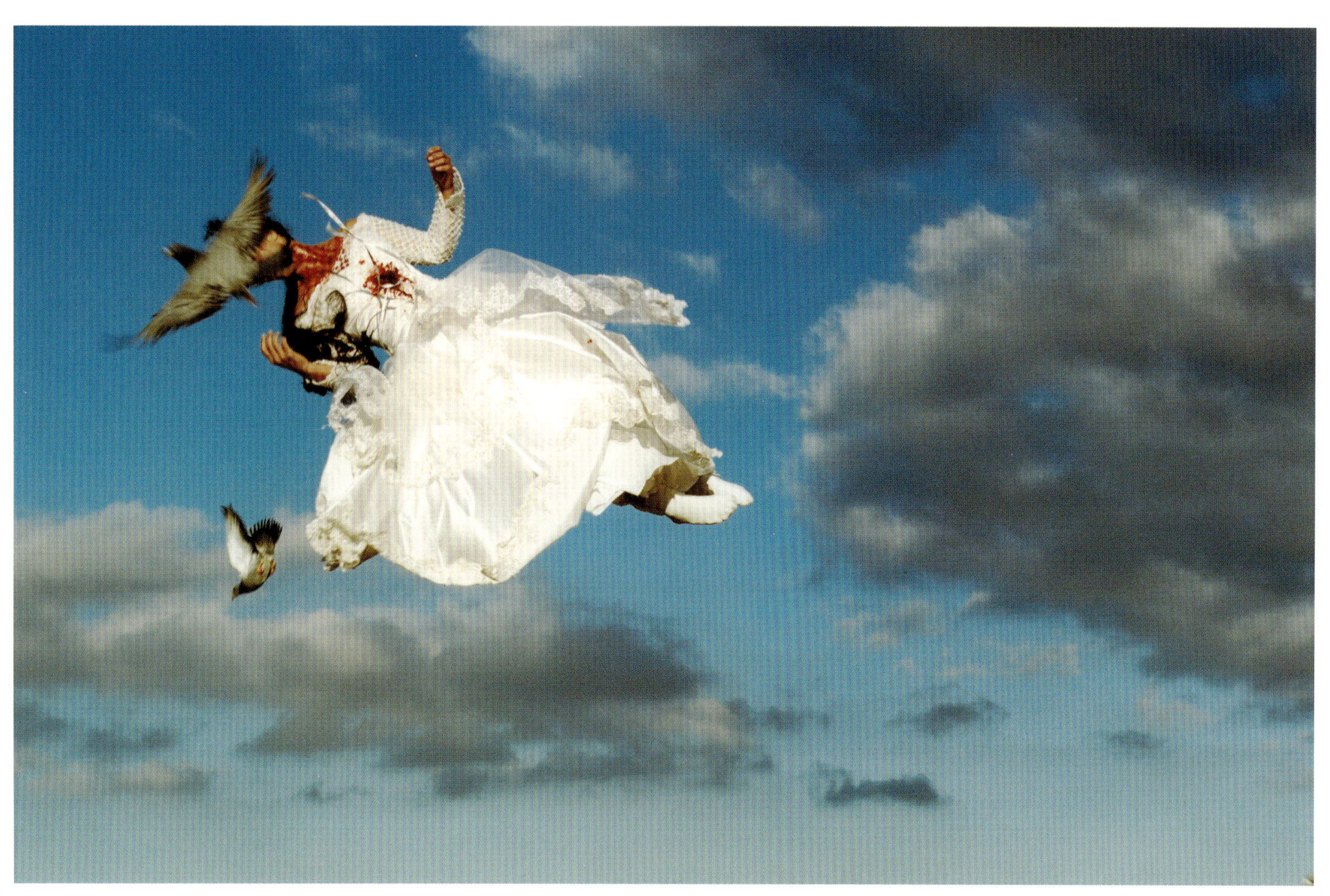

bulletproofglass #7, 2002
27½ x 44⅛ in. (70 x 112 cm)

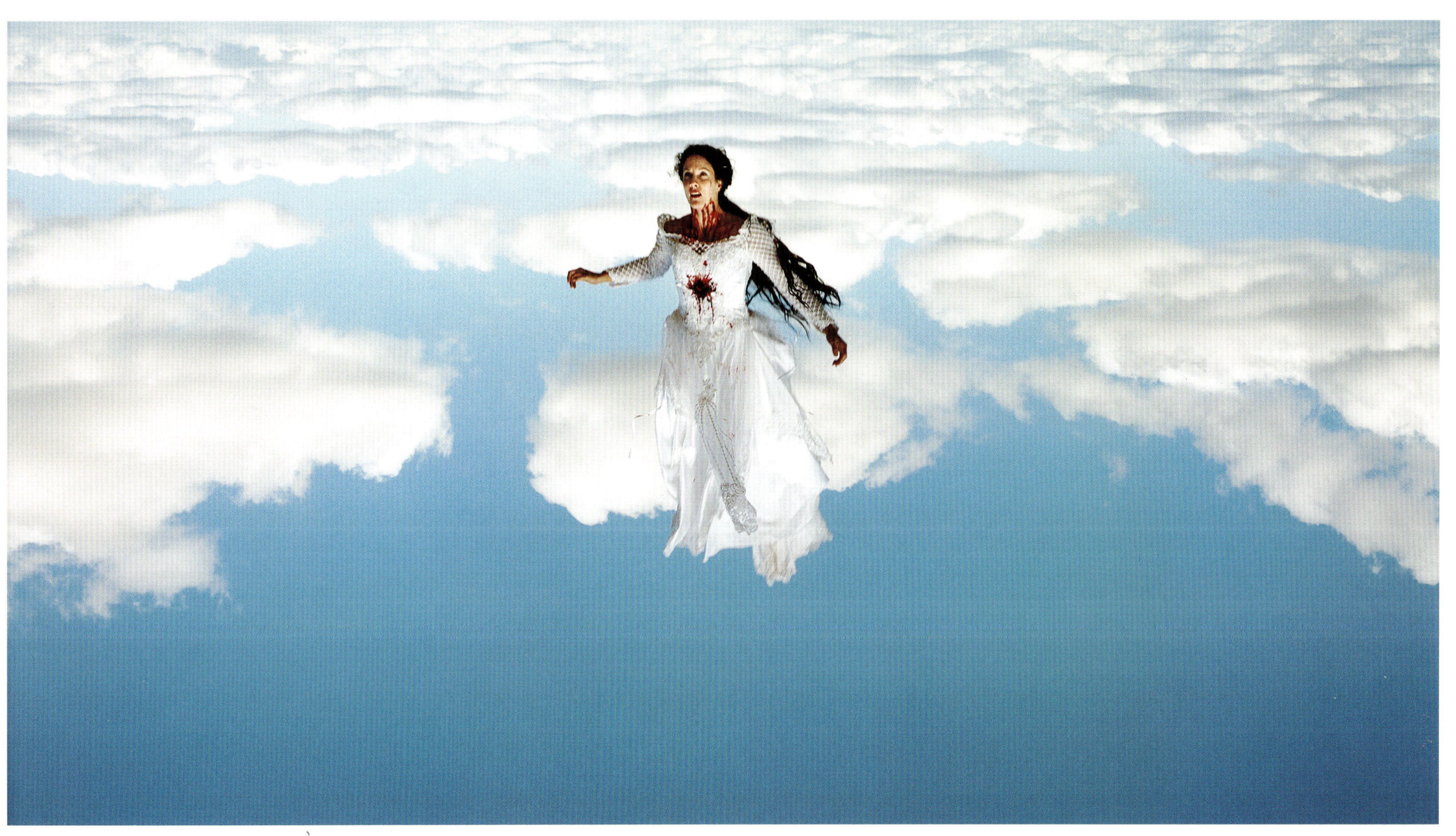

bulletproofglass #1, 2002
47¼ x 82¼ in. (120 x 209 cm)

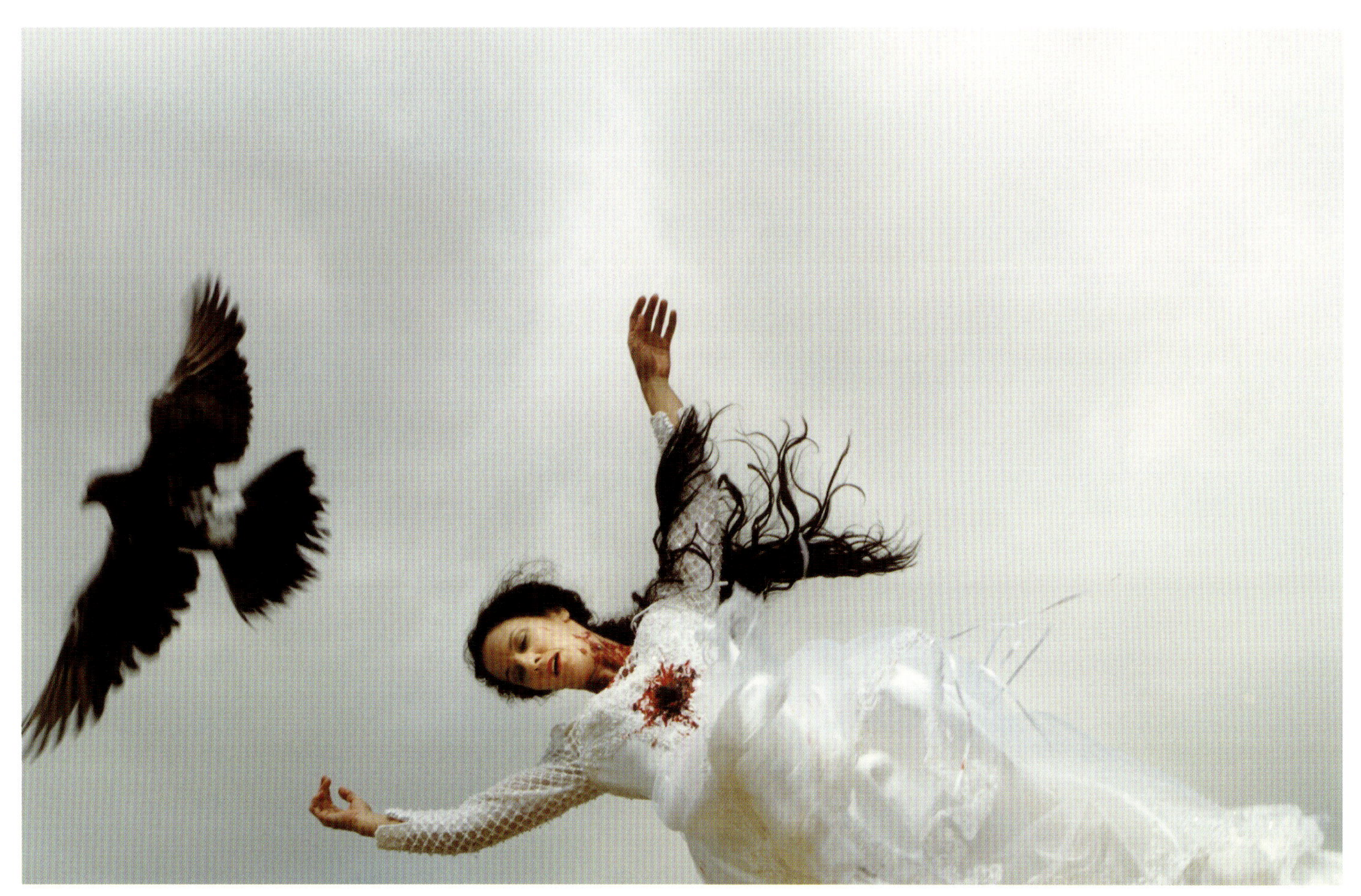

bulletproofglass #4, 2002
27½ x 44⅛ in. (70 x 112 cm)

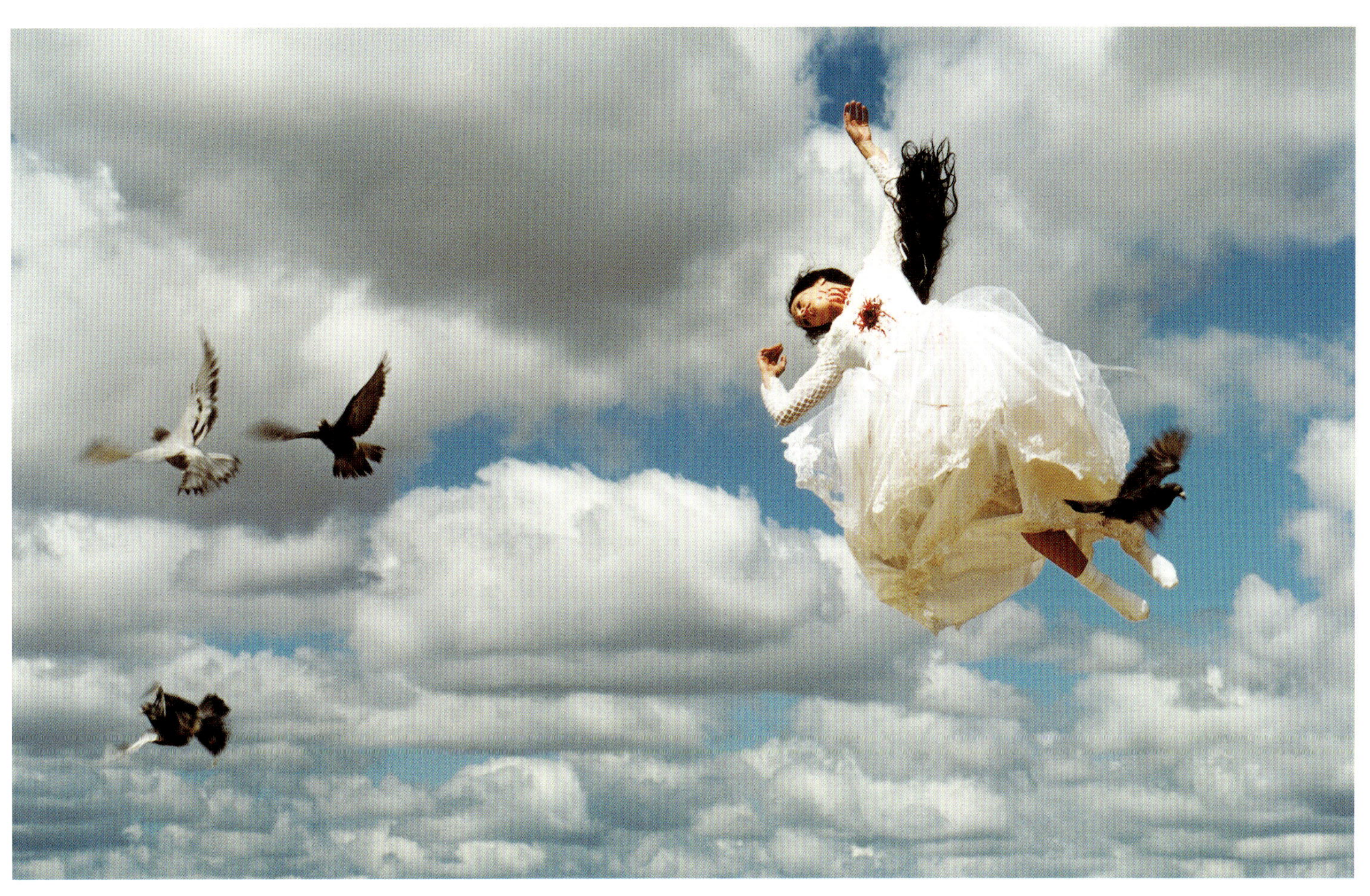

bulletproofglass #8, 2002
27½ x 44⅞ in. (70 x 114 cm)

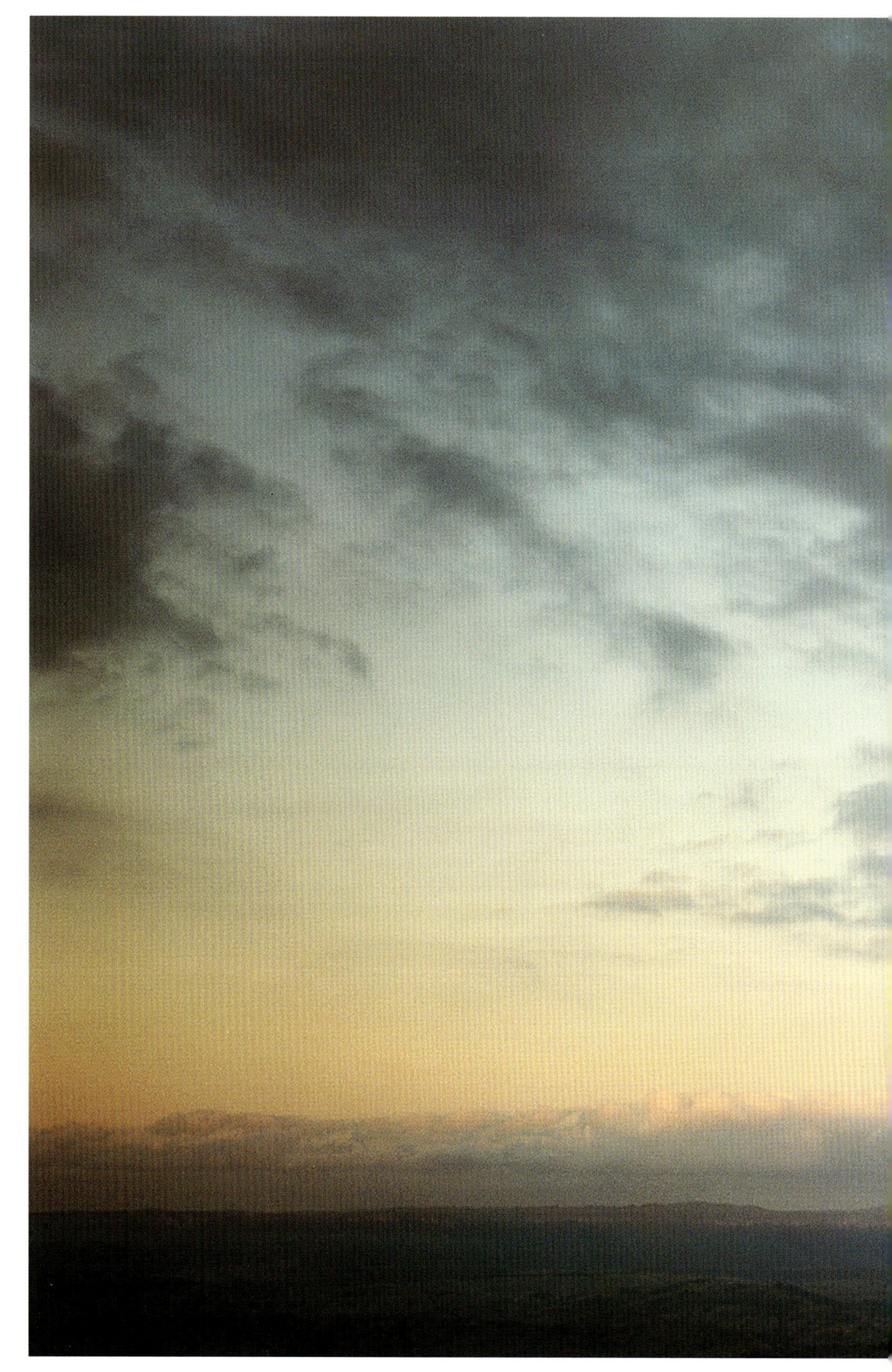

bulletproofglass #2, 2002
Type-C metallic photographic paper
47¼ x 99⅝ in. (120 x 253 cm)

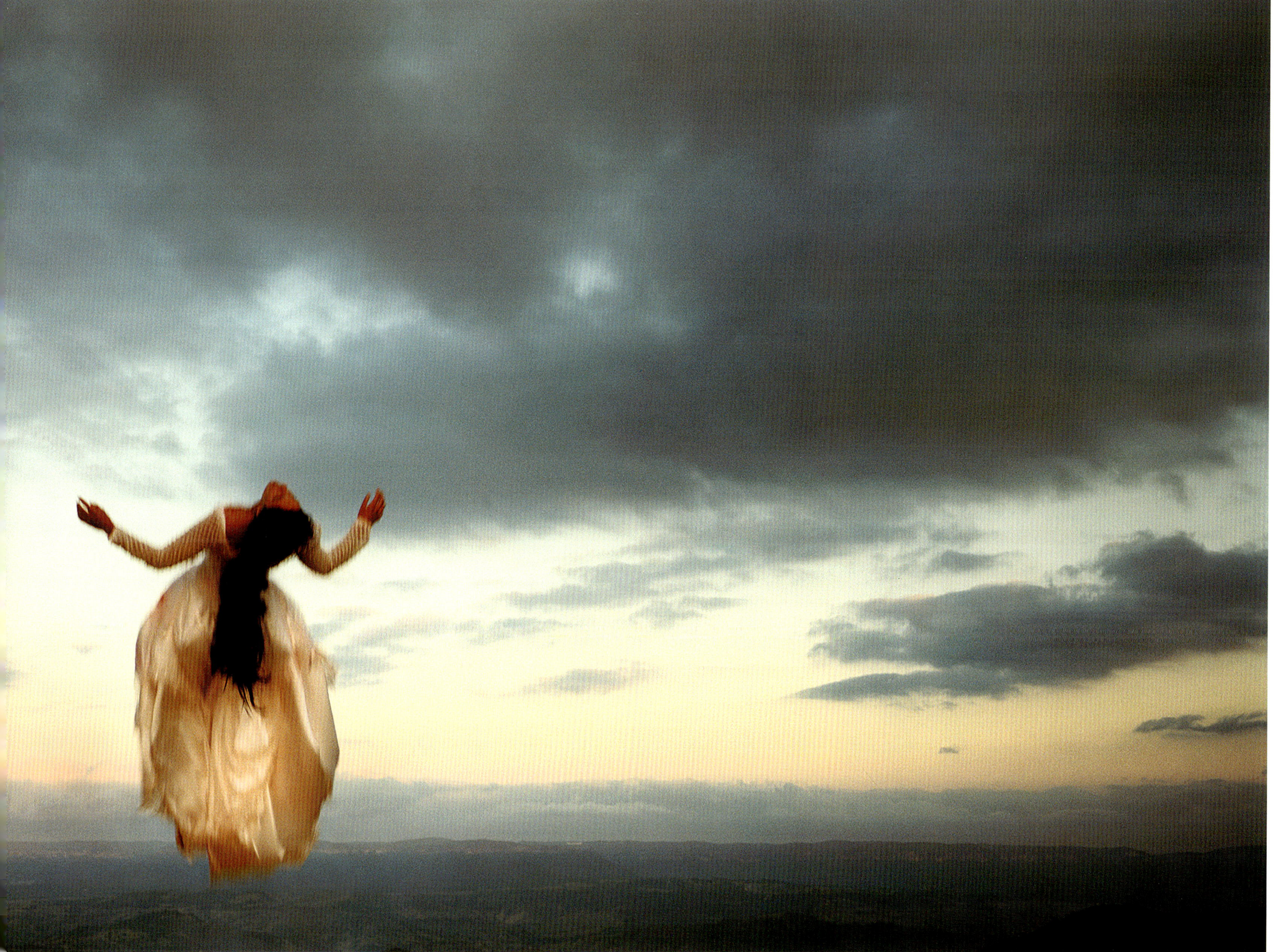

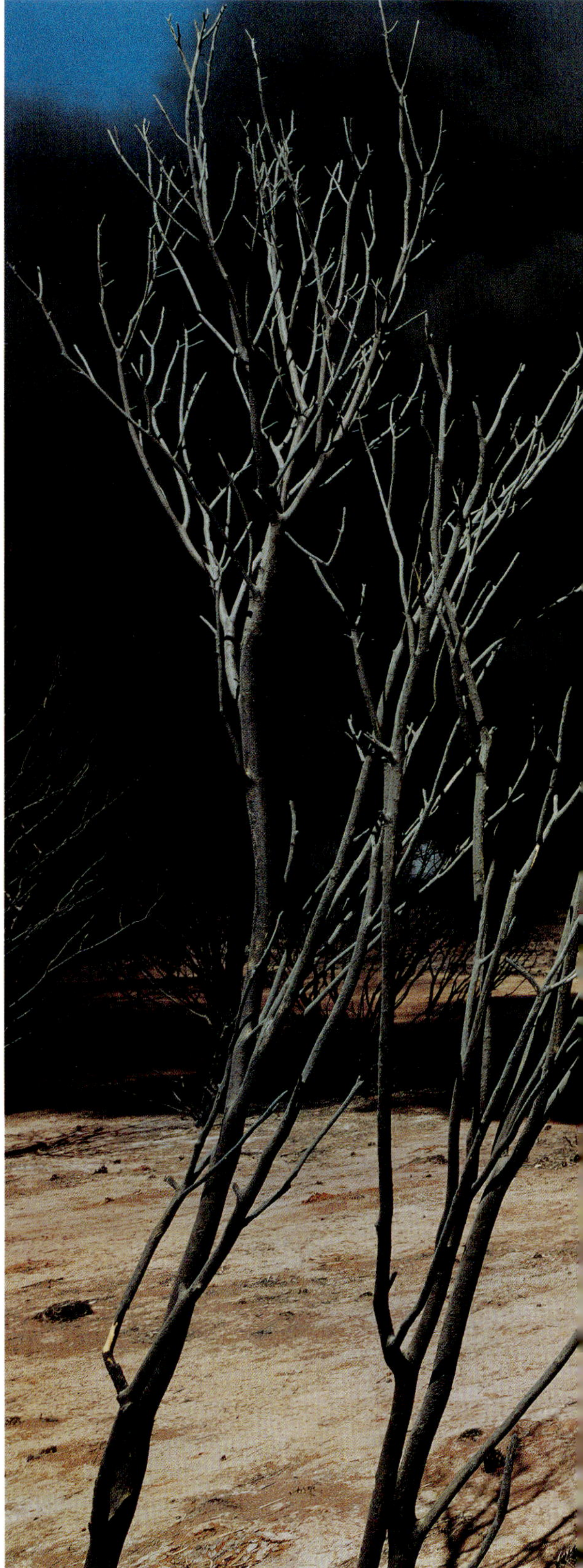

one dozen unnatural disasters in the Australian landscape #2, 2003
43¼ x 81 in. (110 x 205.7 cm)

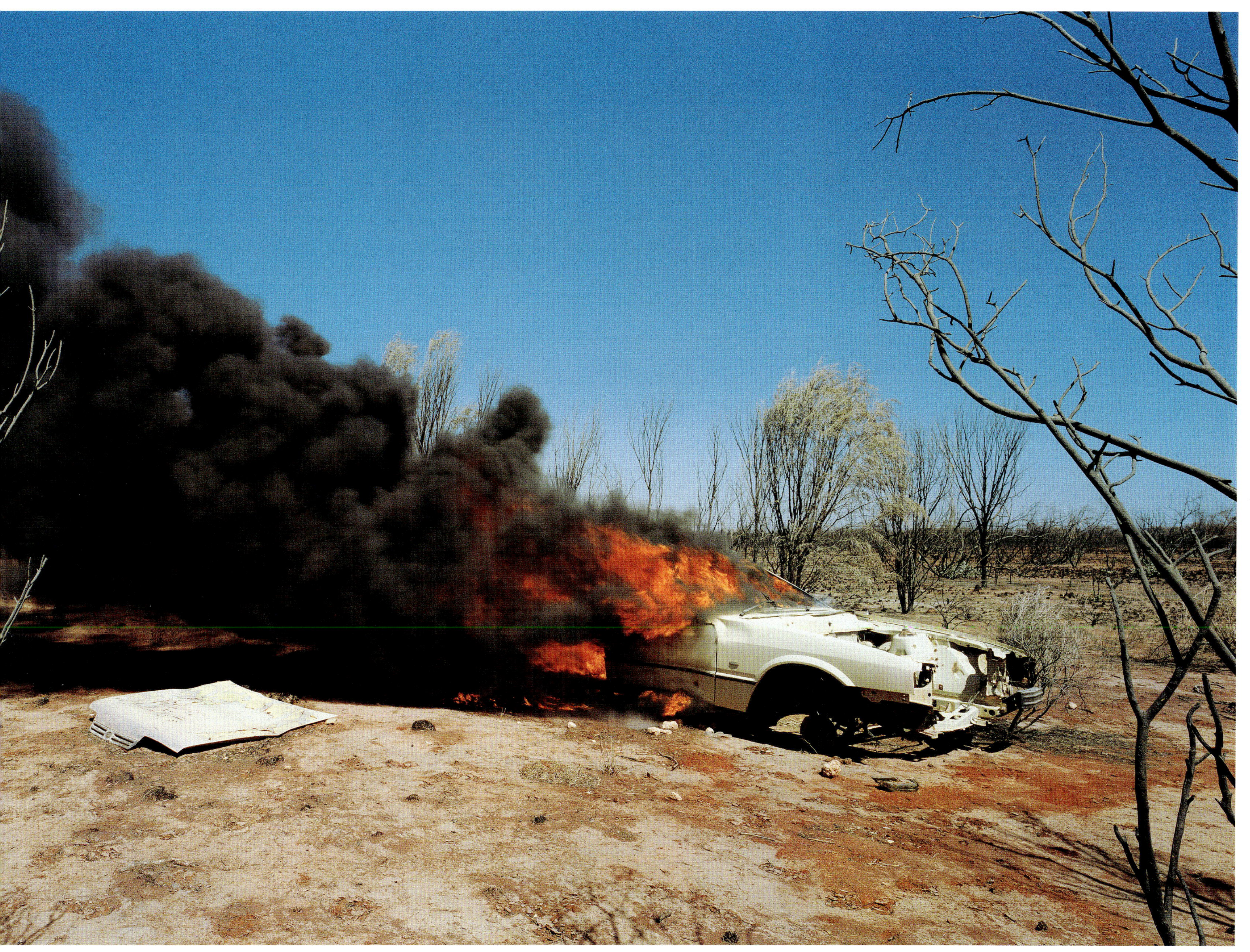

third day of a five day muster, 2003
43¼ x 81⅜ in. (110 x 206.6 cm)

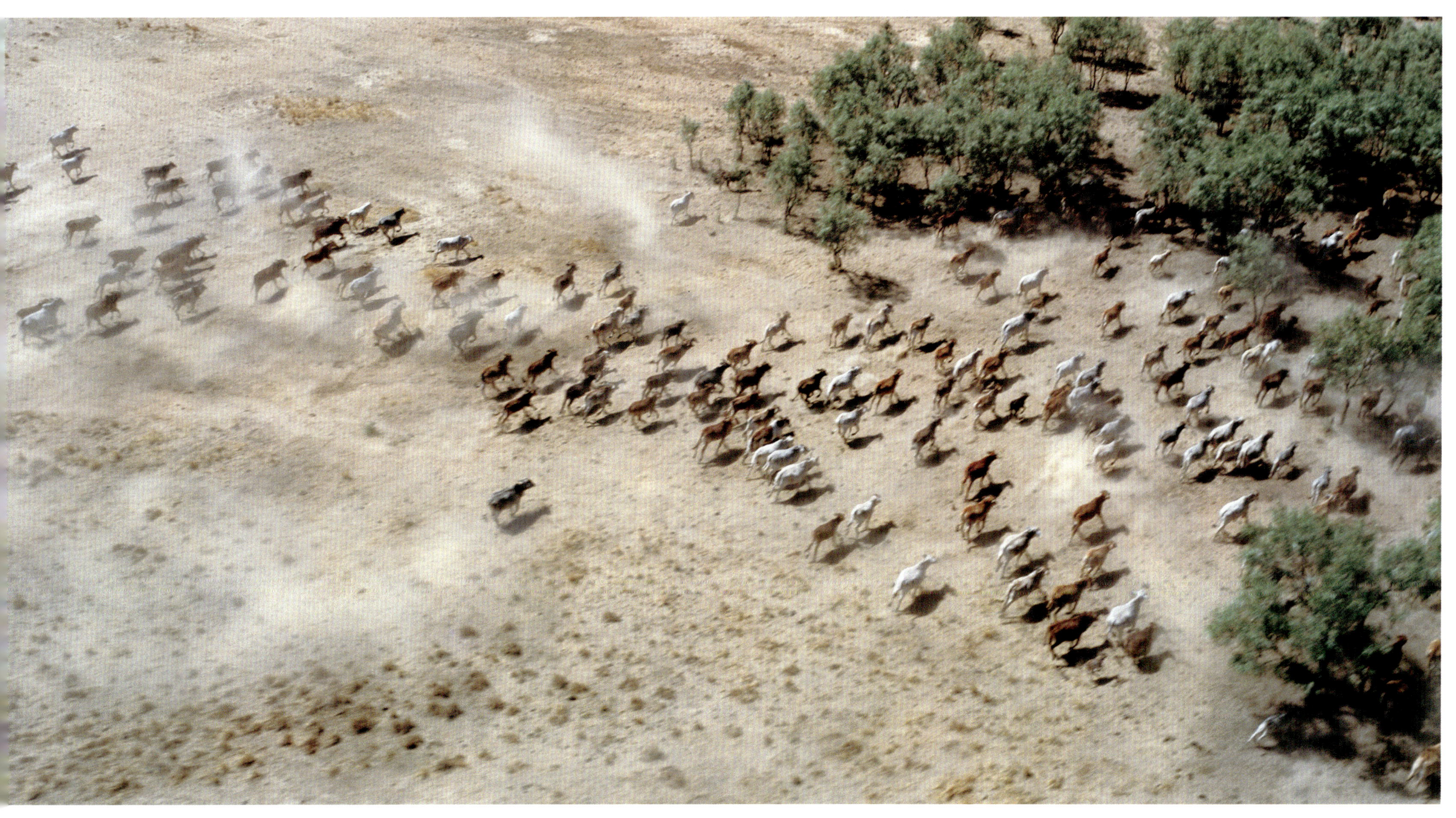

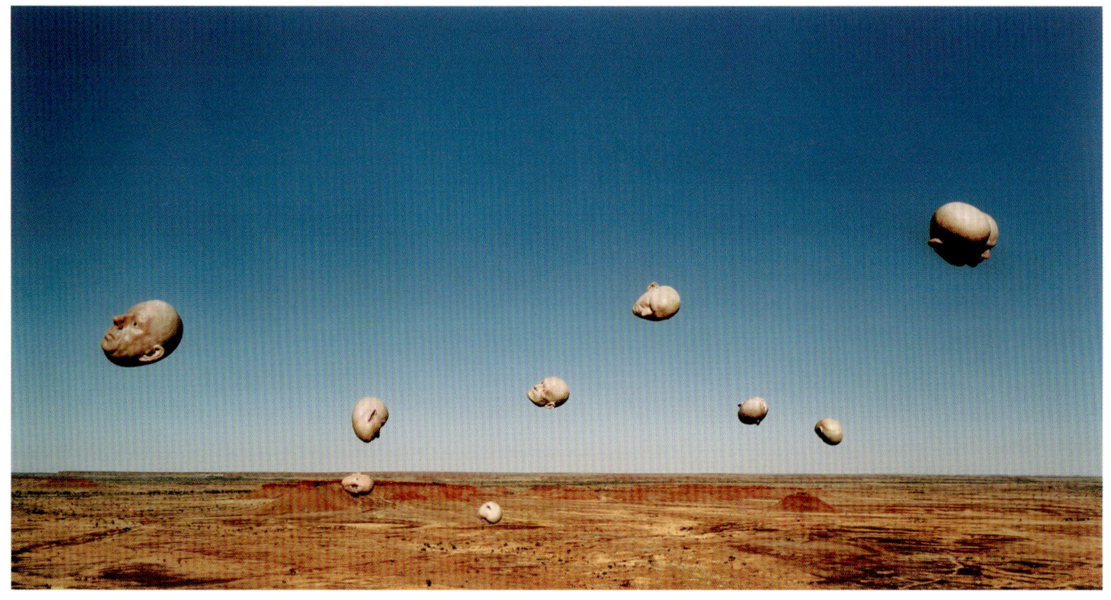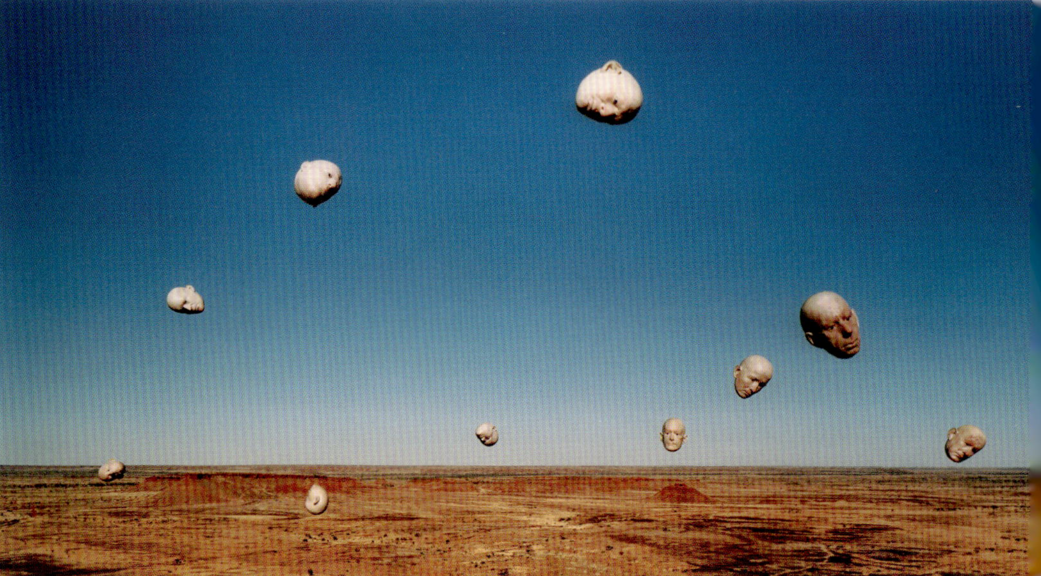

between a rock and a place with no fish, a collaboration with Stephen Birch, 2003
Sequence of four Type-C photographs, each 27½ x 53⅛ in. (70 x 135 cm)

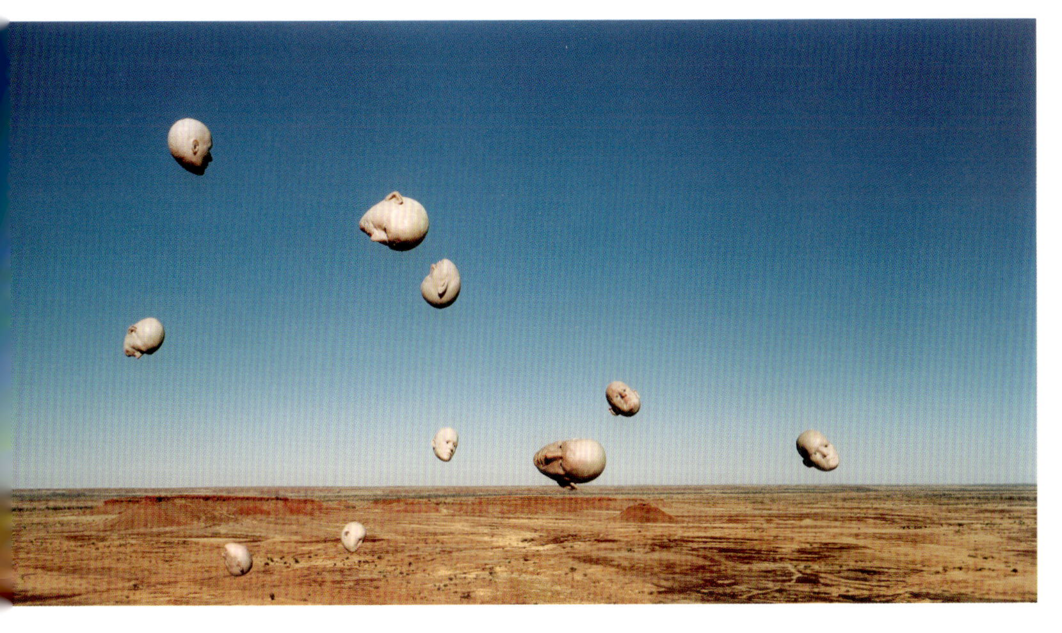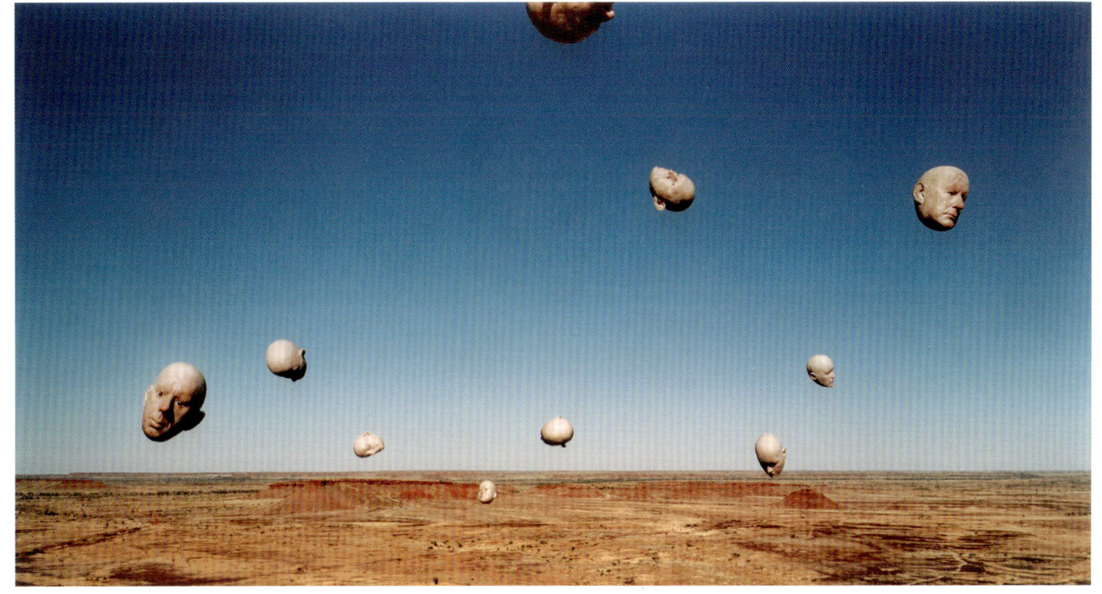

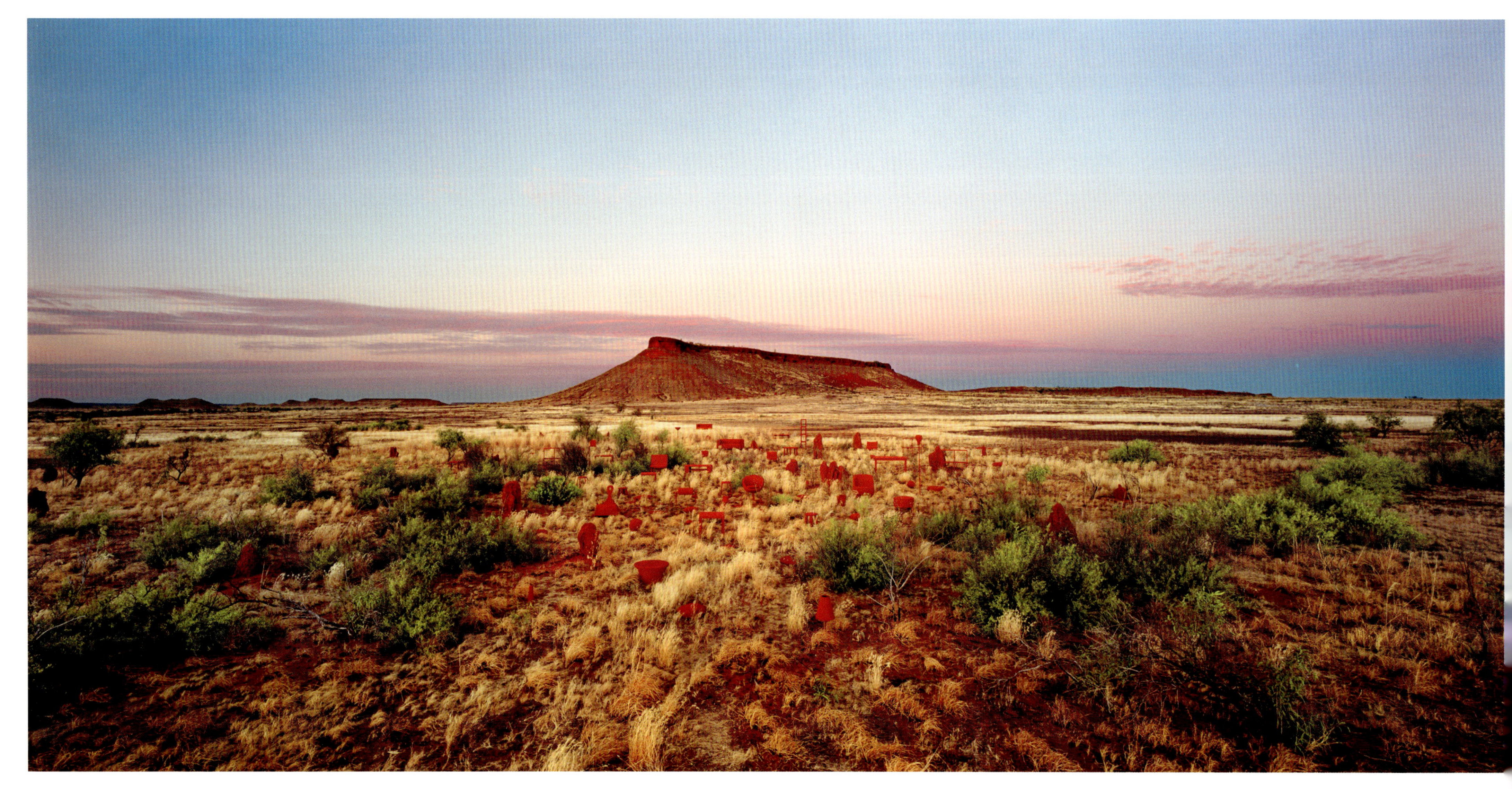

brumby mound #5, 2003
43¼ x 87⅜ in. (110 x 222 cm)

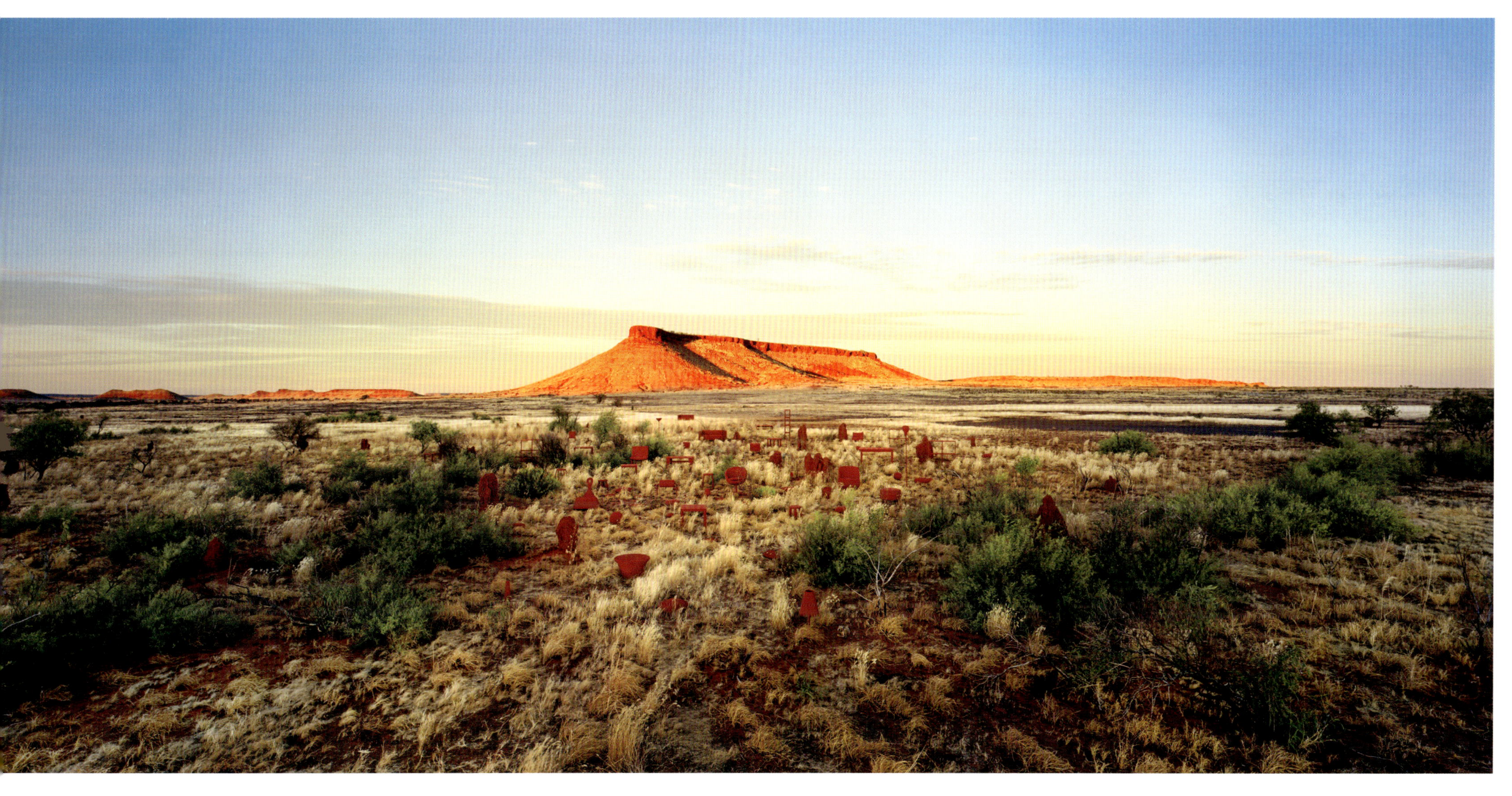

brumby mound #6, 2003
43¼ x 88⅝ in. (110 x 225 cm)

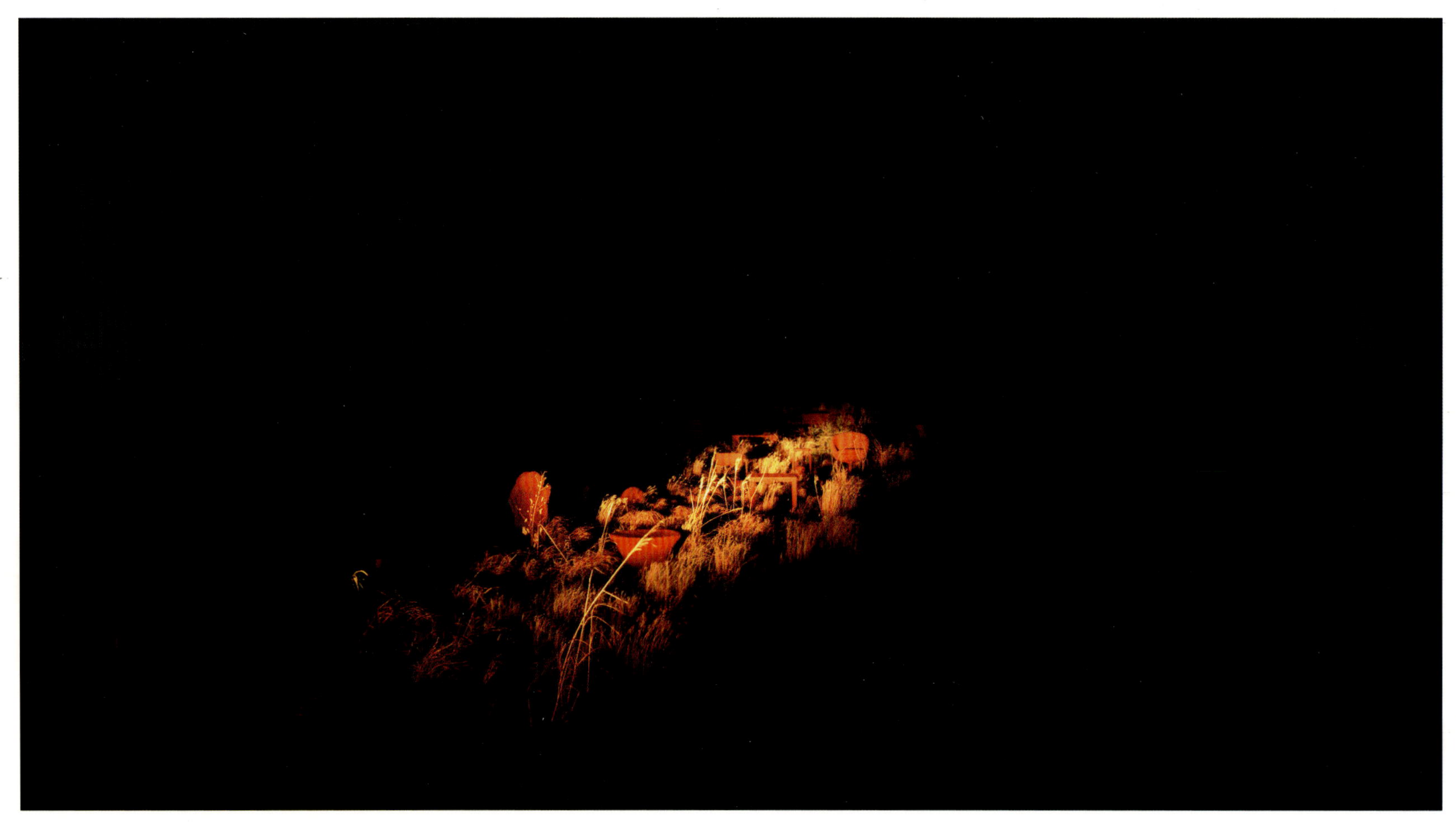

brumby mound #2, 2003
31½ x 58¼ in. (80 x 148 cm)

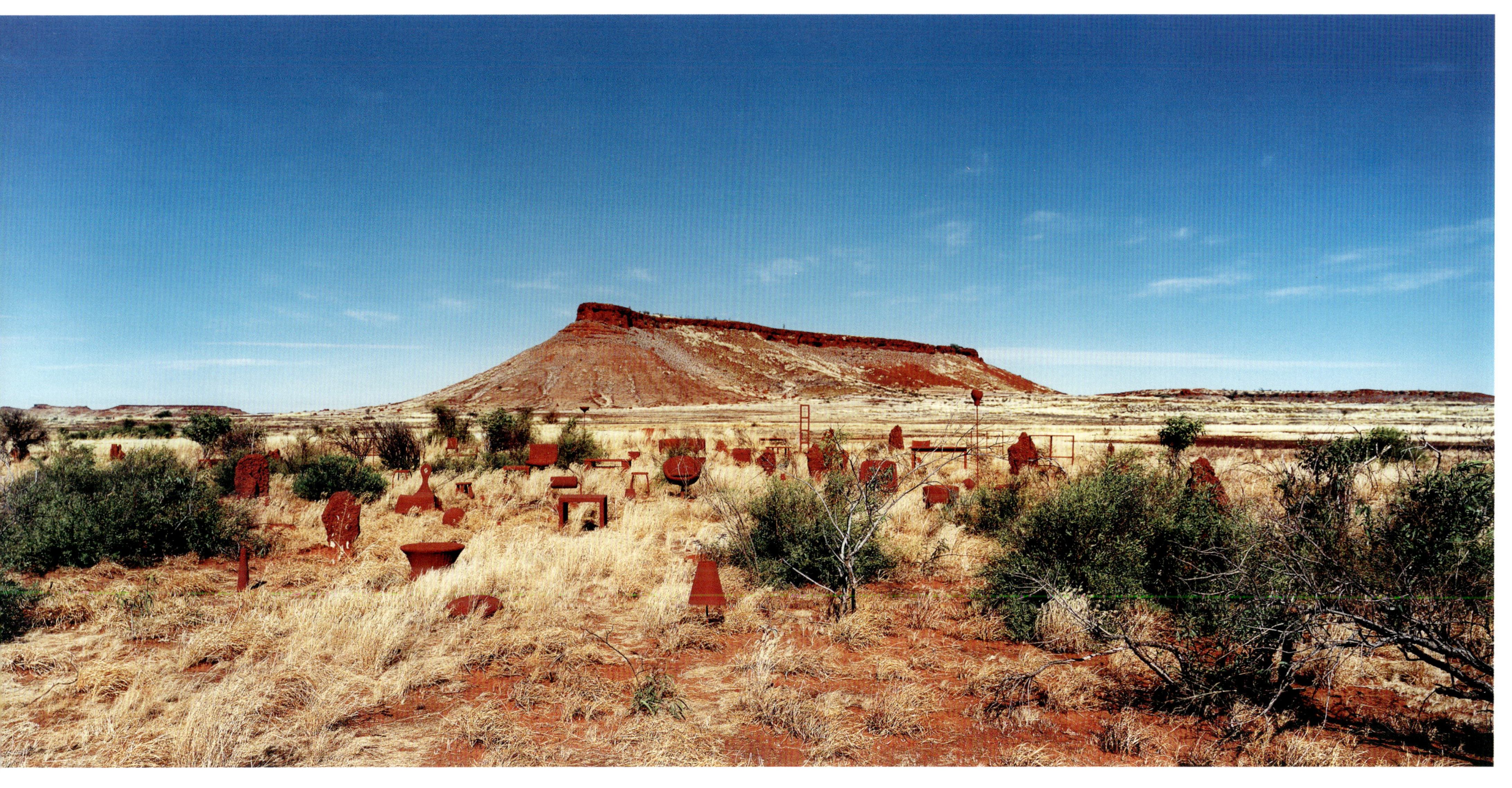

brumby mound #9, 2003

35⅜ x 73 in. (90 x 185.5 cm)

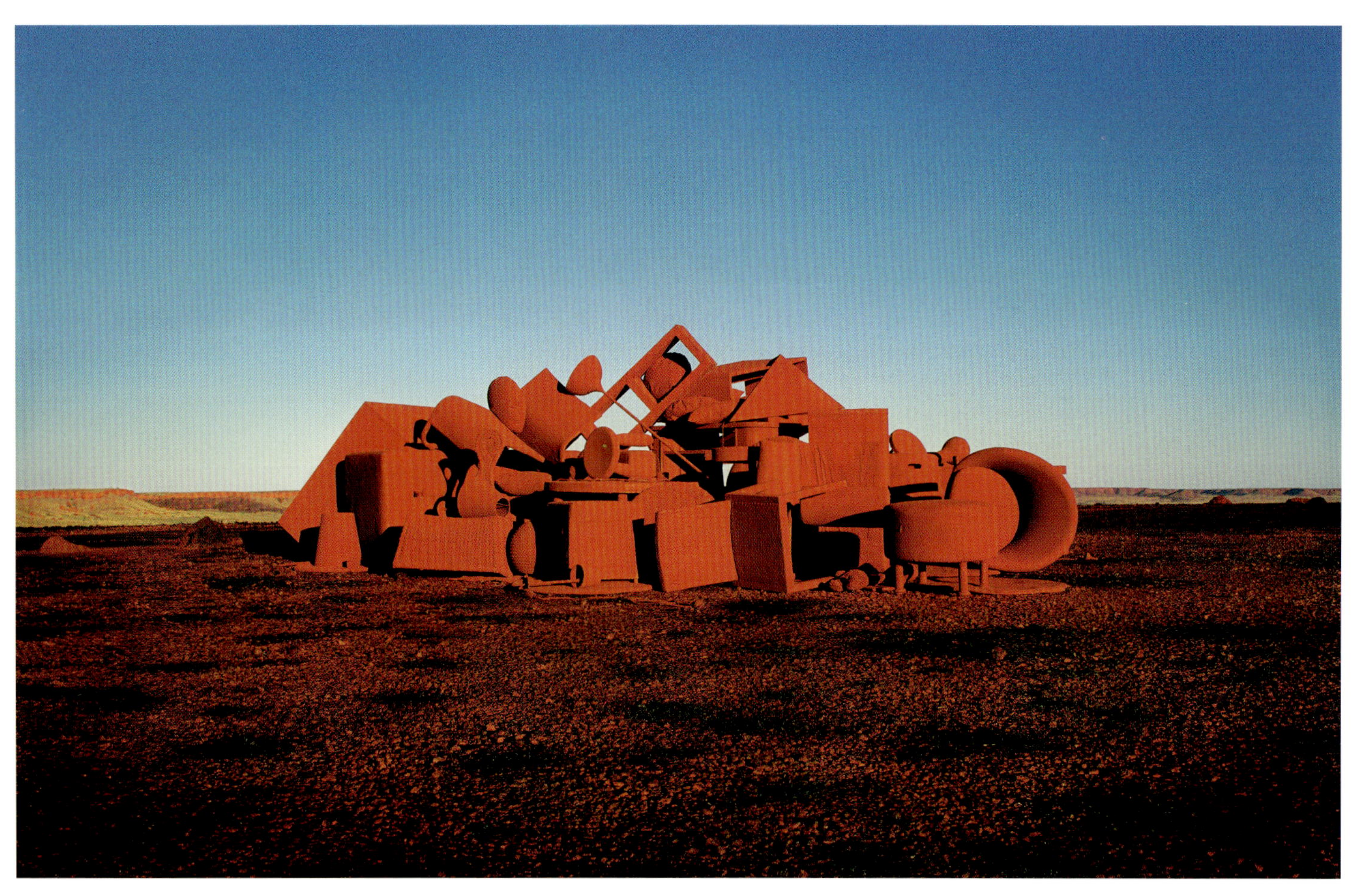

burning Ayer #1, 2003
33½ x 53⅜ in. (85 x 135.7 cm)

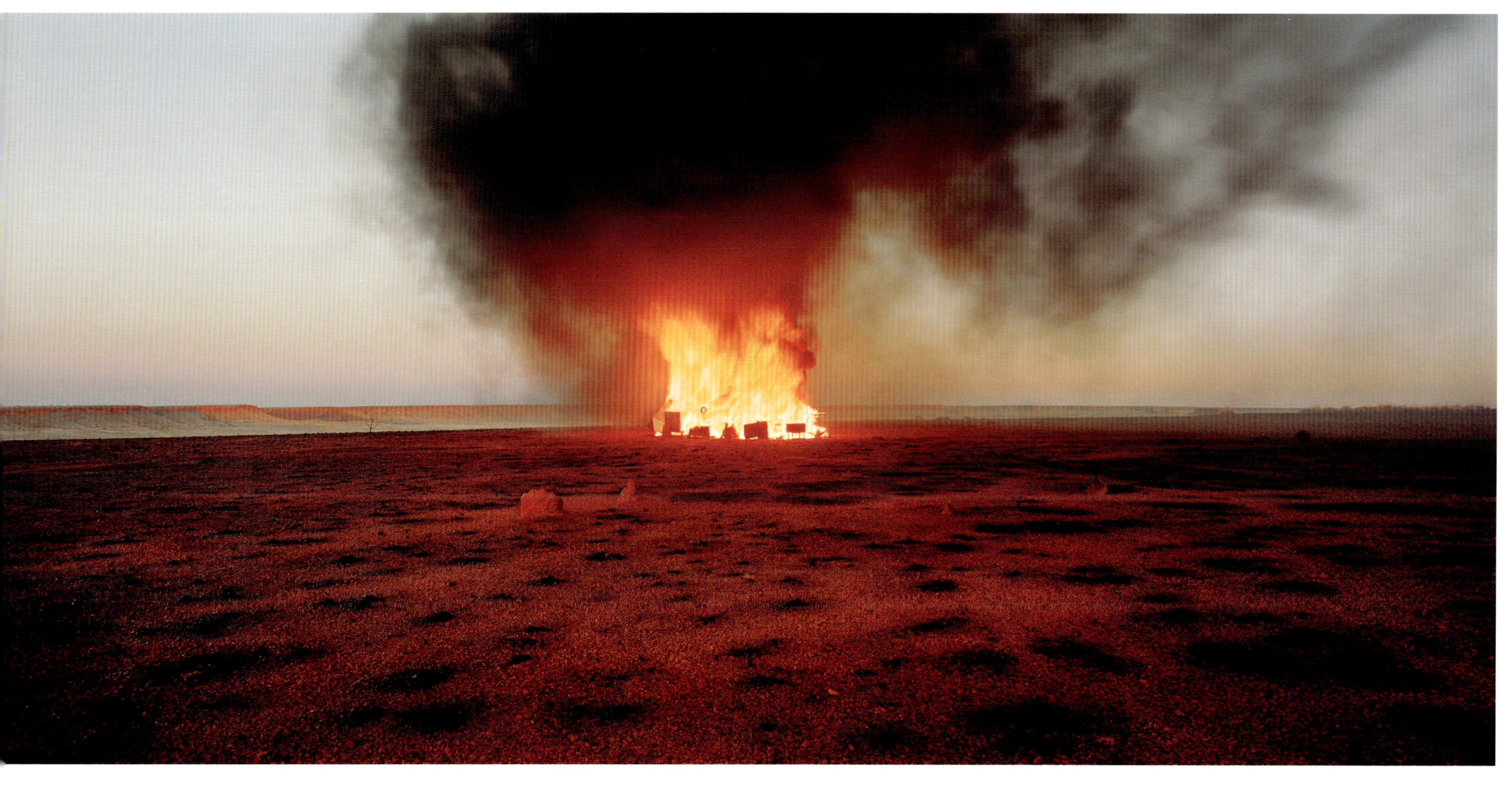

burning Ayer #6, 2003
43¼ x 88¼ in. (110 x 224 cm)

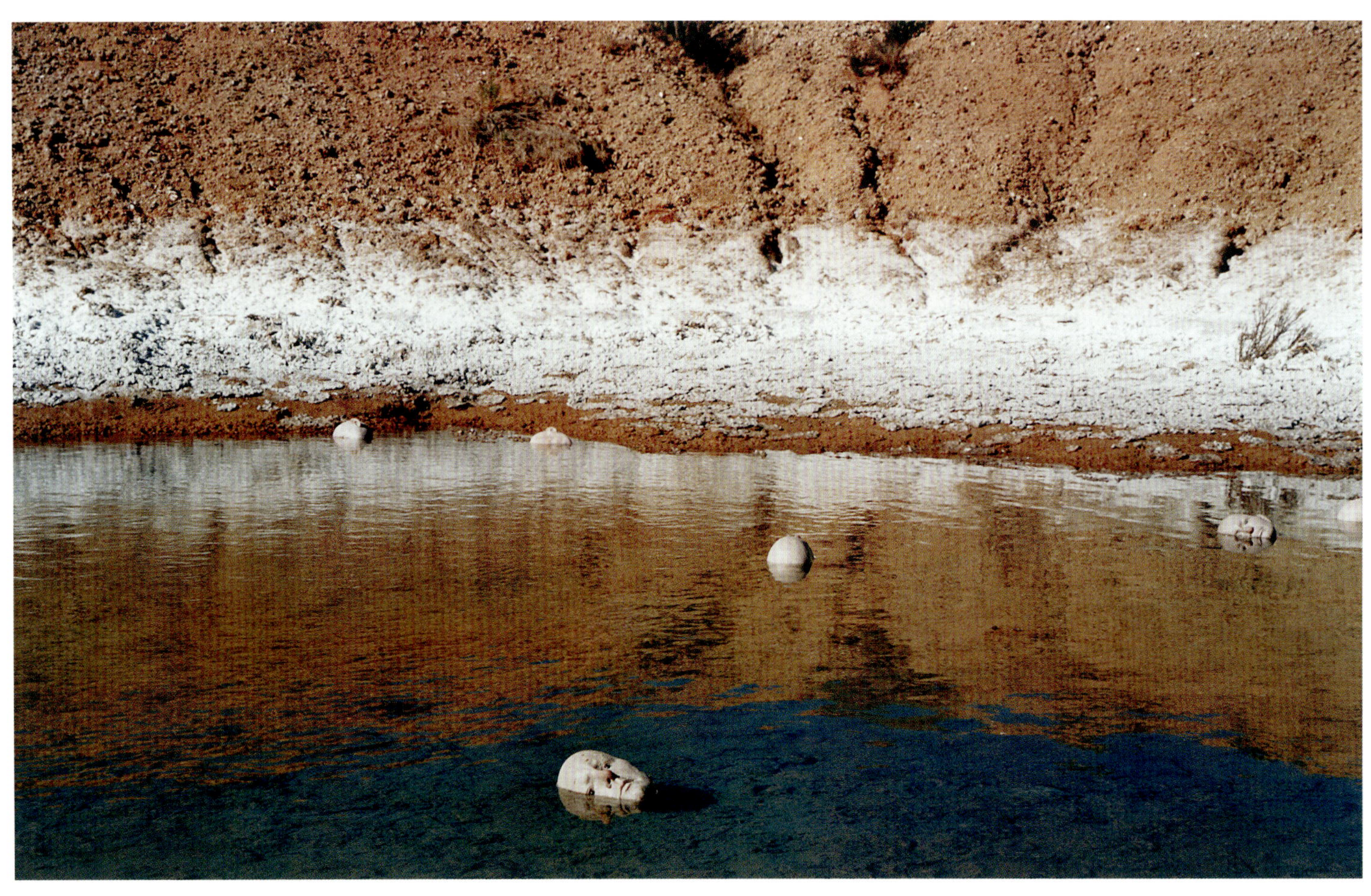

remembering Babylon #6, a collaboration with Stephen Birch, 2003
19⁵/₈ x 31⁷/₈ in. (50 x 81 cm)

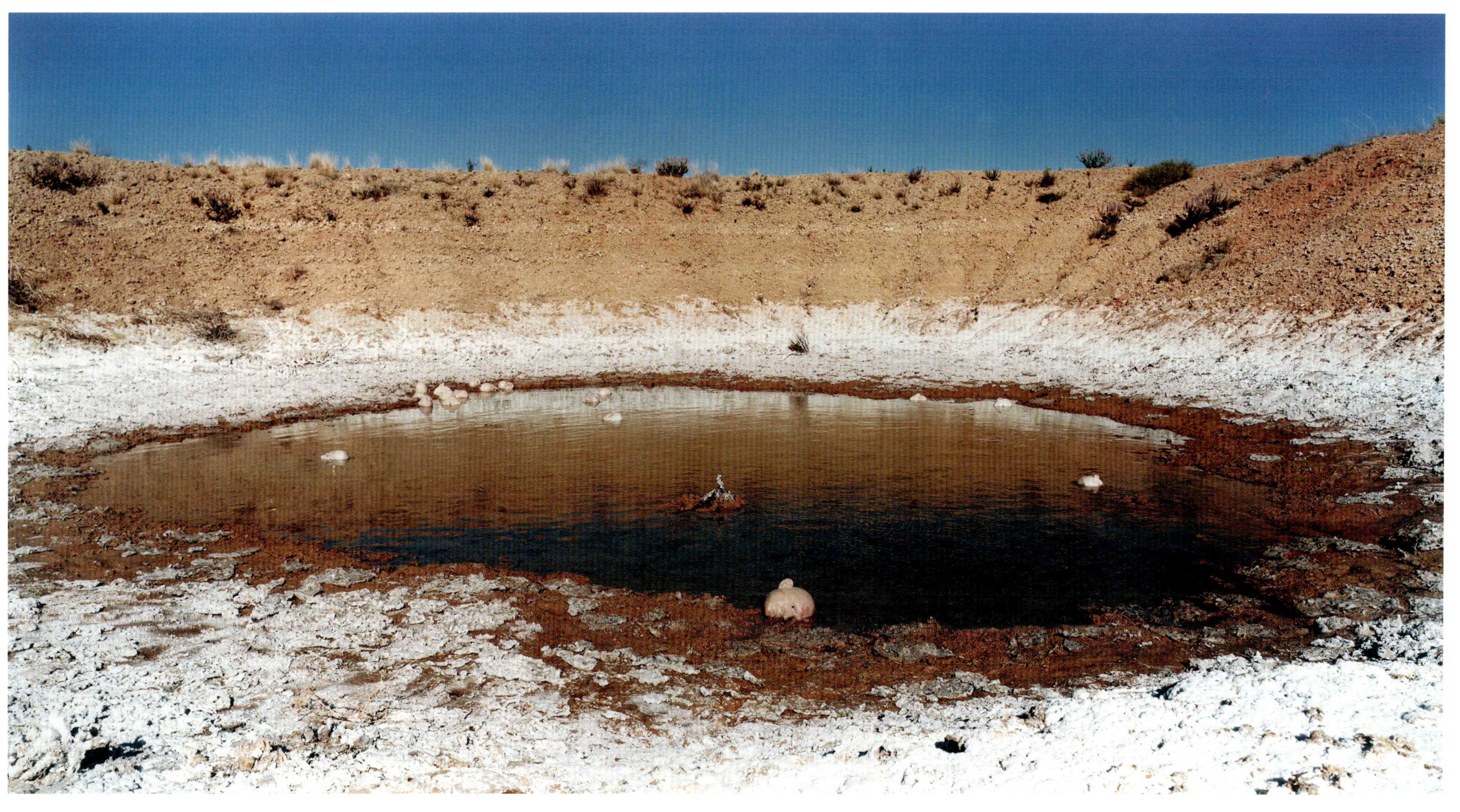

remembering Babylon #5, a collaboration with Stephen Birch, 2003
39³⁄₈ x 74¼ in. (100 x 188.5 cm)

to walk on a sea of salt, 2004
43¼ x 89¼ in. (110 x 226.7 cm)

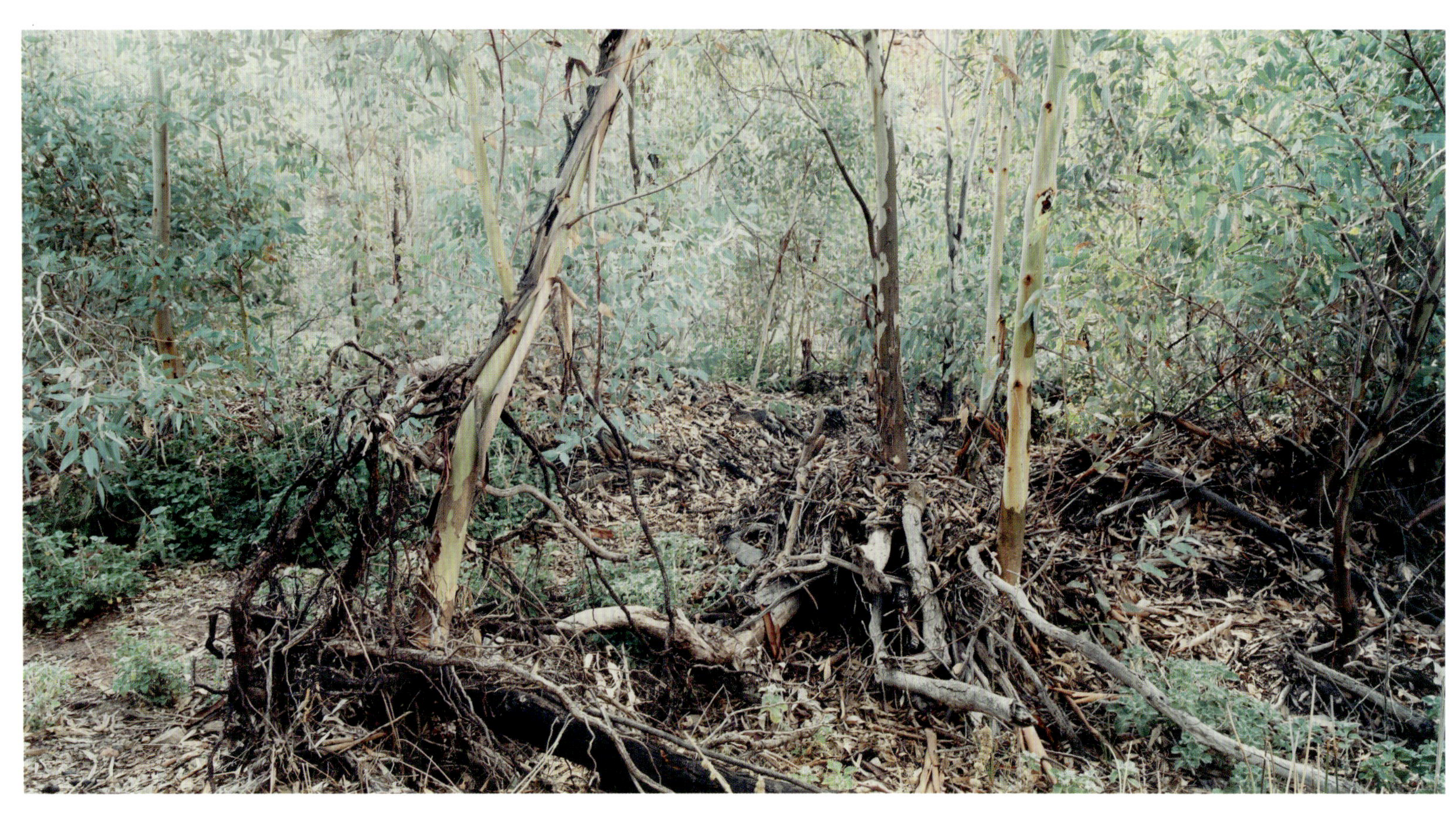

opposite Cazneaux, 2004
33½ x 64½ in. (85 x 164 cm)

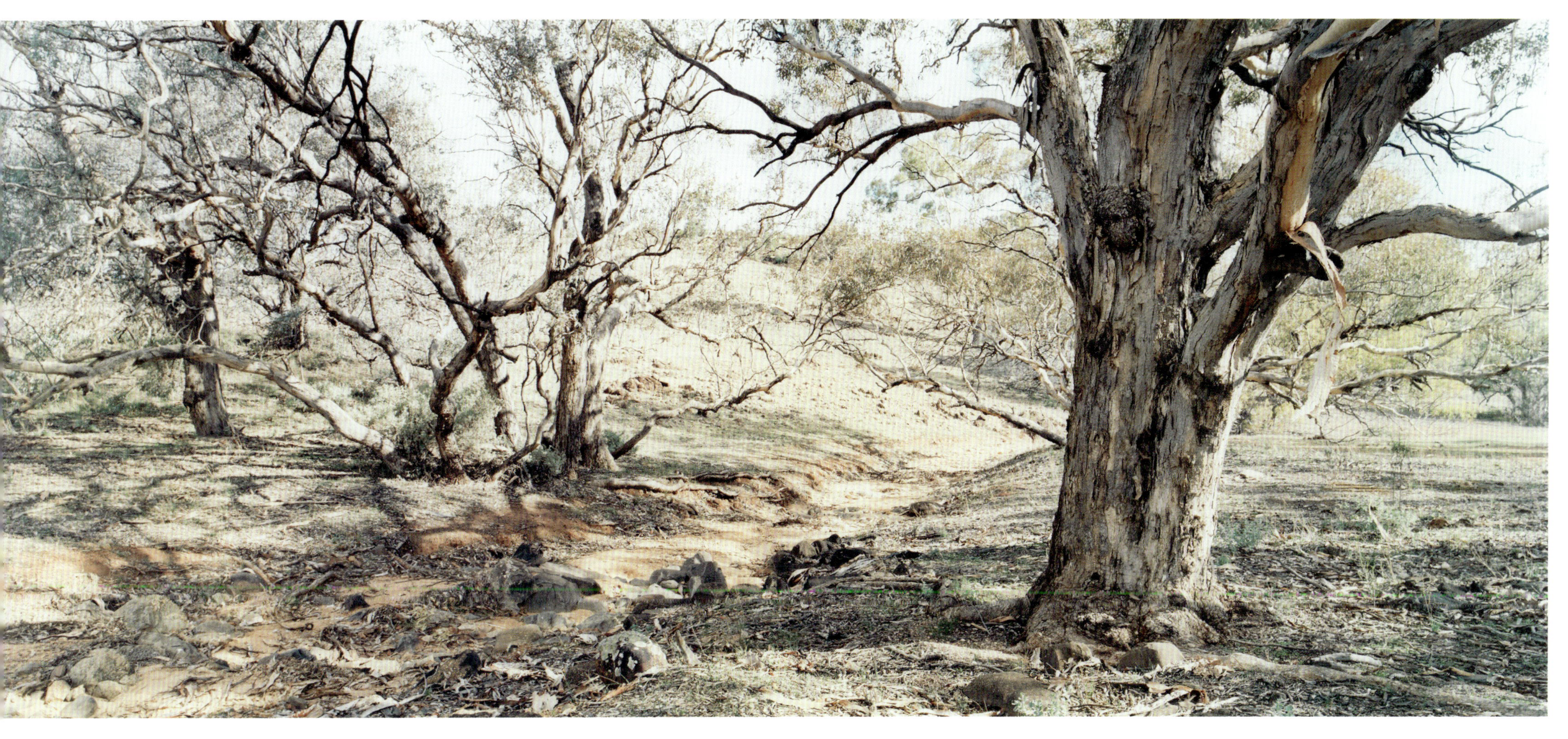

after Heysen, 2004
43¼ x 99¼ in. (110 x 252 cm)

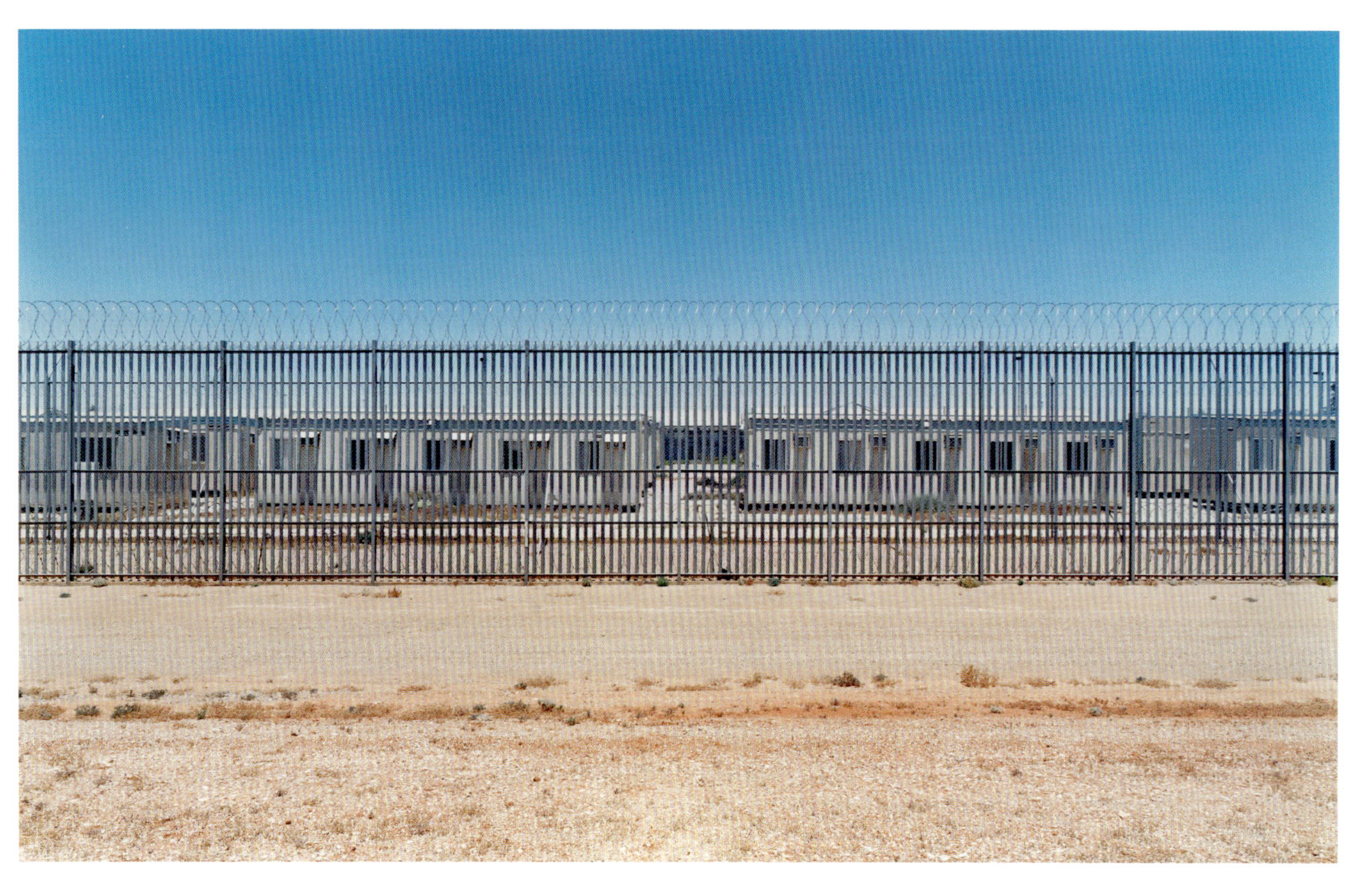

and you can even pay later, 2004
33½ x 55⅛ in. (85 x 140 cm)

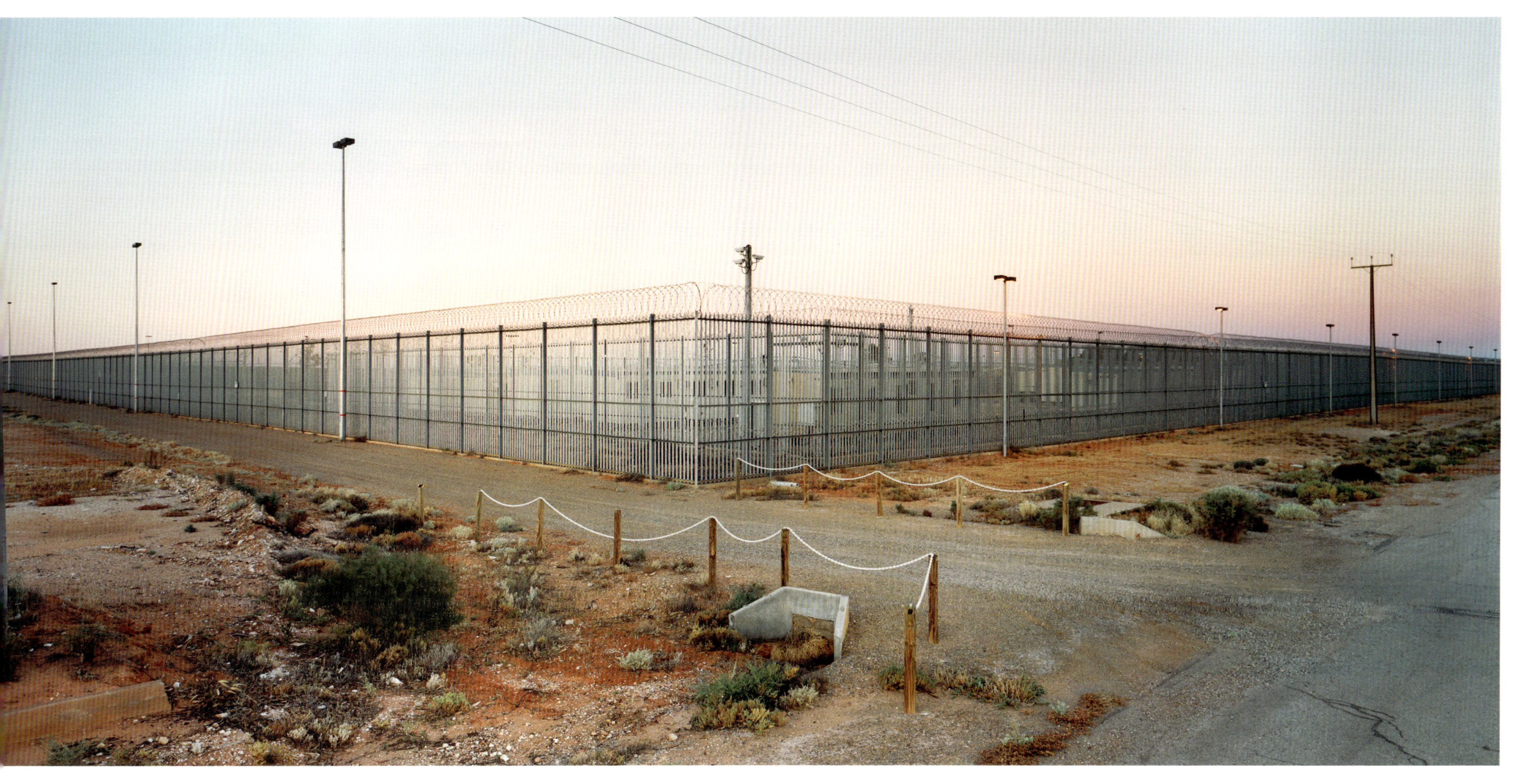

welcome to Australia, 2004
43¼ x 88¼ in. (110 x 224 cm)

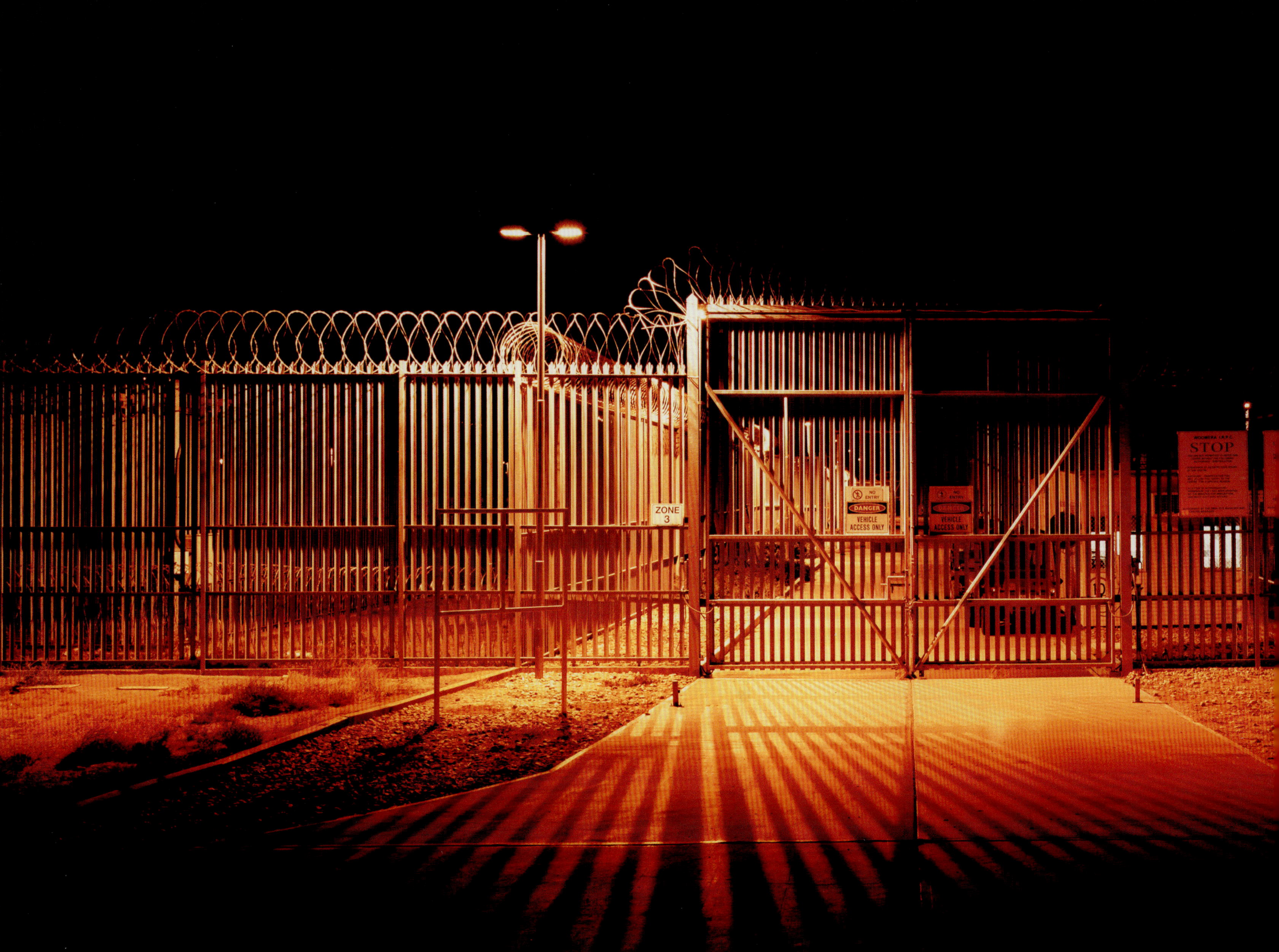
ZONE
3
NO ENTRY
DANGER
VEHICLE
ACCESS ONLY
NO ENTRY
VEHICLE
ACCESS ONLY
STOP

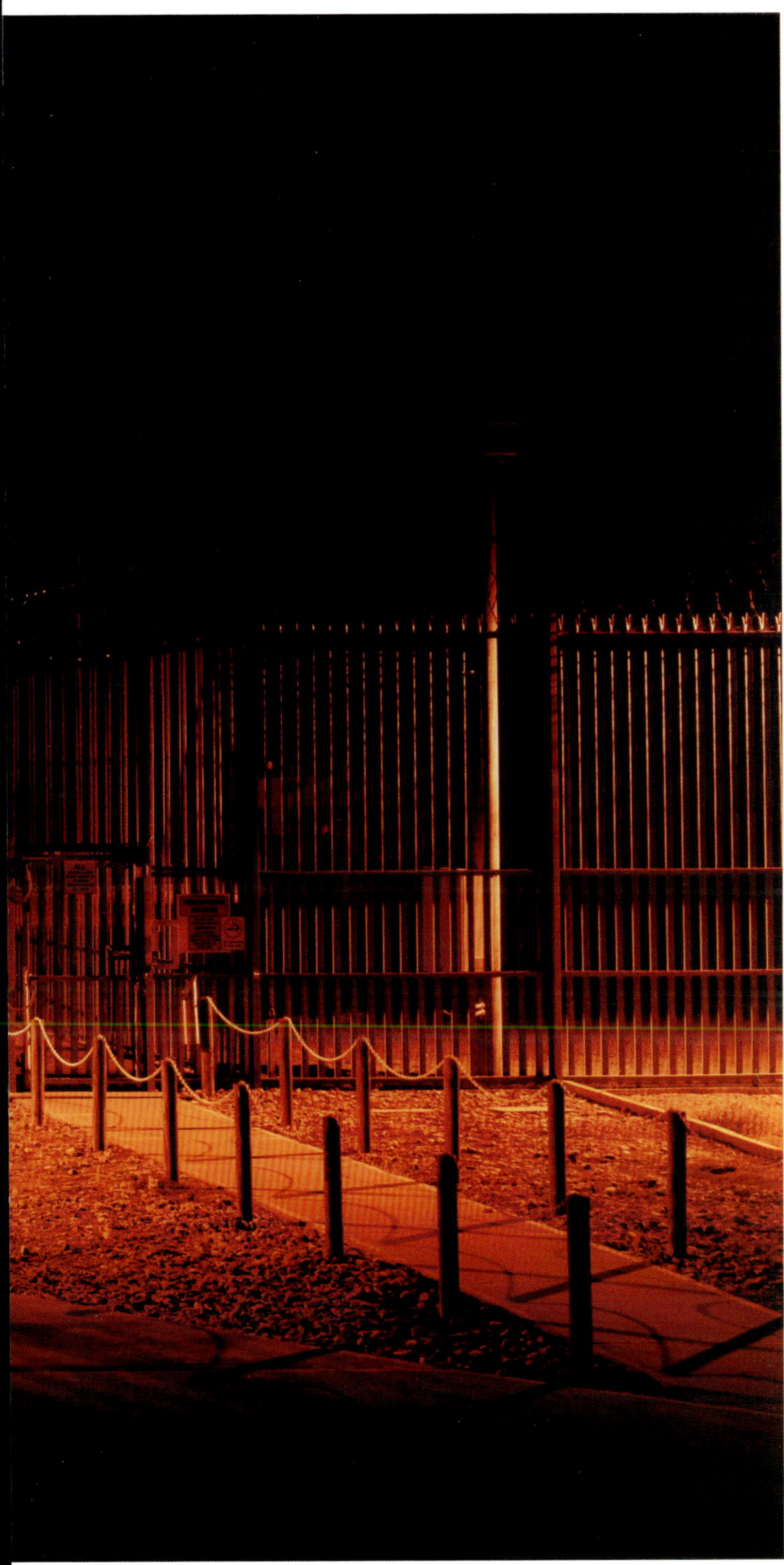

5.10 am, 15th December 2004, 2004
33½ x 66¾ in. (85 x 169.5 cm)

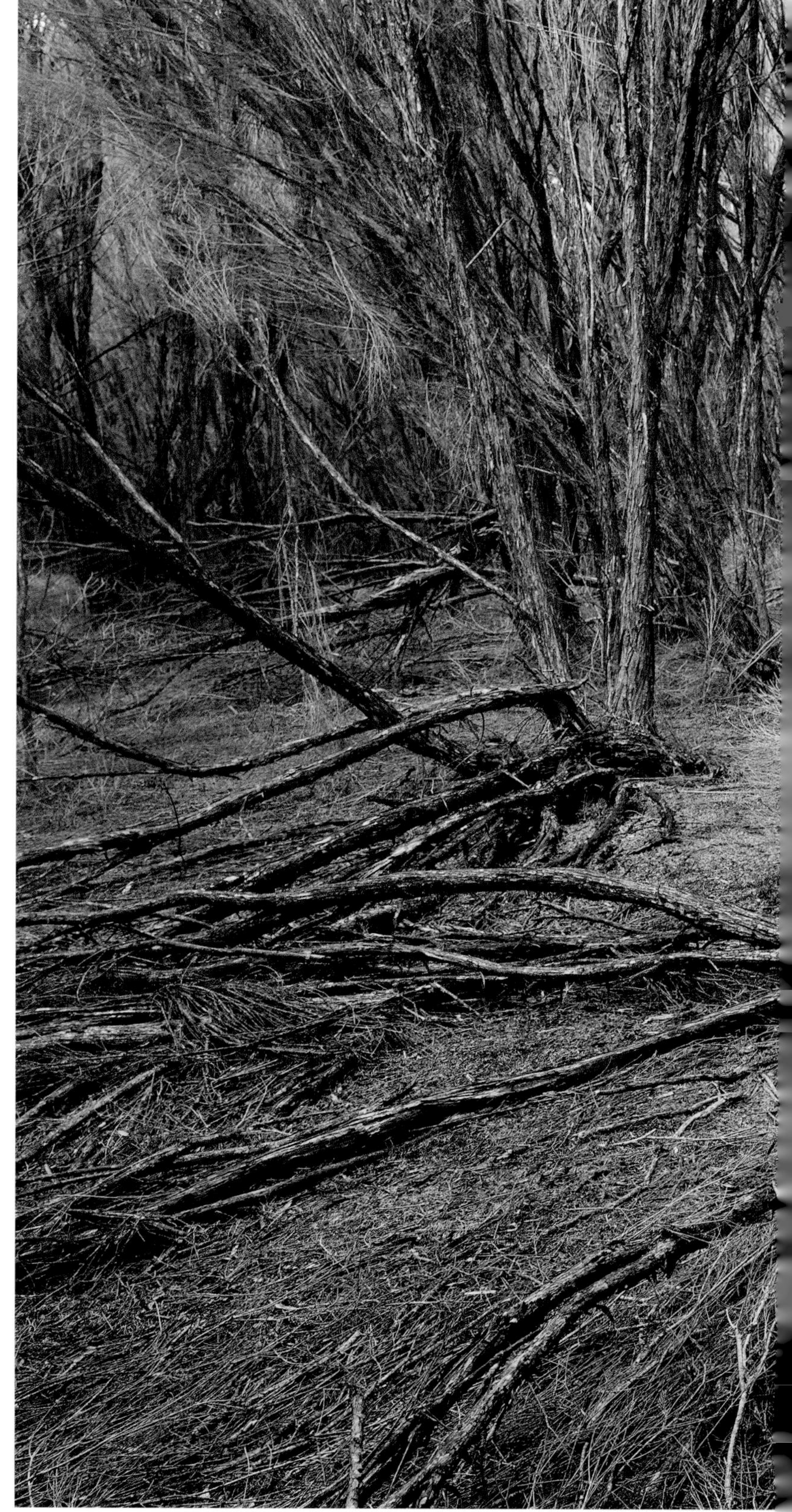

weather (Eden) #1, 2006
43¼ x 87¼ in. (110 x 221.5 cm)

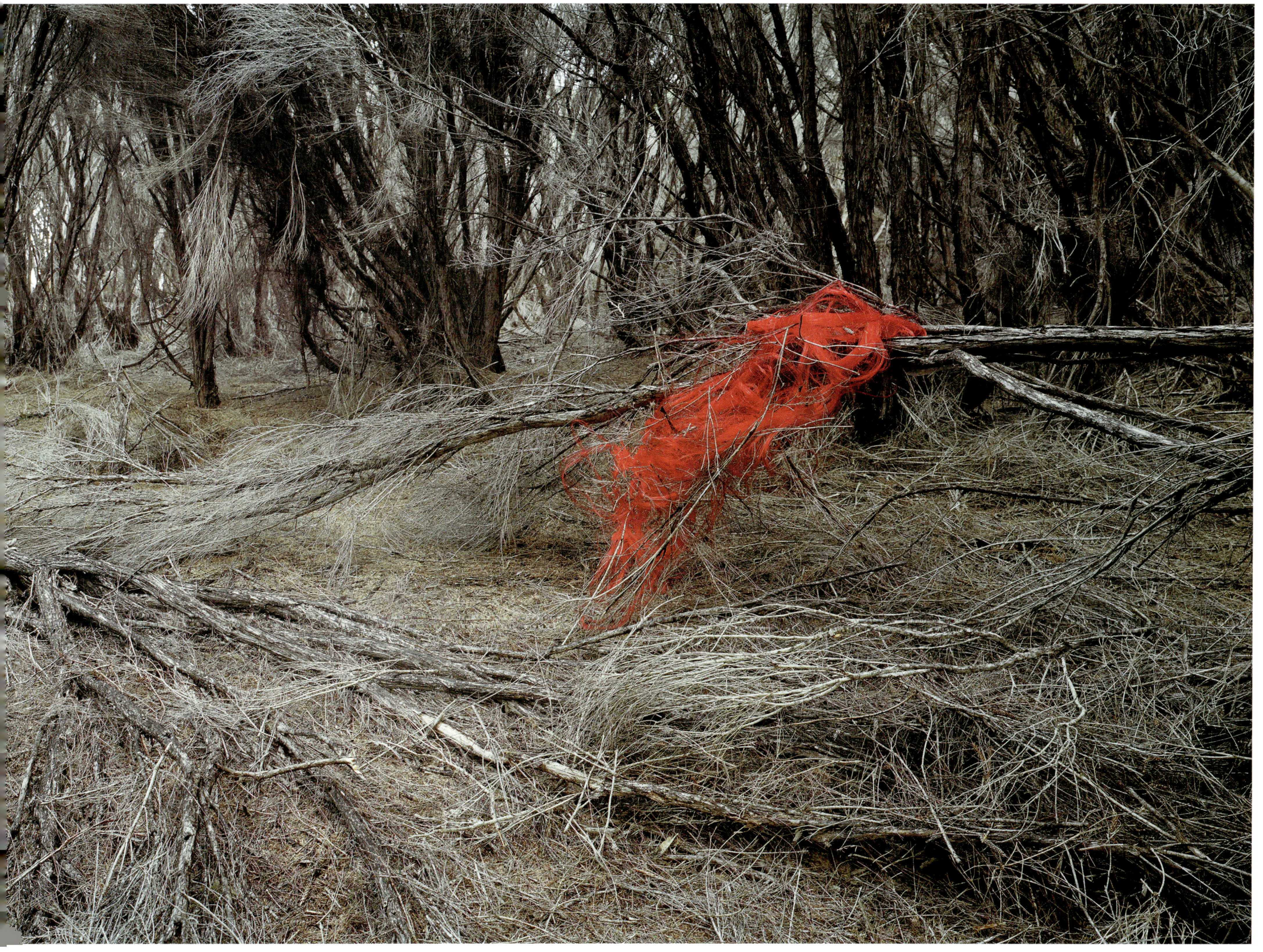

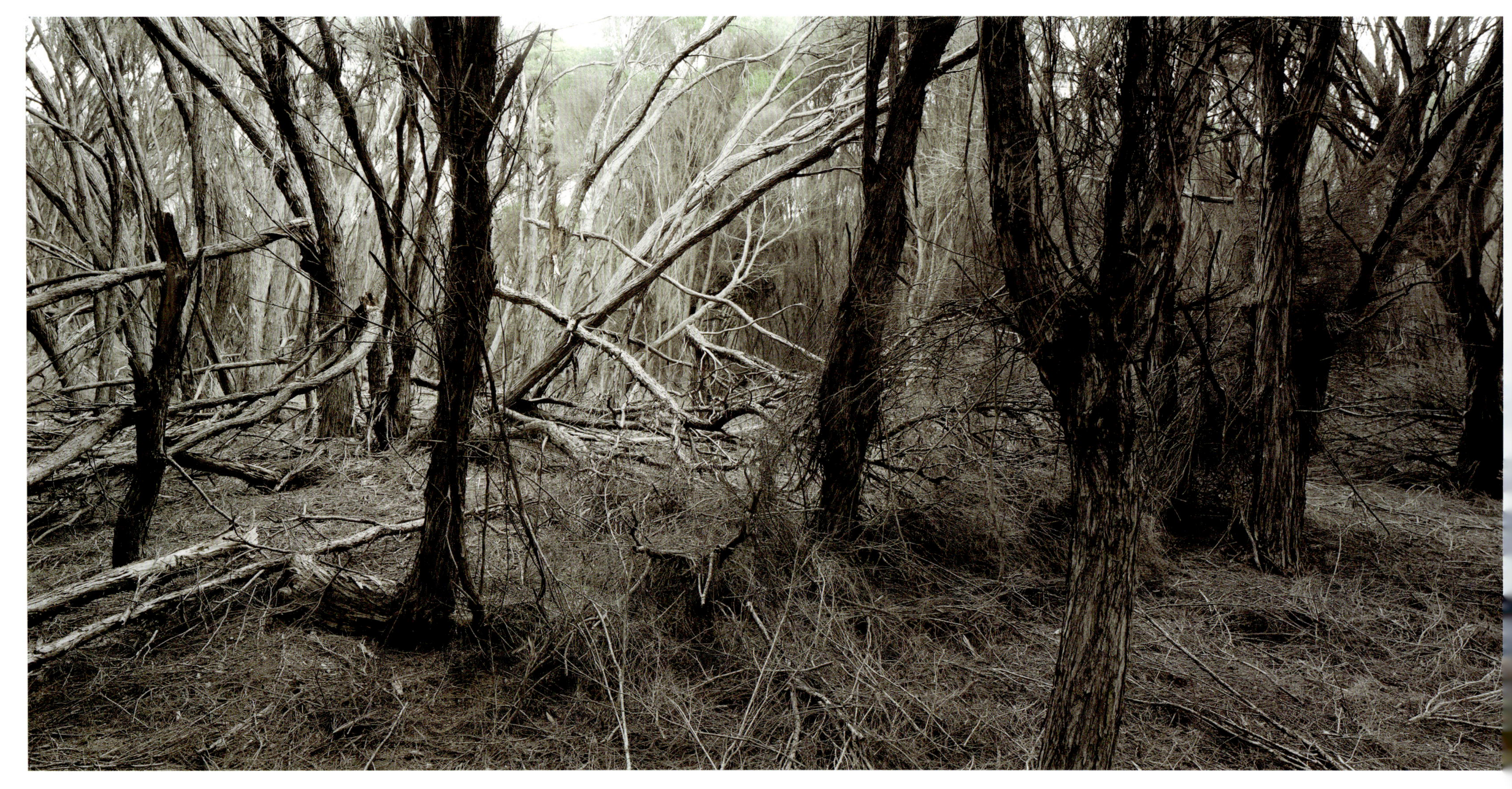

weather (Eden) #2, 2006
43¼ x 87¼ in. (110 x 221.5 cm)

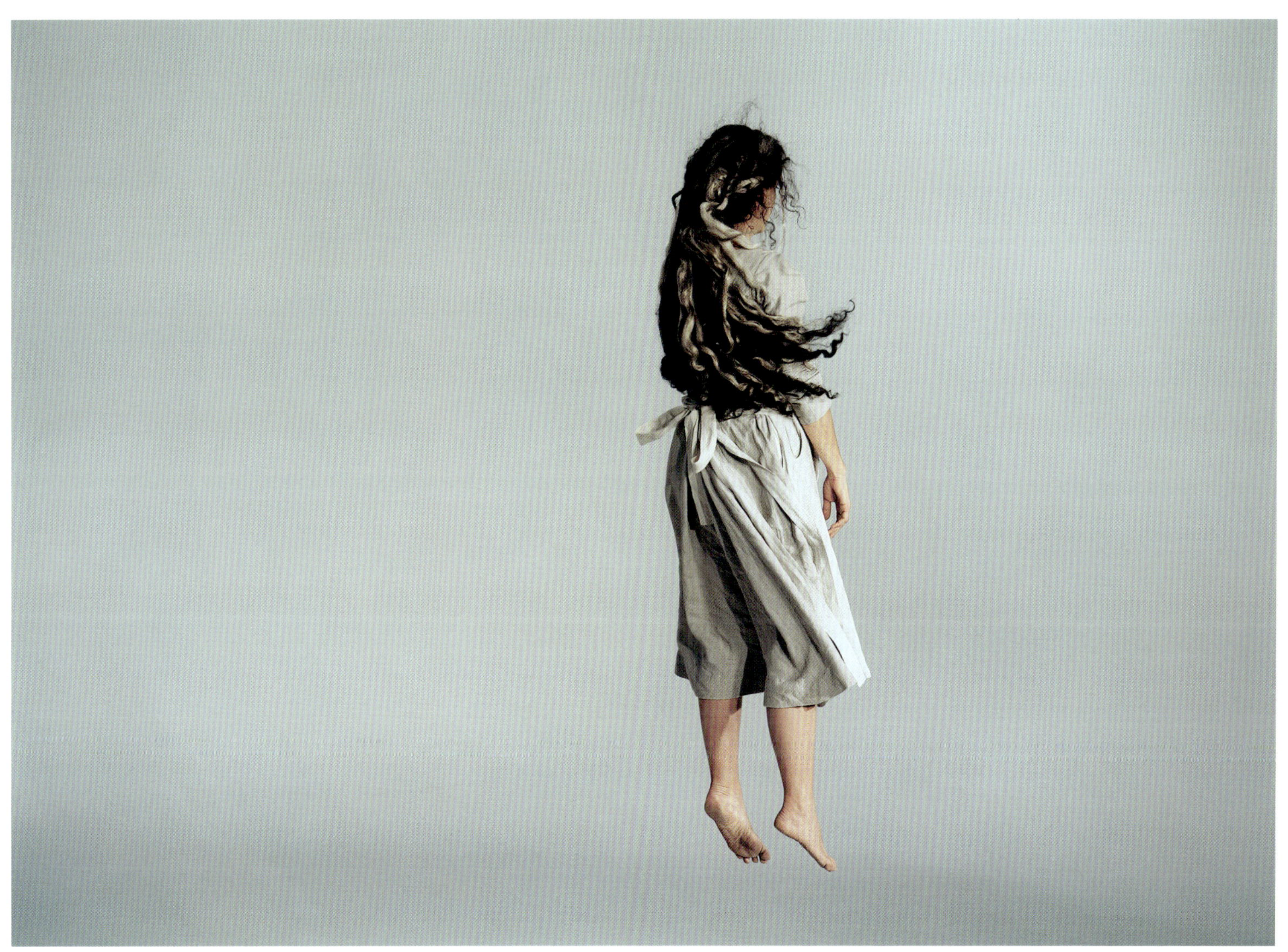

weather #5, 2006
43¼ x 60⅞ in. (110 x 154.5 cm)

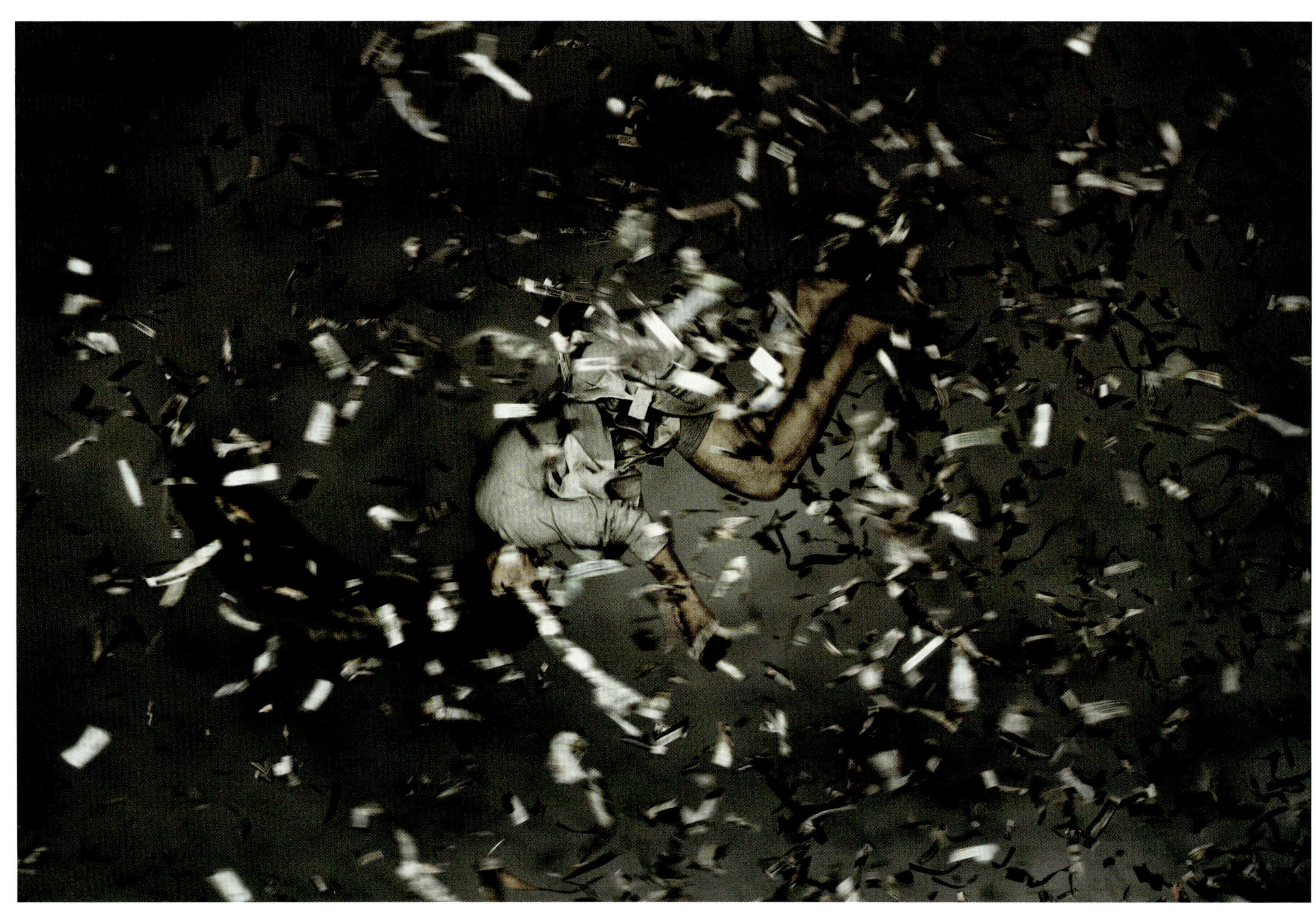

weather #3, 2006
43¼ x 65⅜ in. (110 x 166 cm)

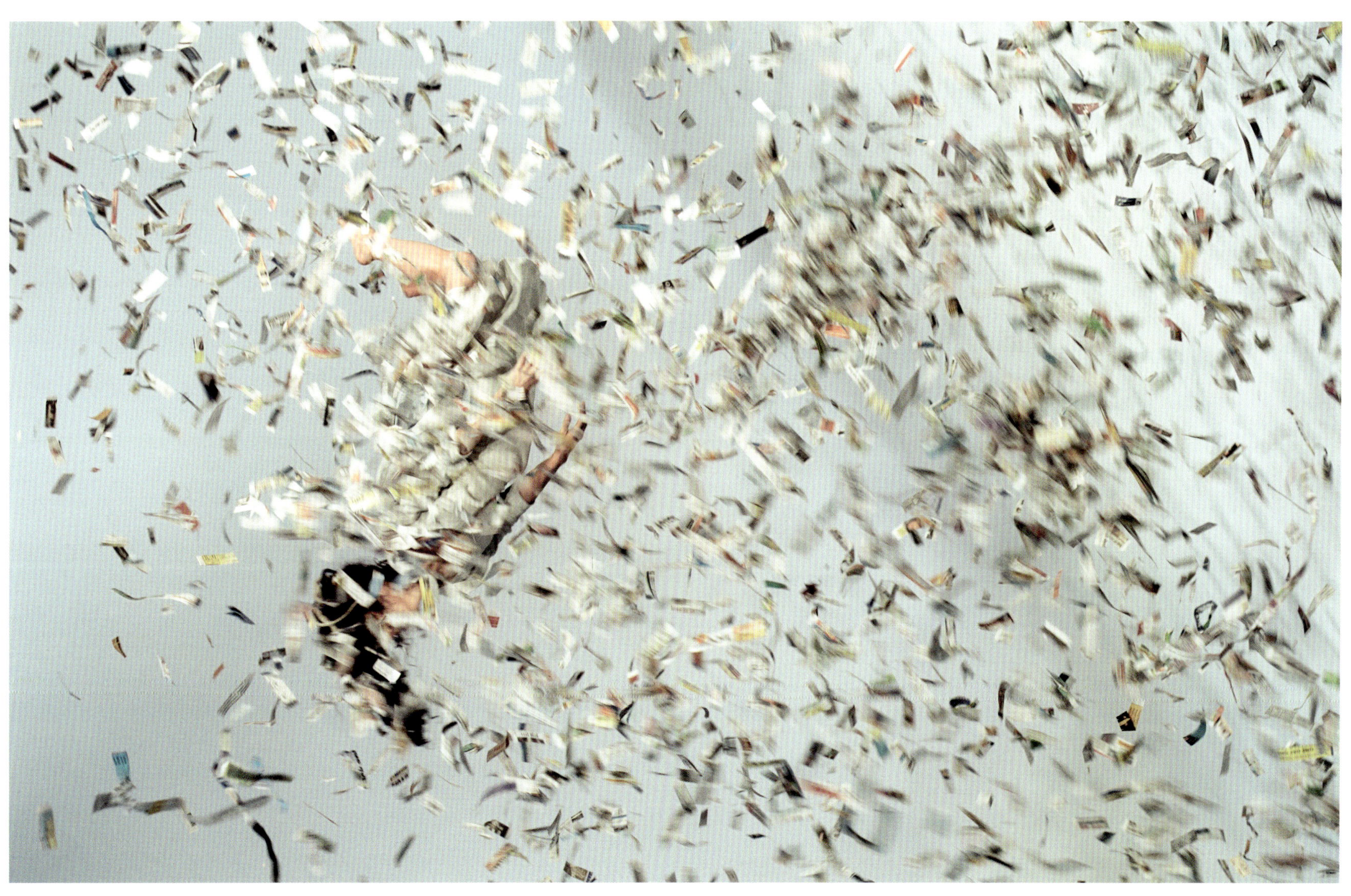

weather #6, 2006
43¼ x 68⅞ in. (110 x 175 cm)

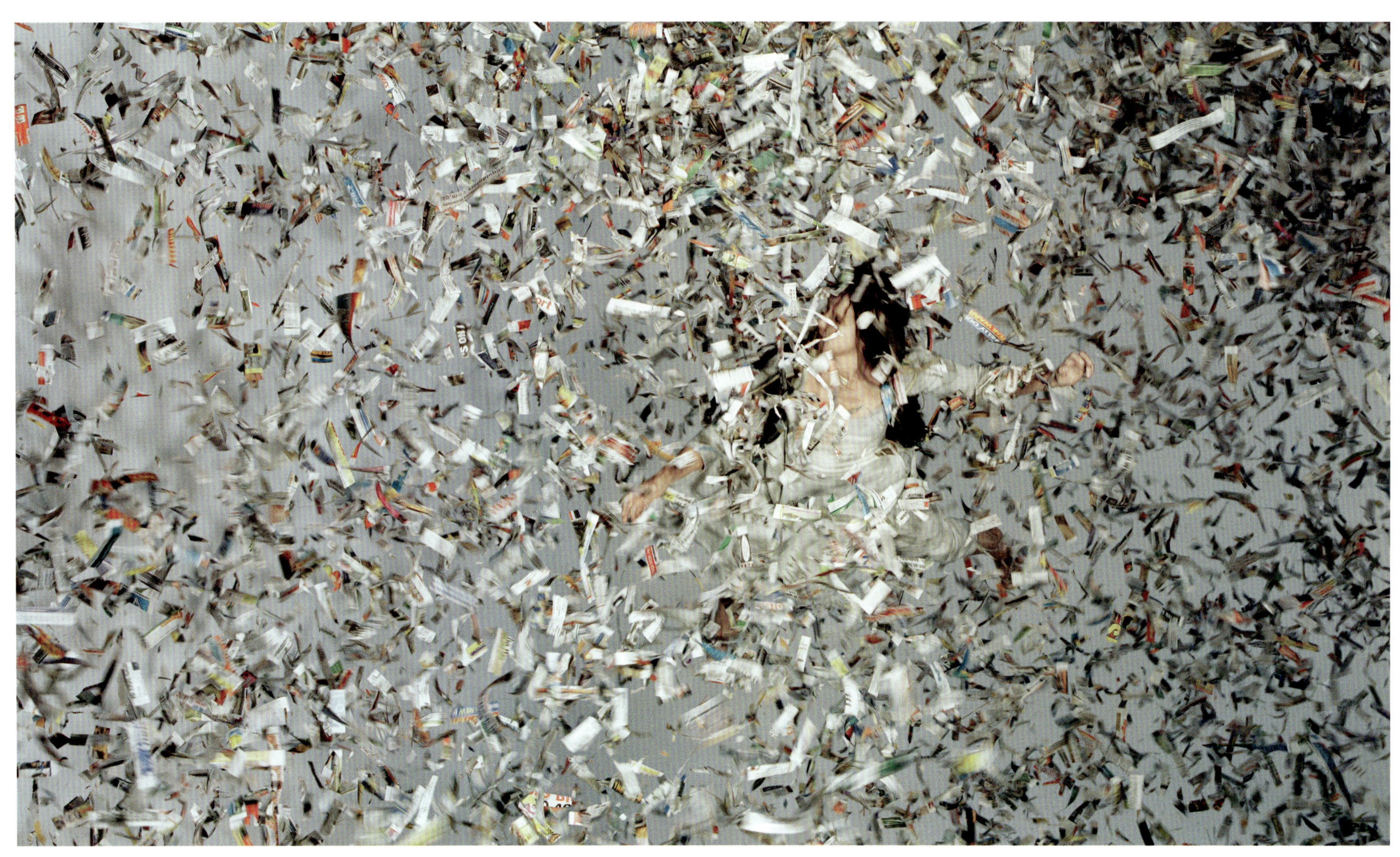

weather #10, 2006
43¼ x 74¼ in. (110 x 188.5 cm)

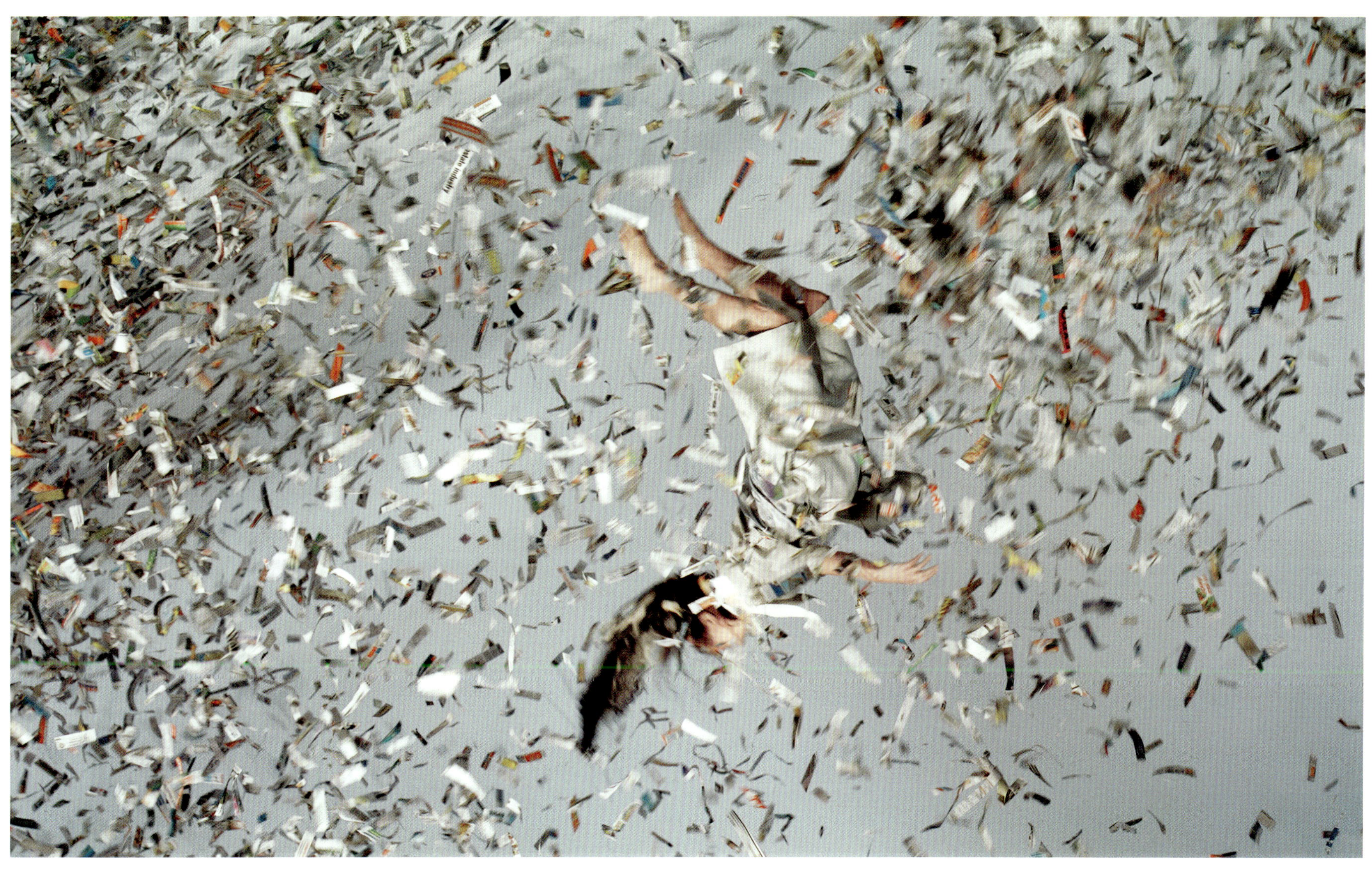

weather #12, 2006
43¼ x 71⅝ in. (110 x 182 cm)

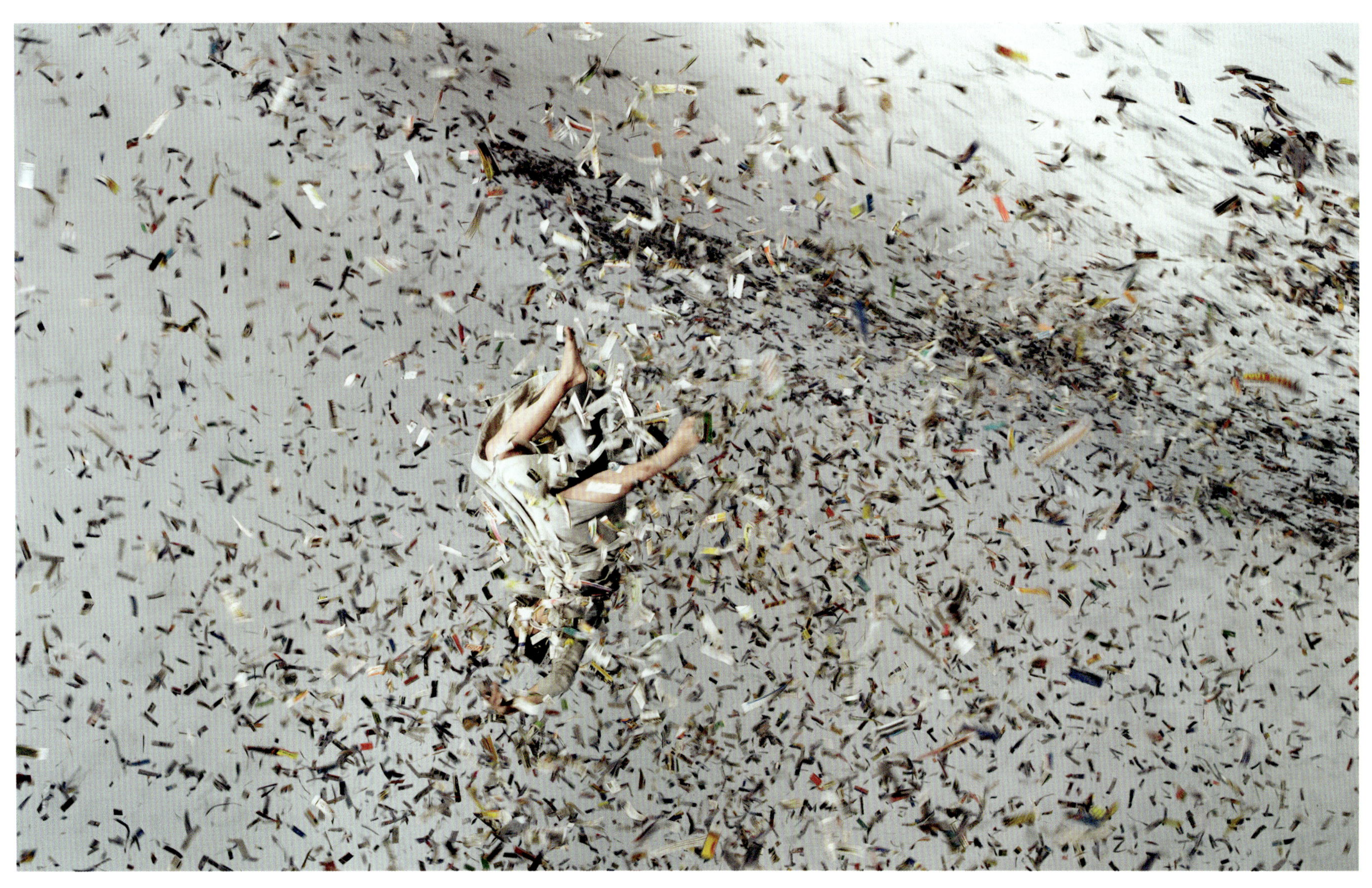

weather #15, 2006
43¼ x 70½ in. (110 x 179 cm)

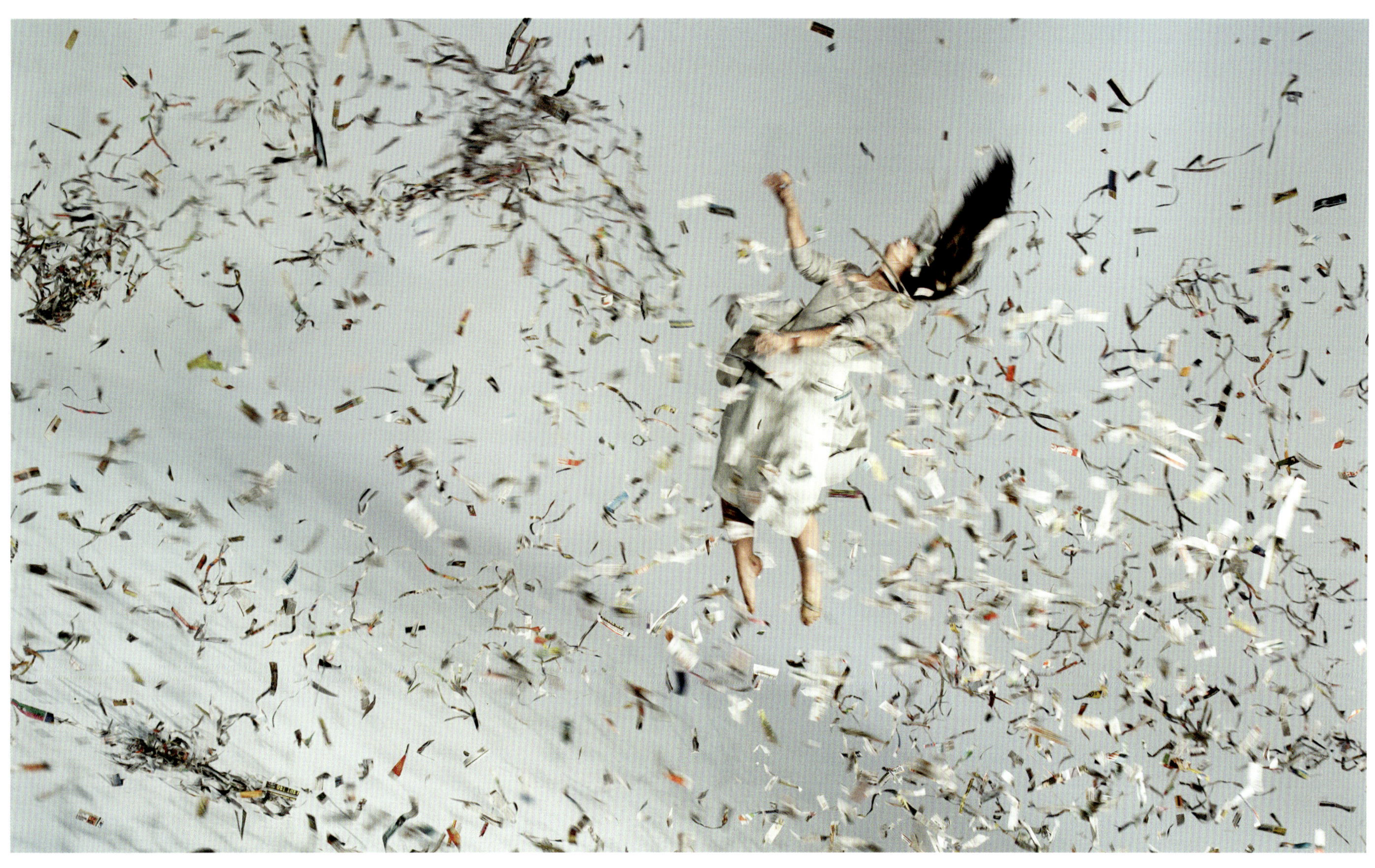

weather #4, 2006
43¼ x 72½ in. (110 x 184 cm)

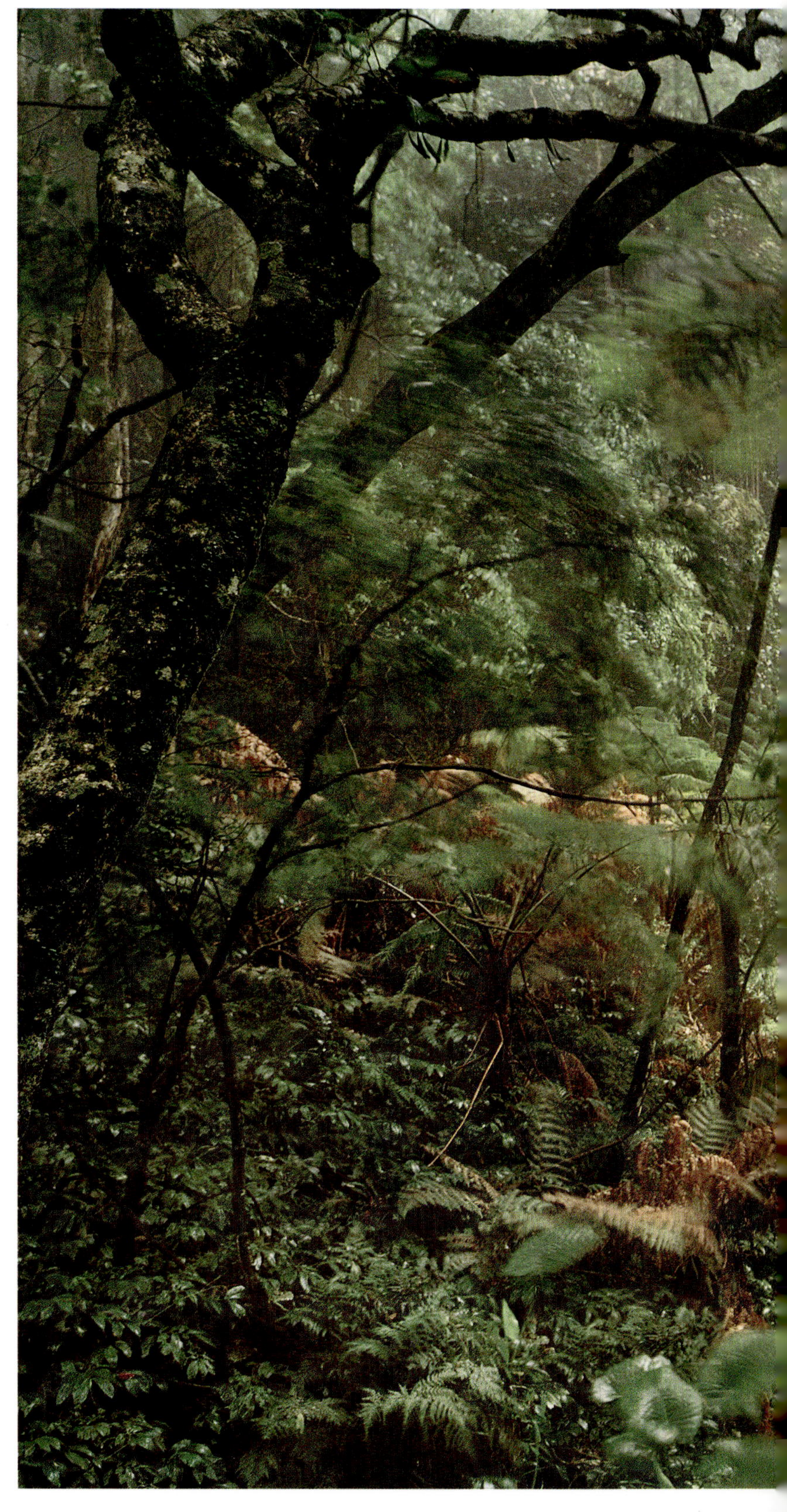

weather (Paradise falls) #14, 2006–07
43¼ x 87½ in. (110 x 222.36 cm)

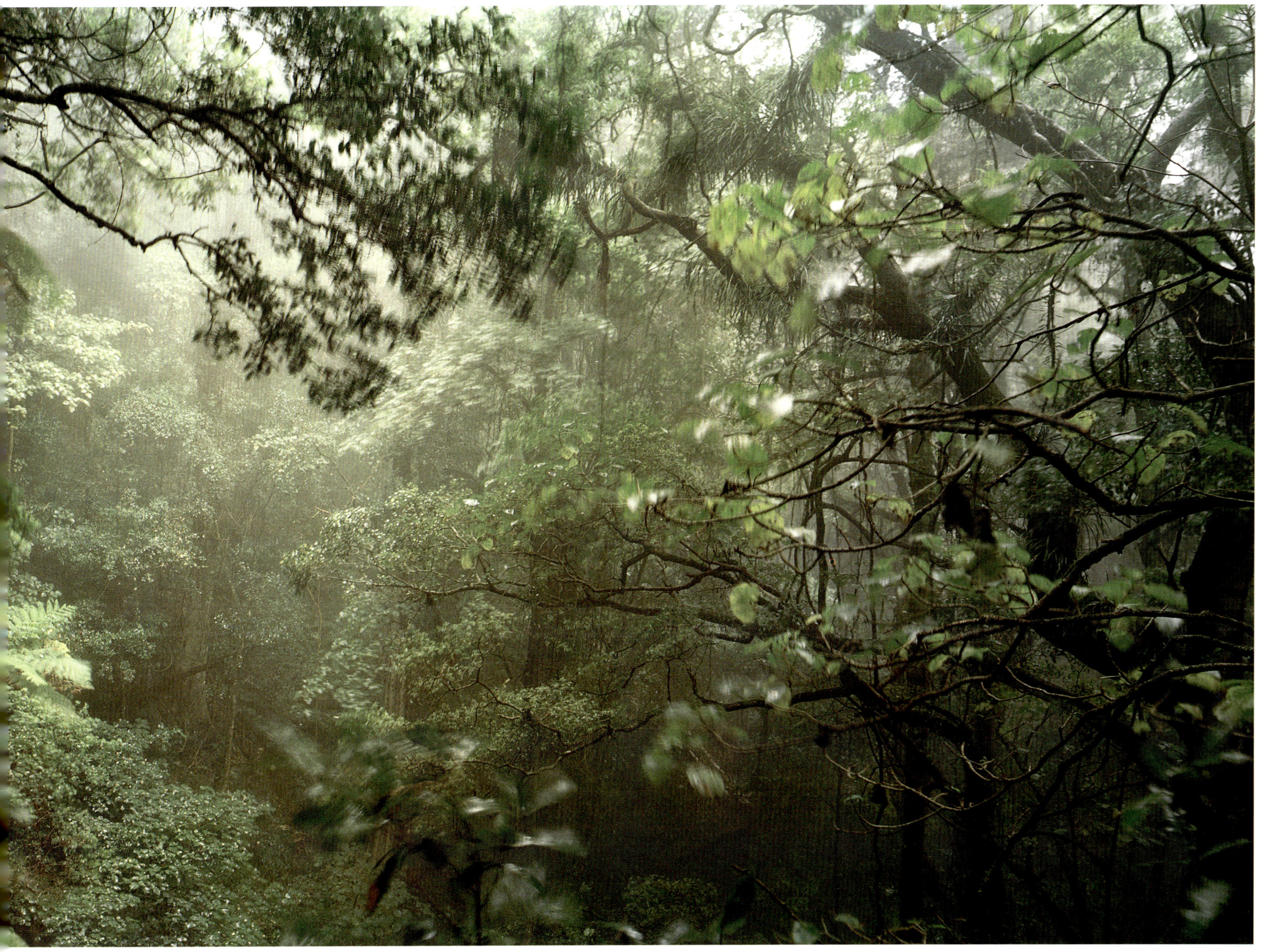

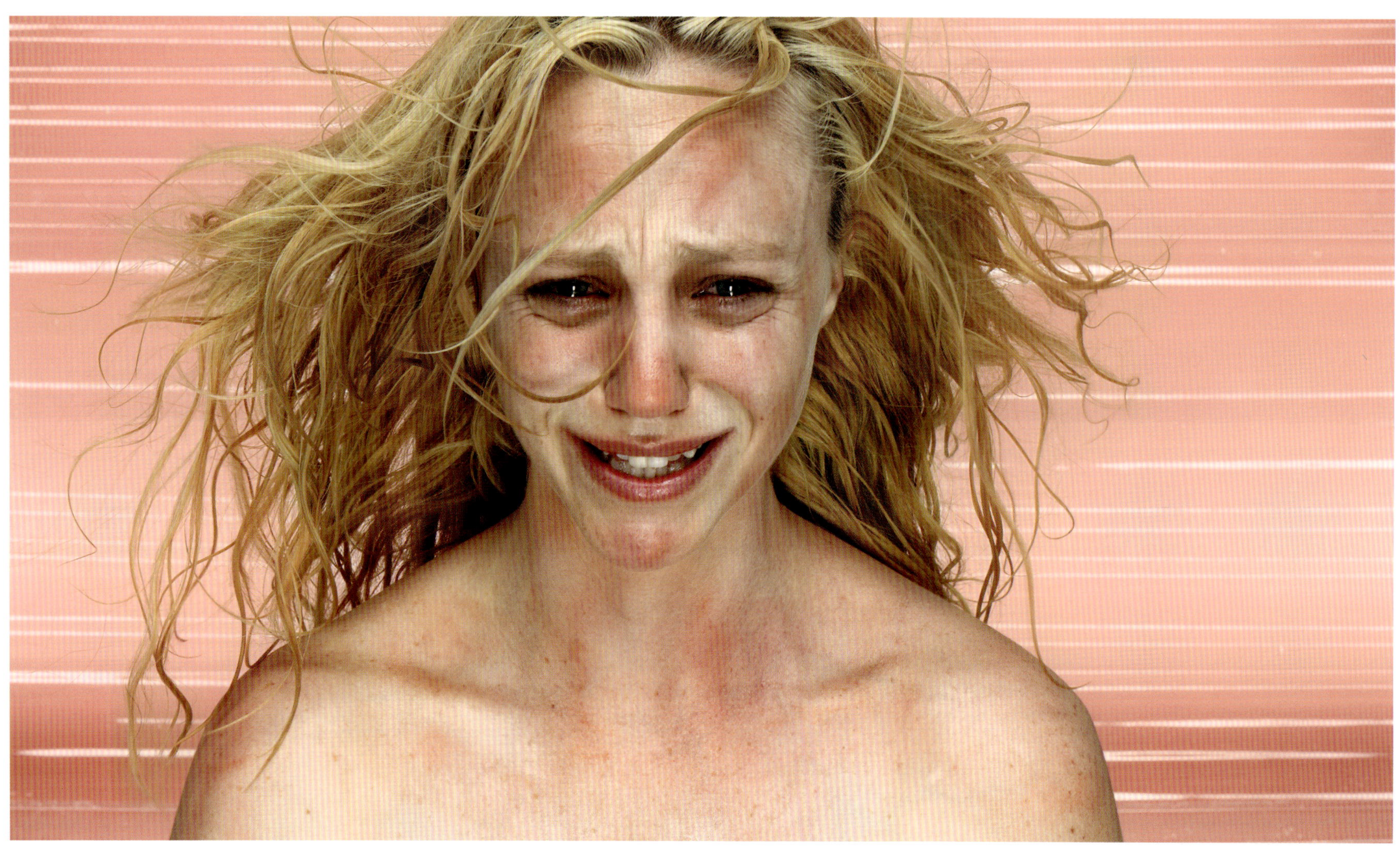

a dozen useless actions for grieving blondes #1, 2009
30¼ x 52⅜ in. (77 x 133 cm)

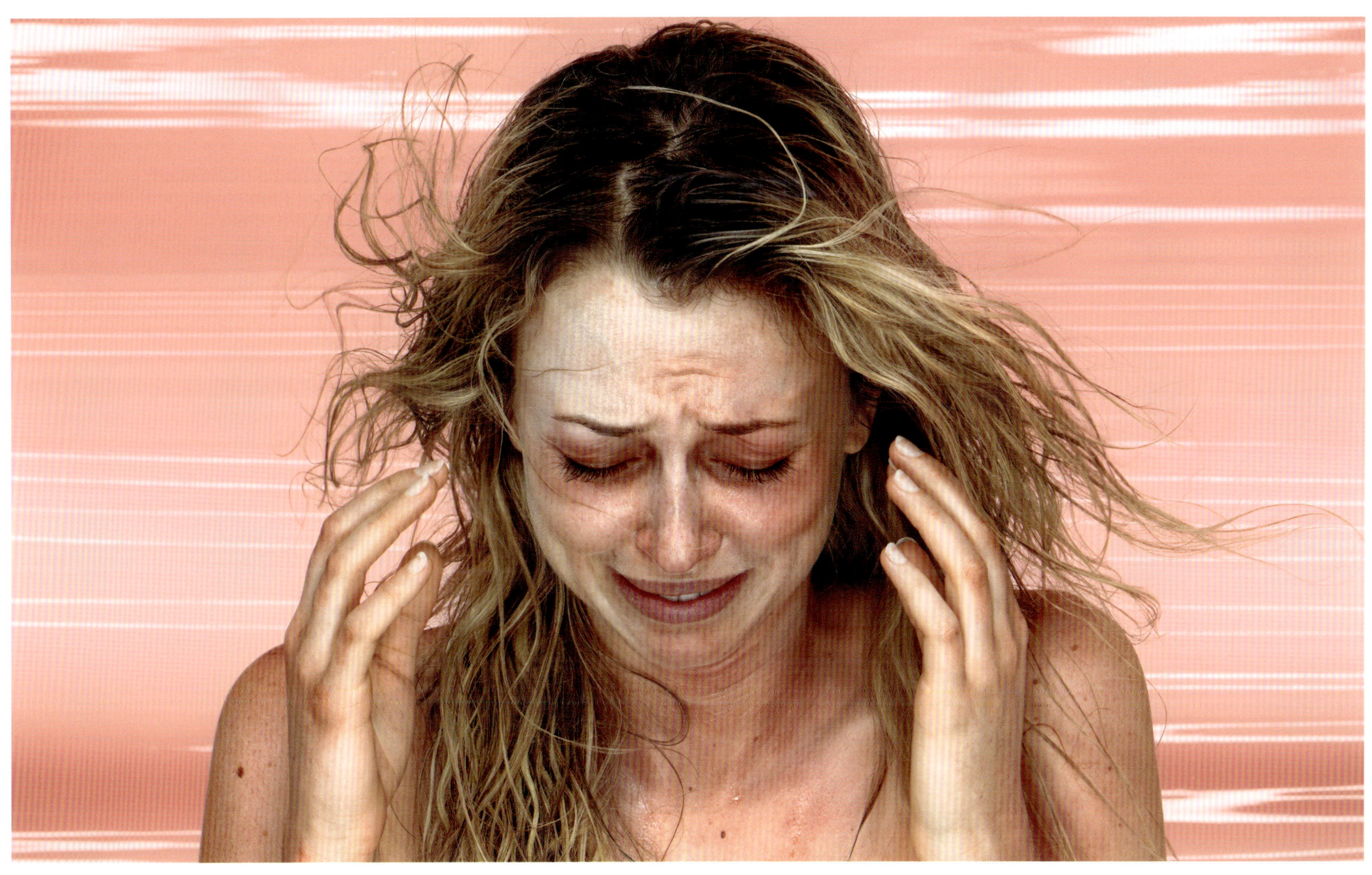

a dozen useless actions for grieving blondes #2, 2009
30¼ x 50 in. (77 x 127 cm)

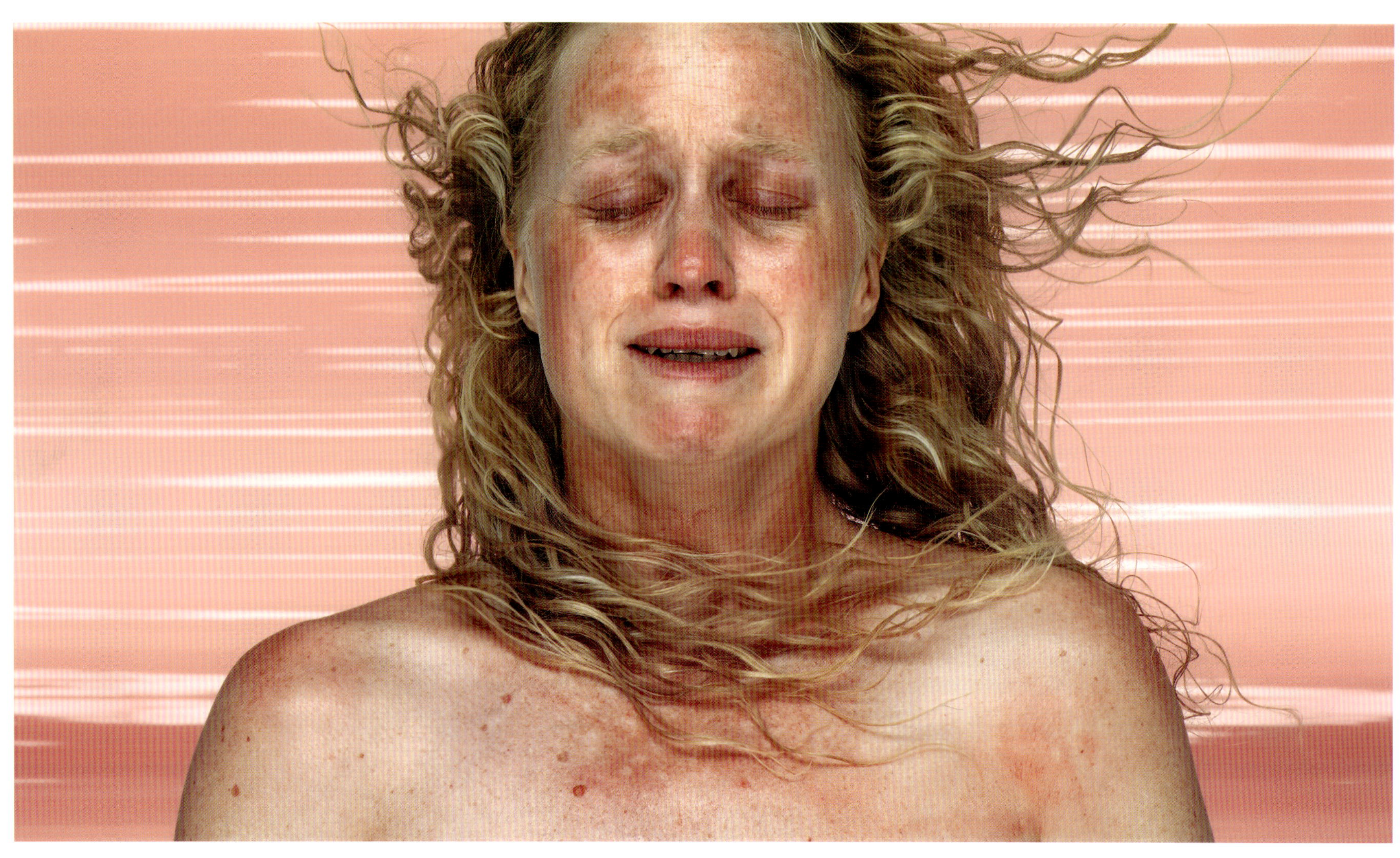

a dozen useless actions for grieving blondes #3, 2009
30¼ x 52⅜ in. (77 x 133 cm)

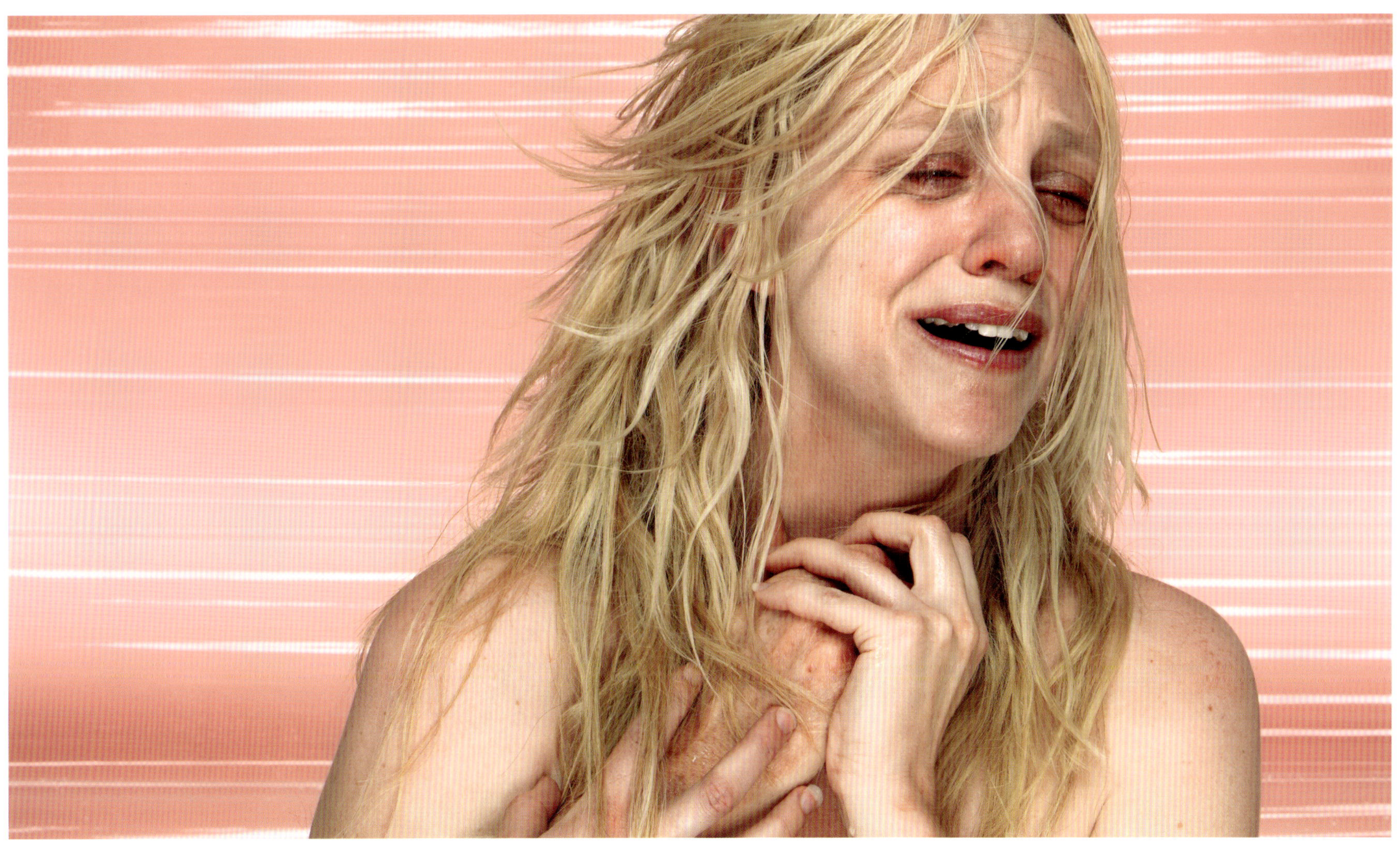

a dozen useless actions for grieving blondes #5, 2009
30¼ x 52⅜ in. (77 x 133 cm)

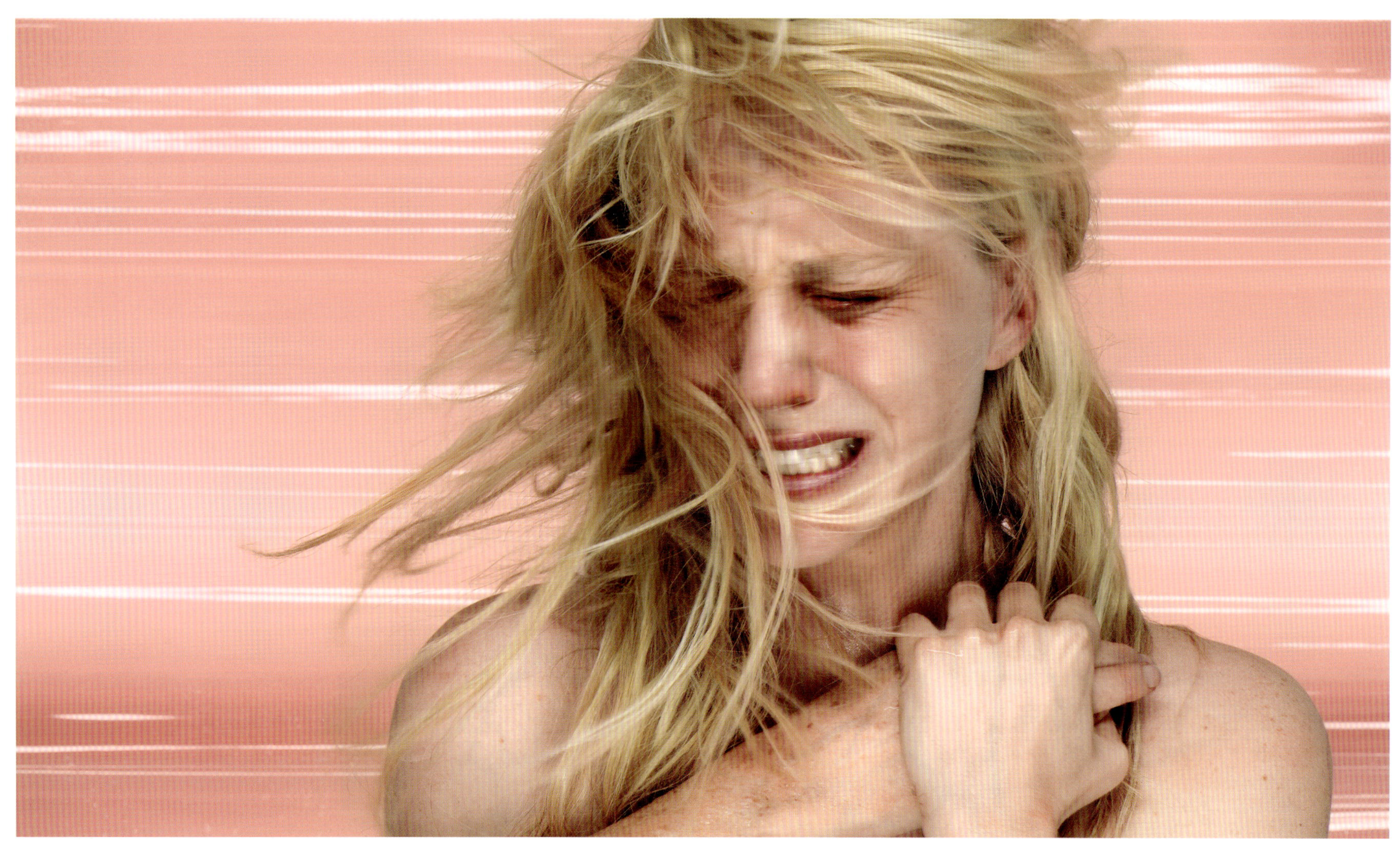

a dozen useless actions for grieving blondes #6, 2009
30¼ x 52⅜ in. (77 x 133 cm)

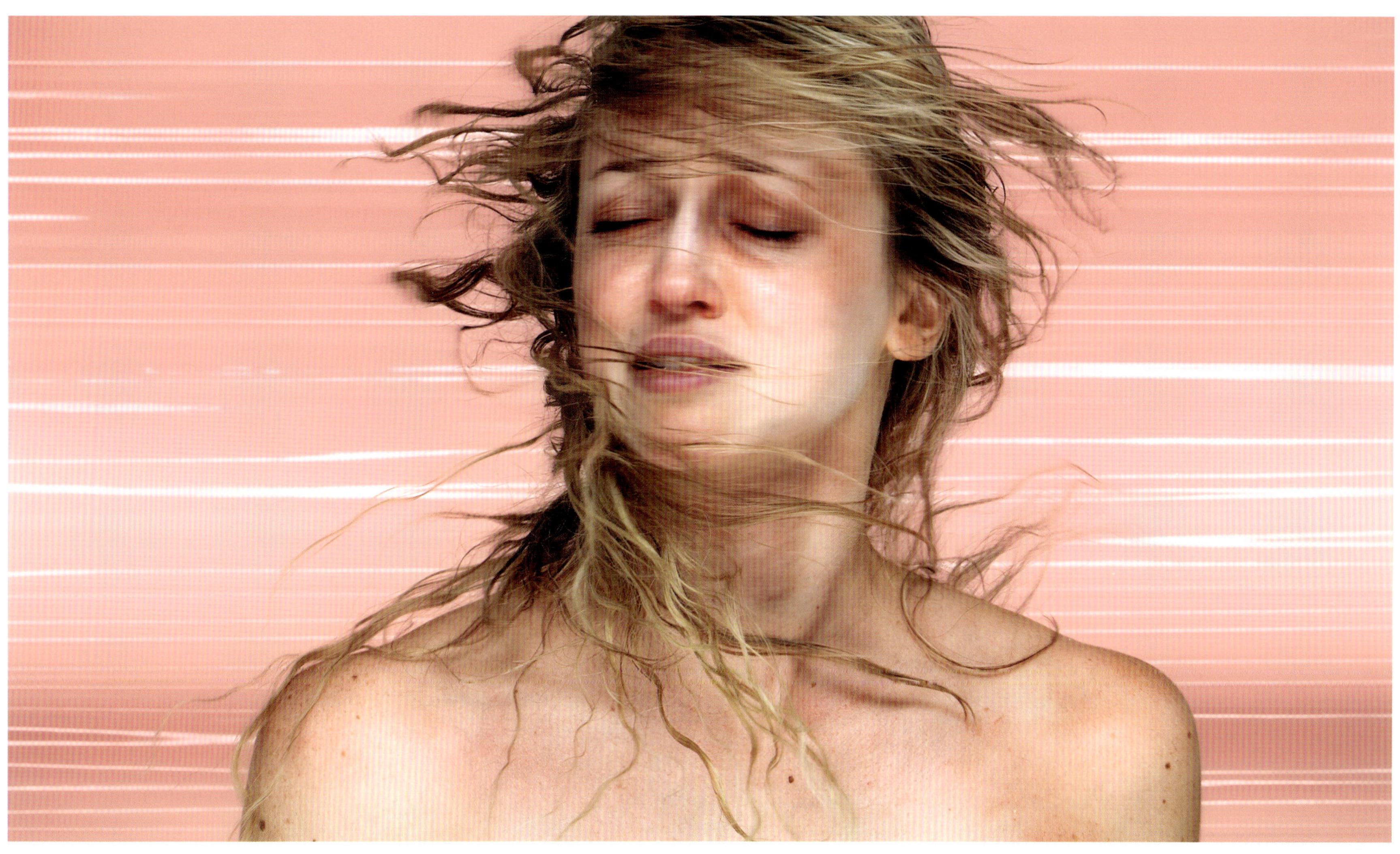

a dozen useless actions for grieving blondes #7, 2009
30¼ x 52⅜ in. (77 x 133 cm)

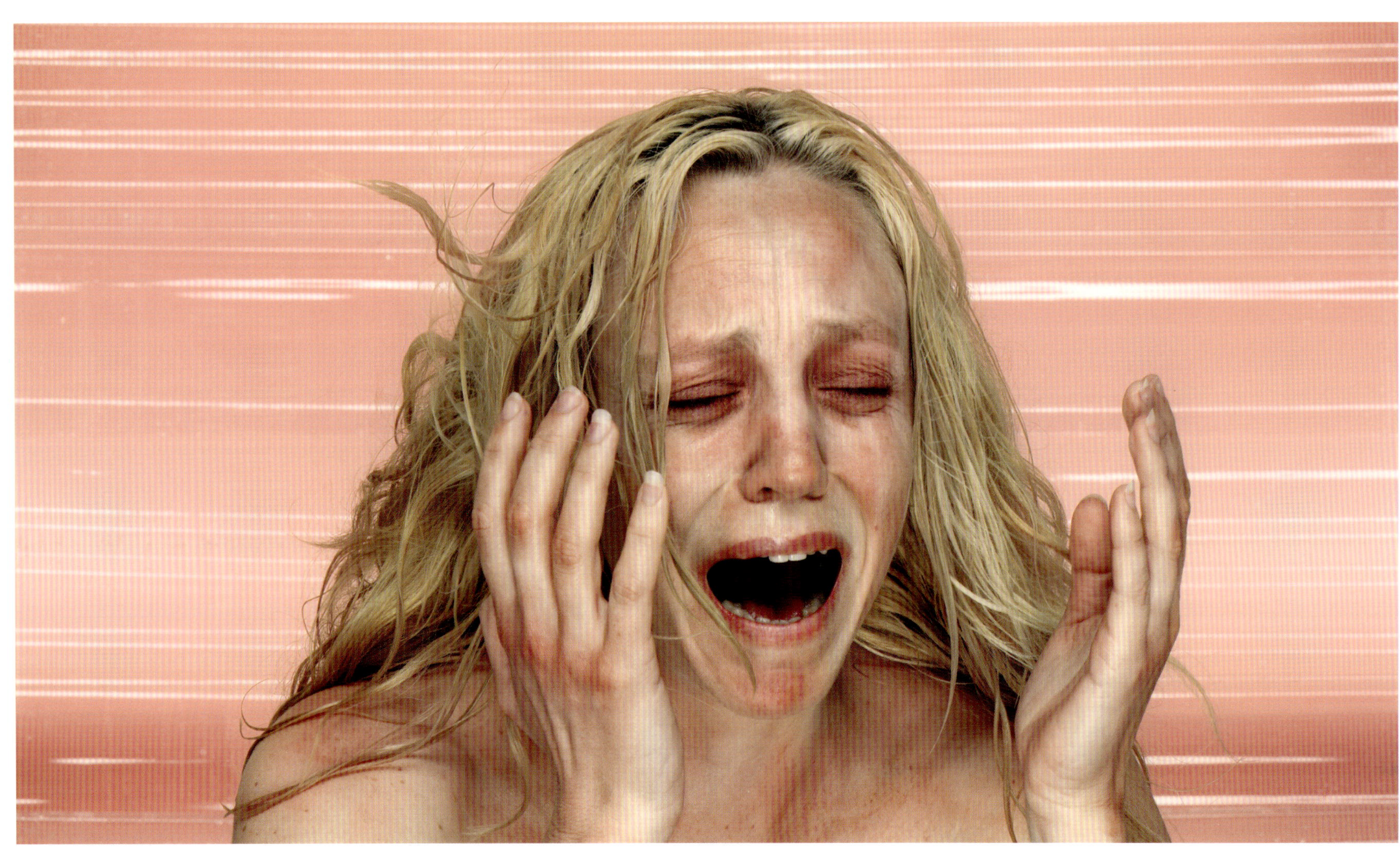

a dozen useless actions for grieving blondes #9, 2009
30¼ x 52⅜ in. (77 x 133 cm)

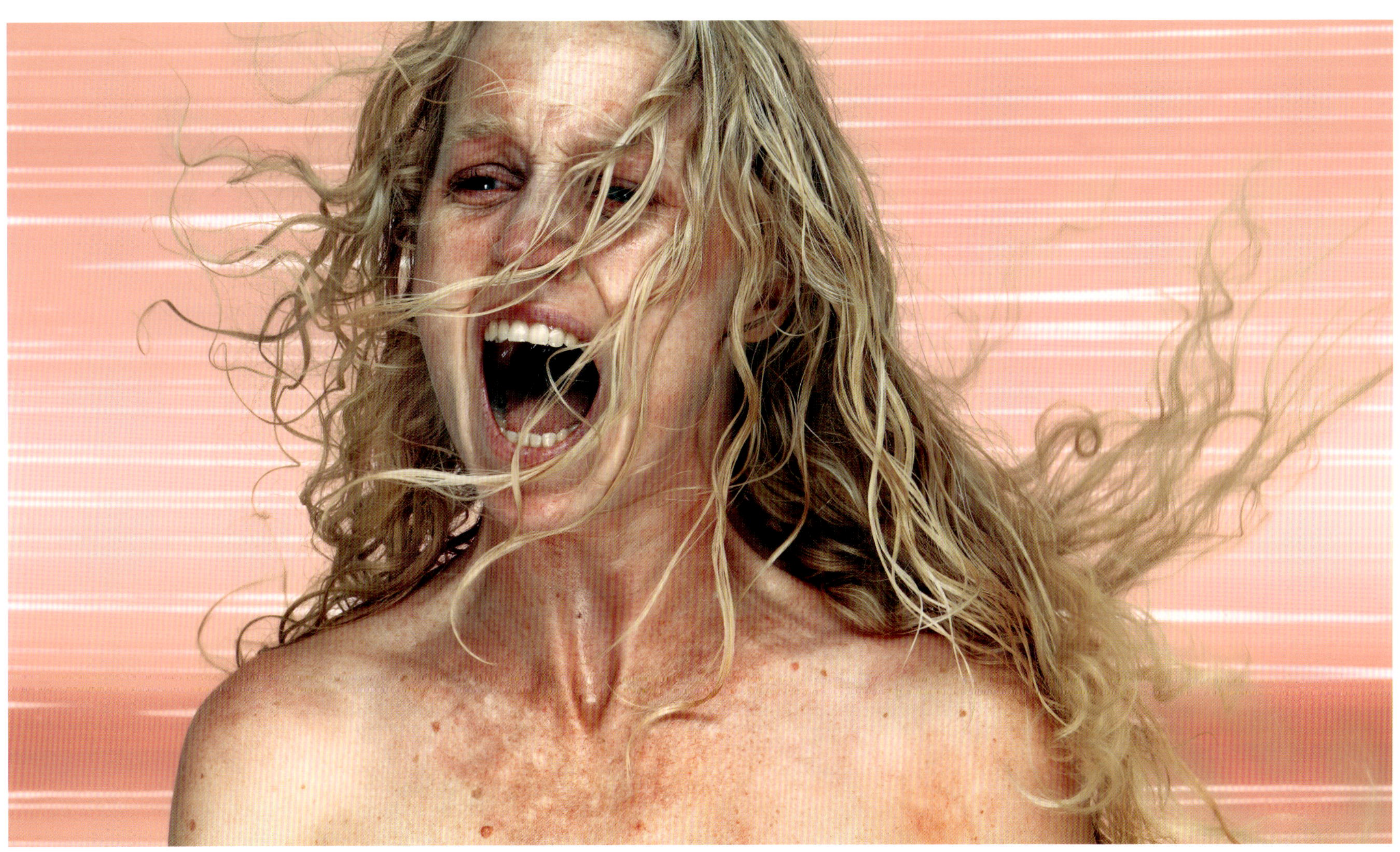

a dozen useless actions for grieving blondes #10, 2009
30¼ x 52⅜ in. (77 x 133 cm)

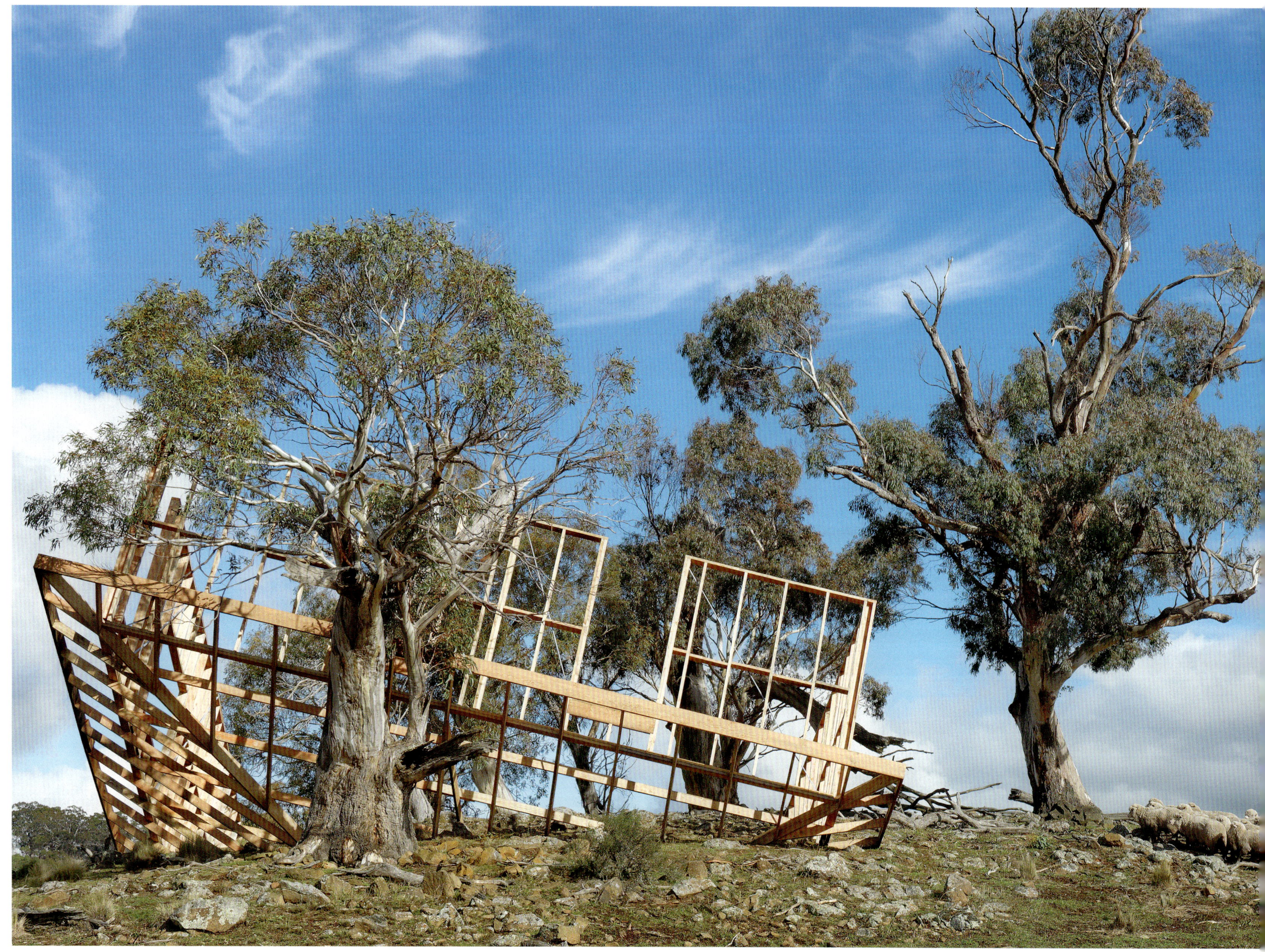

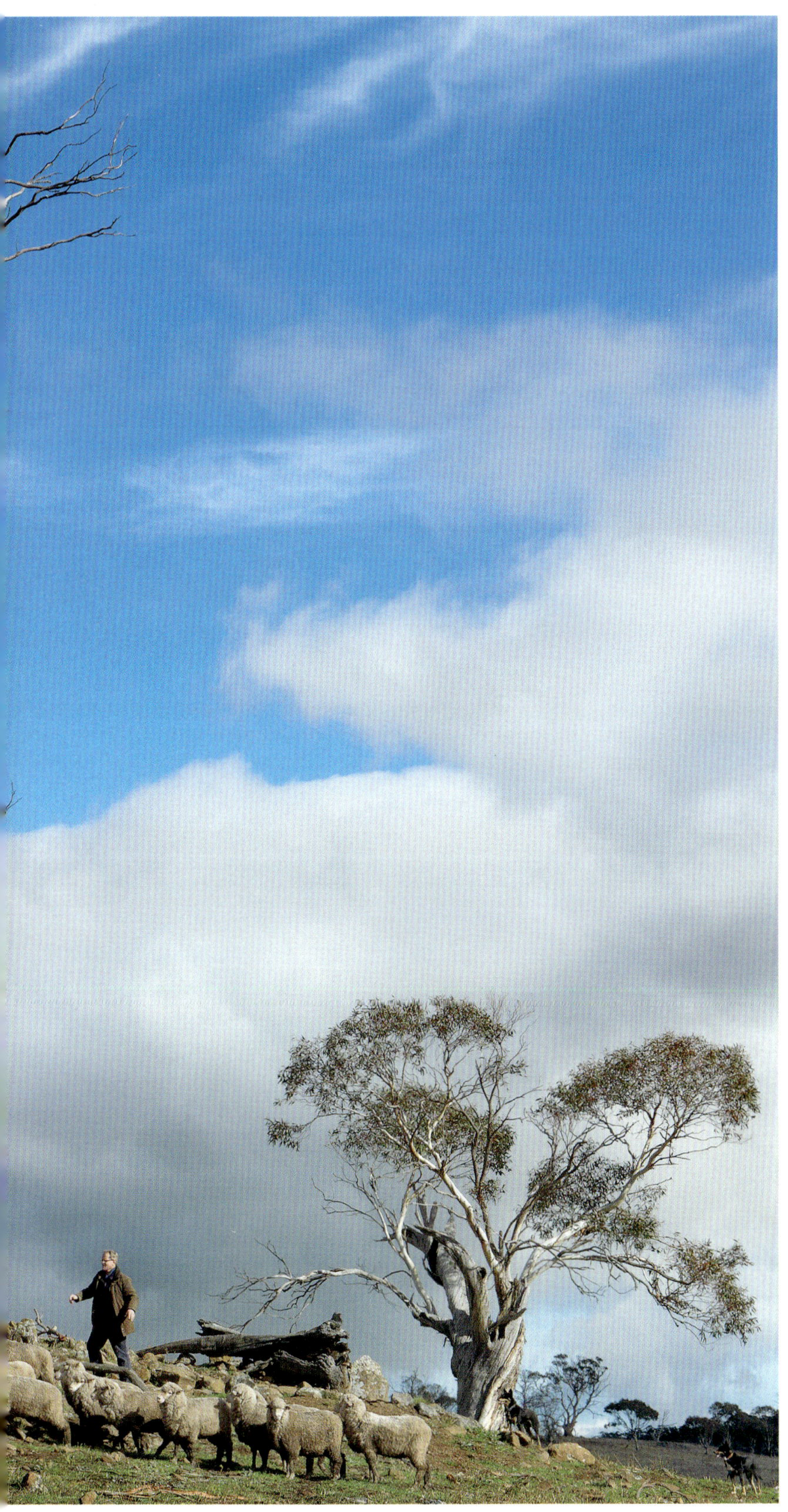

Aristide, 2010
43¼ x 87¾ in. (110 x 223 cm)

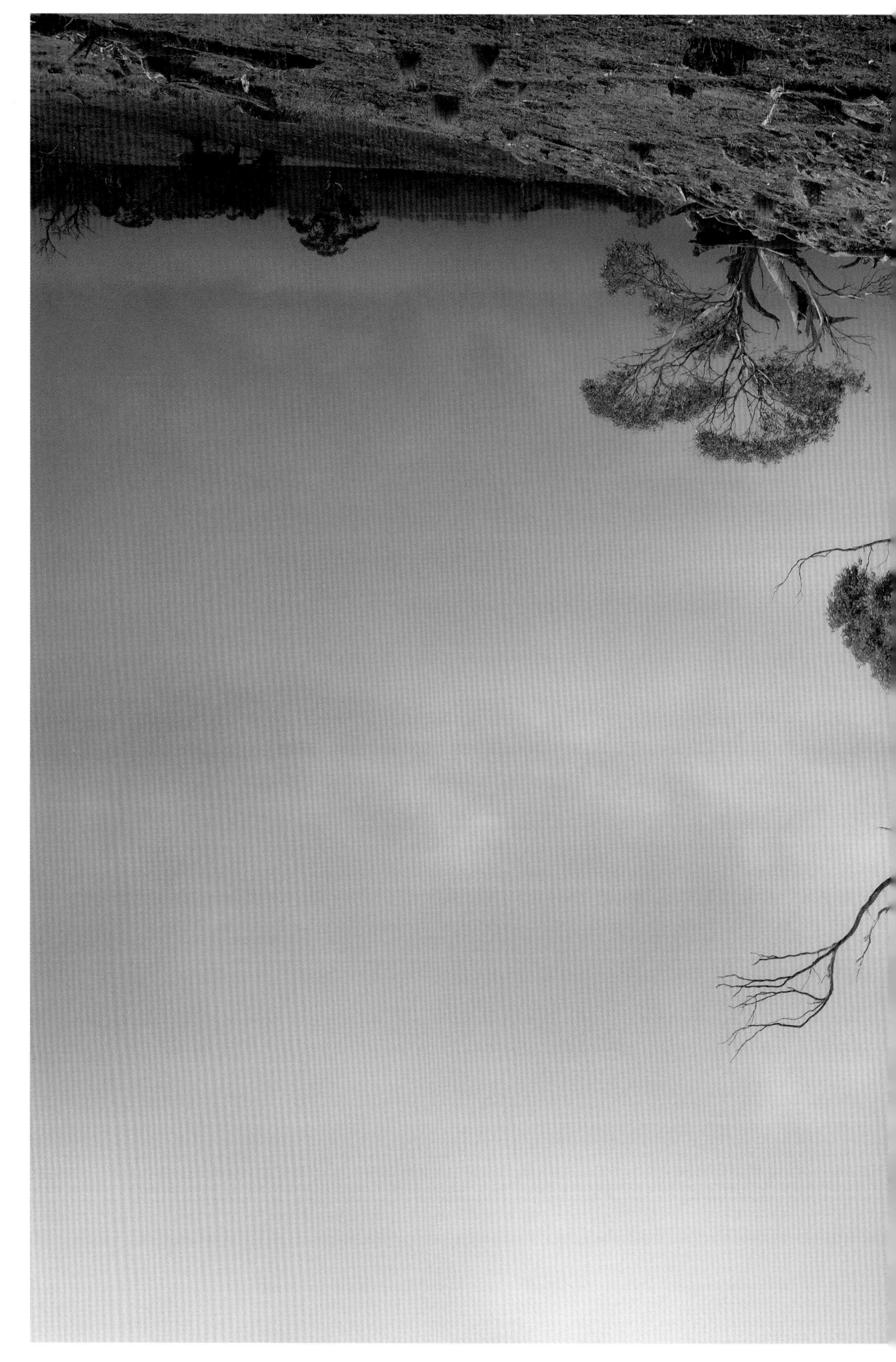

Jim, 2010
43¼ x 93¾ in. (110 x 238 cm)

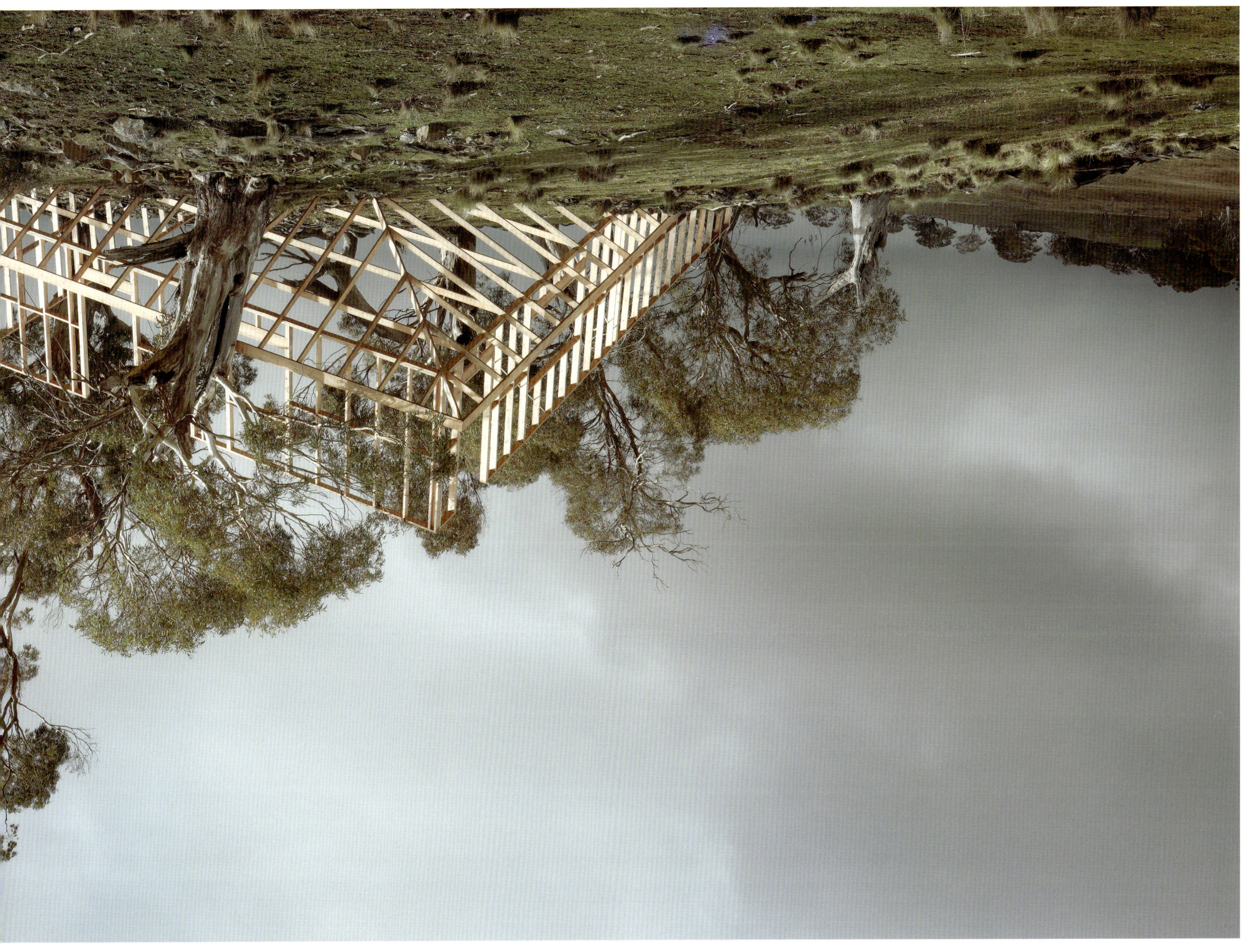

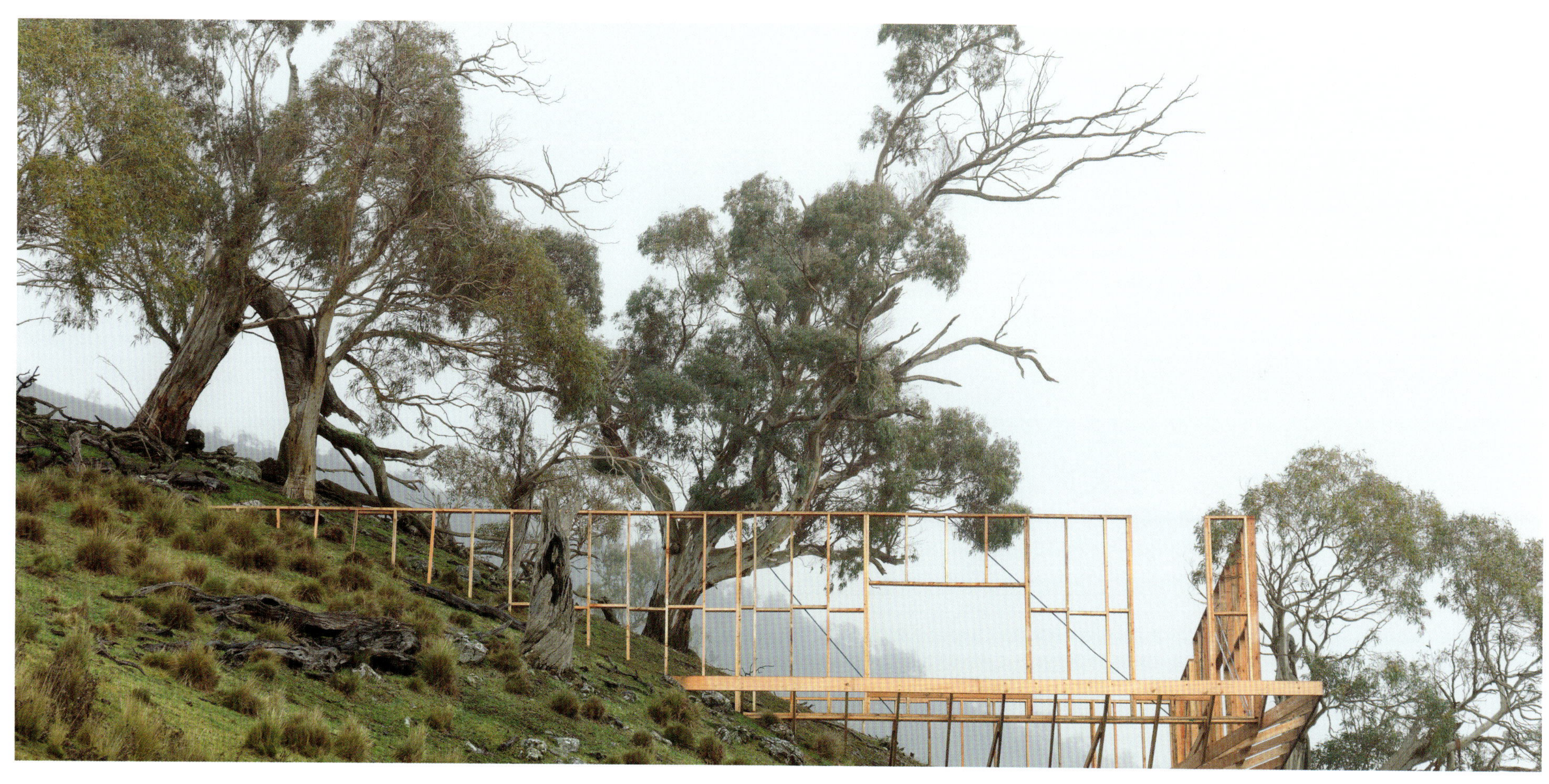

Eudoxia, 2010
39³/₈ x 83½ in. (100 x 212 cm)

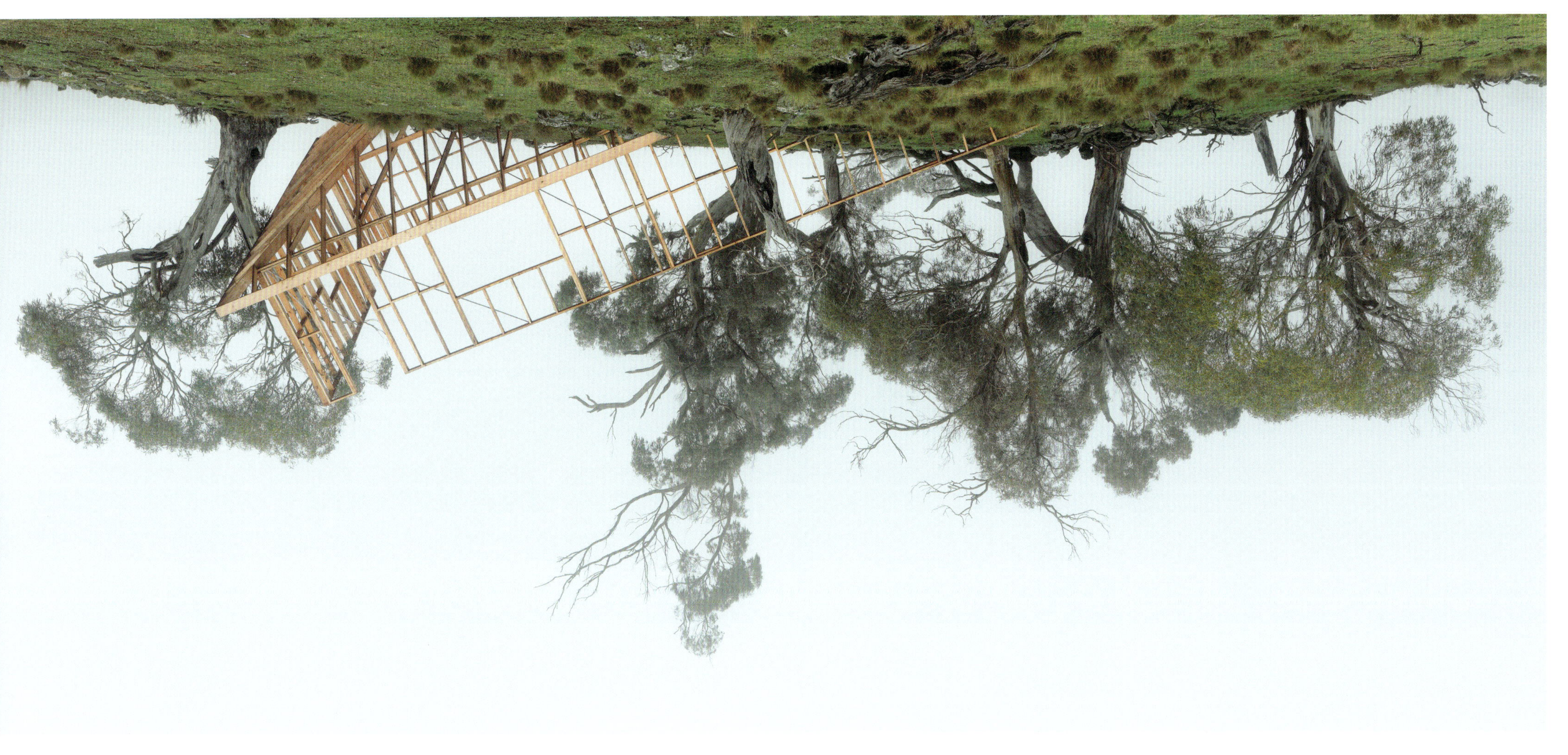

Prowse, 2010
43¼ x 97 in. (110 x 246.5 cm)

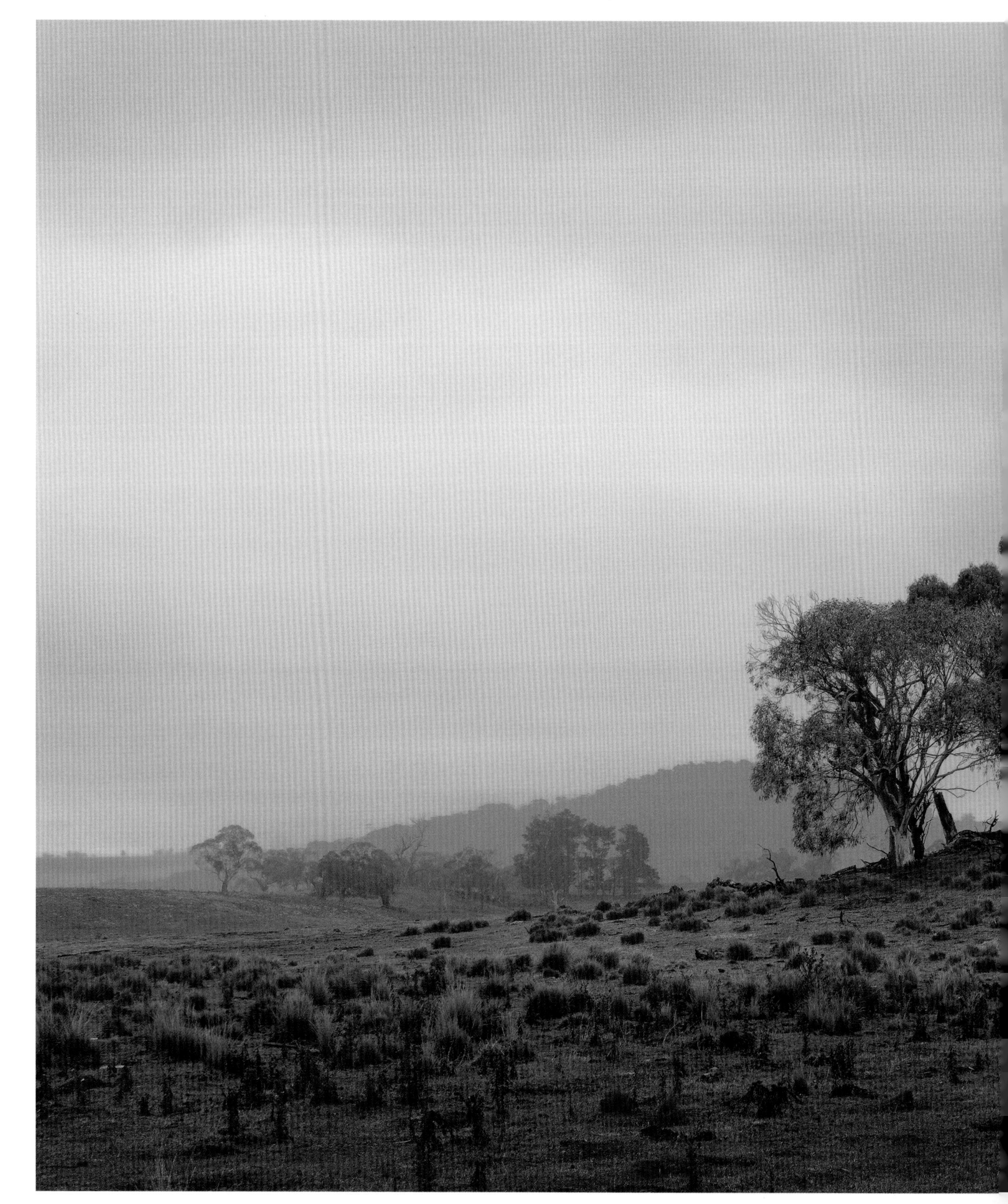

Eddie, 2010
43¼ x 101⅜ in. (110 x 257.5 cm)

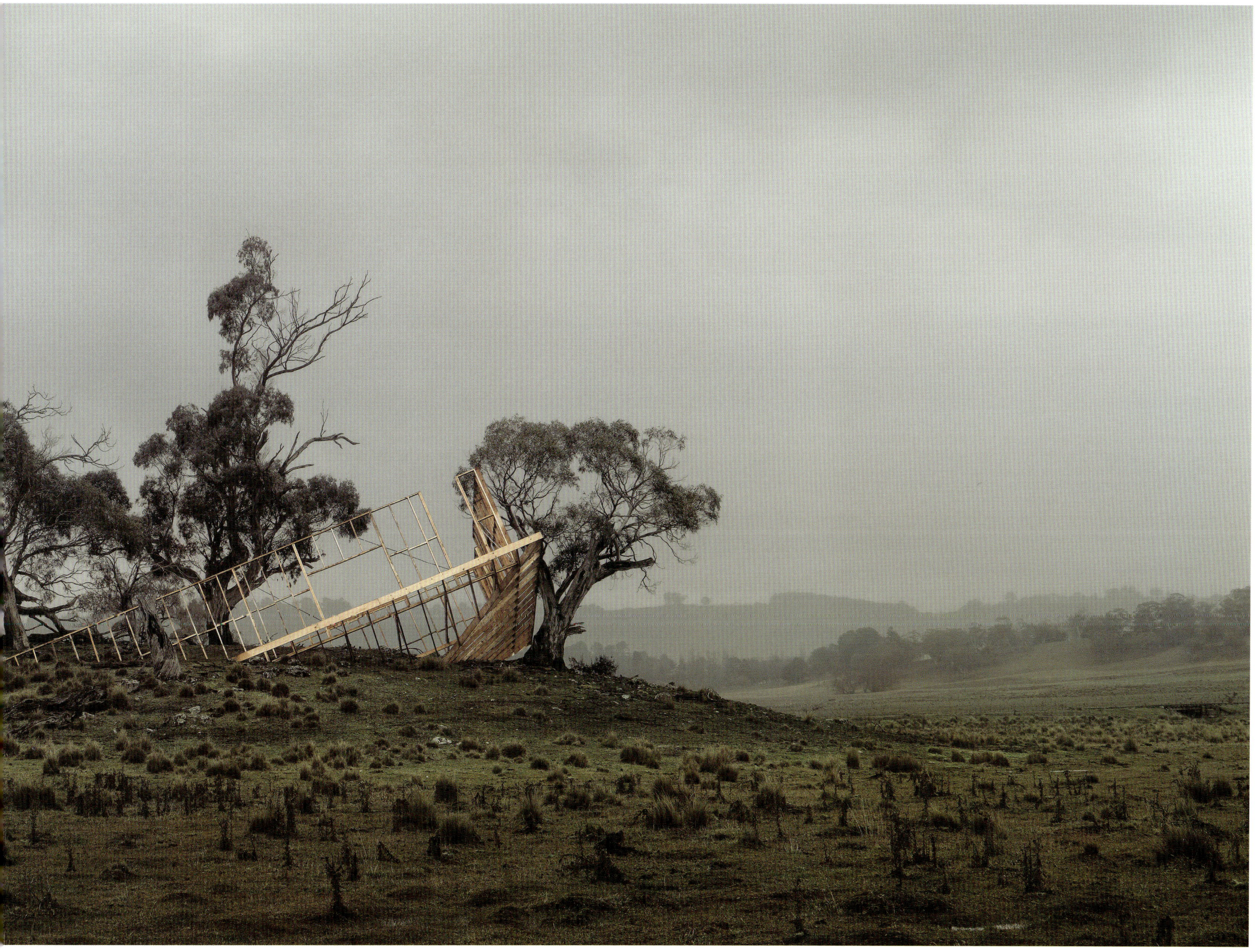

SELECTED SOLO EXHIBITIONS

2012 *leak*, Galerie Lelong, New York

2011 *leak*, Galerie Conrads, Düsseldorf
leak, Tolarno Galleries, Melbourne

2010 *a dozen useless actions for grieving blondes*, Galerie Conrads, Düsseldorf

2009 *prostrate your horses: weather and then some*, The University of Queensland Art Museum, Brisbane
a dozen useless actions for grieving blondes, Galerie Lelong, New York
a dozen useless actions for grieving blondes, Tolarno Galleries, Melbourne

2008 *to walk on a sea of salt*, Contemporary Art Centre of South Australia, Adelaide

2007 *weather*, Filiale, Berlin
Rosemary Laing: Flight, Frist Center for the Visual Arts, Nashville, Tennessee
weather, Galerie Lelong, New York
weather, Tolarno Galleries, Melbourne

2006 *weather*, Galerie Conrads, Düsseldorf

2005 *to walk on a sea of salt*, Tolarno Galleries, Melbourne
groundspeed, Galerie Conrads, Düsseldorf
The Unquiet Landscapes of Rosemary Laing, Museum of Contemporary Art, Sydney; traveled to:
Kunsthallen Brandts Klaedefabrik, Odense, Denmark (2006)
one dozen unnatural disasters in the Australian landscape: a collaboration with Stephen Birch,
GrantPirrie Gallery, Sydney

2004 *Rosemary Laing*, Domus Artium 2002, Salamanca, Spain
one dozen unnatural disasters in the Australian landscape, Galerie Conrads, Düsseldorf
one dozen unnatural disasters in the Australian landscape, Galerie Lelong, New York

2003 *one dozen unnatural disasters in the Australian landscape*, Gitte Weise Gallery, Sydney
Rosemary Laing: A Survey, 1995–2002, Brisbane City Gallery, Brisbane
bulletproofglass, Galerie Conrads, Düsseldorf

2002 *bulletproofglass*, Galerie Lelong, New York
bulletproofglass, Gitte Weise Gallery, Sydney

2001 *groundspeed*, Gitte Weise Gallery, Sydney

2000 *gradience*, Australian Centre for Photography, Sydney
flight research, Gitte Weise Gallery, Sydney

1999 *aero-zone*, National Museum of Art, Osaka; traveled to: Australian Centre for Contemporary Art,
Melbourne; Perth Institute of Contemporary Art, Perth (2000)

1998 *brownwork*, Annandale Galleries, Sydney

1997 *brownwork* (within *Envisioned*), Monash University Gallery, Melbourne

1995 *greenwork*, International Terminal, Sydney (Kingsford Smith) Airport, Federal Airports Corporation,
Sydney
greenwork, Annandale Gallery, Sydney

1993 *blow-out*, Annandale Gallery, Sydney

1992 *from Paradise work*, Queensland Art Gallery, Brisbane

1991 *from Paradise work*, Experimental Art Foundation, Adelaide
from Paradise work, 200 Gertrude Street, Melbourne

1990 *from Paradise work*, First Draft West, Sydney
from Paradise work, Photospace Gallery, Canberra Institute for the Arts, Canberra

1989 *Natural Disasters*, Milburn + Arte Gallery, Brisbane

1988 *Natural Disasters*, Artspace, Sydney

SELECTED GROUP EXHIBITIONS

2012 *Return to Sender*, The University of Queensland Art Museum, Brisbane
Parallel Collisions: 12th Adelaide Biennial of Australian Art, Art Gallery of South Australia, Adelaide
NEW 2011: Selected Recent Acquisitions, The University of Queensland Art Museum, Brisbane
Volume One: MCA Collection, Museum of Contemporary Art, Sydney

2011 *Hängung #7: Art of Australia. Traditional and Contemporary*, Kunstwerk, Eberdingen-Nussdorf, Germany
Arboreal, Macquarie University Art Gallery, Macquarie University, North Ryde, New South Wales
Double Vision, McClelland Gallery + Sculpture Park, Langwarrin, Victoria
Boundary Line, TarraWarra Museum of Art, Healesville, Victoria
Collaborative Witness: Artists' Responses to the Plight of the Asylum Seeker and Refugee, The University
Queensland Art Museum, Brisbane
Interventions in the Landscape, Galerie Lelong, New York
Esk Collection 2001–2011: Collecting Australian Contemporary Art, Academy Gallery, School of Visual
and Performing Art, University of Tasmania, Launceston, Tasmania
New Contemporary Galleries: Featuring the John Kaldor Family Collection, Art Gallery of New South
Wales, Sydney
Small Fires, Sint-Lukasgalerie Brussels, Brussels
Photography and Place: Australian landscape photography 1970s until now, Art Gallery of New South
Wales, Sydney

2010 *LoveArt*, Casula Powerhouse Arts Centre, Casula, New South Wales
Stormy Weather: Contemporary Landscape Photography, The Ian Potter Centre, National Gallery of
Victoria, Melbourne; traveled to: Swan Hill Regional Art Gallery, Victoria (2011–12); Wangaratta
Art Gallery, Victoria (2012)
Change, Monash University Museum of Art, Melbourne
Outside In, McClelland Gallery and Sculpture Park, Langwarrin, Victoria
Anguish, Downtown Gallery, Memphis College of Art, Memphis, Tennessee
Timelines: Photography and Time, National Gallery of Victoria, Melbourne
Be a Star, Play a Model, Cultural Institution, Knokke, Belgium
Reference and Affinity: Art of the 21st Century from the Collection, Kunstmuseum Luzern, Lucerne

2009 *12 Degrees of Latitude: Regional and University Art Collections in Queensland*, QUT Art Museum,
Queensland University of Technology, Brisbane
Almanac: The Gift of Ann Lewis AO, Museum of Contemporary Art, Sydney; traveled to: Goulburn
Regional Gallery (2011), ANU Drill Hall Gallery (2011), Wollongong City Gallery (2011),
Shepparton Art Gallery (2011), New England Regional Art Museum (2011), Wagga Wagga Art
Gallery (2012), Tweed River Art Gallery (2012), Newcastle Regional Art Gallery (2012)
*Les nuages… là-bas… les merveilleux nuages! Autour des études de ciel d'Eugène Boudin, Hommages
et digressions* (*Clouds… over there… marvellous clouds! Around Eugene Boudin's studies of the sky:
tributes and digressions*), Musée Malraux, Le Havre, France
Queensland Art, Pestorius Sweeney House, Hamilton, Queensland
Varios Artistas: Tiempo Suspendido, Domus Artium 2002 Salamanca, Salamanca, Spain
The Edge of Reason: Australian Women Photographers, Bendigo, Victoria Art Gallery, Bendigo, Victoria
Light Sensitive Material: Works from the Verghis Collection, Bathurst Regional Art Gallery, Bathurst,
New South Wales
Manipulating Reality: How Images Redefine the World, Centro di Cultura Contemporanea Strozzina,
Palazzo Strozzi, Florence
Curating the COFA Collection, Ivan Dougherty Gallery, College of Fine Arts, University of New South
Wales, Sydney

Collecting Lines: Selected Works from the Geoff and Vicki Ainsworth Collection, Maitland Regional Art Gallery, Maitland, New South Wales

Reframing Darwin: Evolution and Art in Australia, Ian Potter Museum of Art, University of Melbourne, Melbourne

Silence: A Selection of Works from the Collection, Kunstmuseum Luzern, Lucerne

Other Worlds, Confederation Centre Art Gallery, Charlottetown, Prince Edward Island, Canada

Remote Proximity: >Nature< In Contemporary Art/Ferne Nähe: >Natur< in der Kunst der Gegenwart. Kunstmuseum Bonn, Bonn

Trouble in Paradise: Examining Discord Between Nature and Society, Tucson Museum of Art, Tucson, Arizona

2008 *Primary Views*, Monash University Museum of Art, Melbourne

New: selected recent acquisitions 2007–2008, The University of Queensland Art Museum, St. Lucia, Queensland

Surreale 08, Mimmo Scognamiglio Artecontemporanea, Milan

neo goth: back in black, The University of Queensland Art Museum, St. Lucia, Queensland

Holding on, letting go, Monash Gallery of Art, Wheelers Hill, Victoria

Revolutions–Forms That Turn: 16th Biennale of Sydney, Museum of Contemporary Art, Sydney

FX in Contemporary Photography, McClelland Gallery and Sculpture Park, Langwarrin, Victoria

Depth of field: contemporary photography from The University of Queensland Art Collection, The University of Queensland Art Museum, Queensland

2007 *Garden of Eden: The Garden in Art Since 1900*, Kunsthalle Emden, Emden, Germany

Lives and Times: A Selection of Works from the Victorian Foundation for Living Australian Artists, National Gallery of Victoria; traveled to: Regional Australian Galleries (2007–08)

Janus. Photography's Double Face, Museo Nacional Centro de Arte Reina Sofia, Madrid

Think with the Senses, Feel with the Mind: Art in the Present Tense–52nd International Art Exhibition, Venice Biennale

New Nature, Govett Brewster Art Gallery, Taranaki, New Zealand

June Bride, Yossi Milo Gallery, New York

Grey Water, Institute Modern Art, Brisbane

The BIG Picture, North Carolina Museum of Art, Raleigh, North Carolina

2006 *Prism: Contemporary Australian Art*, Bridgestone Museum of Art, Tokyo

Art, Life and Confusion: 47th October Salon, Belgrade Cultural Centre, Belgrade

Scary Tales, Filiale, Berlin

Dresscode, Historisches + Völkerkundemuseum, St. Gallen, Switzerland

The Genius of Place, Museum of Western Virginia, Roanoke, Virginia

Shifting Terrain: Contemporary Landscape Photography, Wadsworth Atheneum, Hartford, Connecticut

Mite! Okayama Prefectural Museum of Art, Okayama, Japan

Strange Cargo: Contemporary Art as a State of Encounter, Newcastle Region Art Gallery, Newcastle, New South Wales; traveled to Broken Hill City Art Gallery (2007); Bendigo Art Gallery (2007); Orange Regional Gallery (2007); Wagga Wagga Art Gallery (2007); Tweed River Regional Gallery (2007); and Ipswich Art Gallery (2008)

Artbank: Celebrating 25 Years of Australian Art, Artbank, Sydney; traveled to: Redland Art Gallery, Queensland; Carnegie Gallery, Tasmania; Latrobe Regional Gallery, Victoria; Artspace Mackay, Queensland; Perc Tucker Regional Gallery, Queensland (2006–07); New England Regional Art Museum, New South Wales (2007); Bathurst Regional Art Gallery, New South Wales (2007); Cairns Regional Art Gallery, Queensland (2007); Noosa Regional Gallery, Queensland (2007); Geelong Gallery, Victoria (2007–08)

Decade Acquisitions 1996–2006, Bendigo Regional Art Gallery, Bendigo, Victoria

2005 *The Forest: Politics, Poetics and Practice*, Nasher Museum of Art, Duke University, Durham, North Carolina

Points of View: Australian Photography 1985–95, Art Gallery of New South Wales, Sydney

Beyond Real. Part 2: Making A Scene, Australian Centre of Photography, Sydney

Time's Arrow, Twelve Random Thoughts on Beauty, BRIC Rotunda Gallery, Brooklyn

A Kind of Magic: The Art of Transforming, Kunstmuseum Luzern, Lucerne

Points of View: Landscape and Photography, Galerie Lelong, New York

Out There: Landscape in the New Millennium, Museum of Contemporary Art Cleveland (MOCA), Cleveland, Ohio

Picturing the Landscape, Deloitte Touche Tohmatsu, Grosvenor Place Building, Sydney

Art Almanac: Cover Stories 269, Sir Hermann Black Gallery, University of Sydney, Sydney

After Nature, Lake Macquarie City Art Gallery, Lake Macquarie, New South Wales

2004 *Revealing Secret Treasures: Women Artists from the Reg & Sally Richardson Collection*, Mosman Art Gallery, Sydney

The Nature Machine: Contemporary Art, Nature and Technology, Queensland Art Gallery, Brisbane

Apparemment léger: Semaines européennes de l'image (Apparently Light), Galerie Nei Liicht, Dudelange, Luxembourg

Femina, Galerie Les Filles du Calvaire, Paris; traveled to: Galerie Les Filles du Calvaire, Brussels

Clouded Over, Lawrence Wilson Art Gallery, University of Western Australia, Perth

2004: Australian Culture Now, National Gallery of Victoria, Melbourne

Adrift, Queensland Centre for Photography, Brisbane

Penumbra: Images of darkness and light, McClelland Gallery + Sculpture Park, Langwarrin, Victoria

Flock and Fable: Animals and Identity in Contemporary Art, Chelsea Art Museum, New York

2004 Busan Biennale: Chasm–NET, "Point of Contact," Busan Metropolitan Art Museum, Busan, Korea

More Easily Imagined, Crossings of the Blue Mountains, Bathurst Regional Art Gallery, Bathurst, New South Wales

Breathtaking, Art Institute of Boston, Main Gallery, Lesley University, Boston

Arquitecturas Urbanas, Centro Municipal de las Artes de Alcorcón, Madrid, and Centro Nacional de Fotografía Torrelavega, Santander, Spain

Paisaje & Memoria/Landscape & Memory, La Casa Encendida, Madrid

Rendezvous mit Gitte: Volume 4, Gitte Weise Gallery, Sydney

Living together is easy, Art Tower Mito, Tokyo, Japan; traveled to National Gallery of Victoria, Melbourne

2004 Adelaide Biennal of Australian Art: Contemporary Photomedia, Art Gallery of South Australia, Adelaide

2003 *Defying Gravity: Contemporary Art and Flight*, North Carolina Museum of Art, Raleigh, North Carolina

L'attimo fuggente fra fotografia e cinema (The Fleeting Moment Between Photography and Cinema), Pinacoteca Giovanni e Marella Agnelli, Turin, and Museo Nazionale del Cinema of Turin

Face Up: Contemporary Art from Australia, Nationalgalerie im Hamburger Bahnhof, Museum for the Present, Berlin

Hothouse: The flower in contemporary art, Monash University Museum of Art, Melbourne; traveled to: State Library of Victoria; Ballarat Fine Art Gallery; McCelland Gallery and Sculpture Park, Langwarrin, Victoria; Geelong Art Gallery; National Library of Australia, Canberra; Gippsland Art Gallery, Victoria; Keith Murdoch Gallery, Melbourne

Nature and Nation: Vaster than Empires, Hastings Museum and Art Gallery, Hastings, U.K.; traveled to: Worcester City Museum and Art Gallery, Worcester, U.K.; Yard Gallery, Wollaton Park, Nottingham, U.K.; Lethaby Gallery, Central Saint Martins College of Art and Design, London

Himmelschwer. Transformationen der Schwerkraft, Landesmuseum Joanneum, Kulturzentrum bei den Minoriten, Graz, Austria; traveled as *Himmel Falden* to: Kunsthallen Brandts Klædefabrik, Odense, Denmark

Rendezvous mit Gitte volume 3, Gitte Weise Gallery, Sydney

Picturing Paradise, Mori Gallery, Sydney

2002 *2002: The Year in Art*, S.H. Ervin Gallery, Sydney

out of the dark, Adelaide Perry Gallery, Presbyterian Ladies College, Sydney

A Silver Lining & A New Beginning, Ivan Dougherty Gallery, College of Fine Arts, University of New South Wales, Sydney

Tales of the Unexpected, National Gallery of Australia, Canberra

10th Anniversary Exhibition, Gitte Weise Gallery, Sydney

Sahte/Gerçek (Faux/Real), Borusan Art Gallery, Istanbul

Gold Coast Ulrick Schubert Photographic Art Award, Gold Coast City Gallery, Surfers Paradise, Queensland

2001 *Staged!*, Worcester Art Museum, Worcester, Massachusetts

Stellar: Contemporary Art Auction, Centre for Contemporary Photography, Melbourne

Shoot, Gold Coast City Gallery, Surfers Paradise, Queensland; traveled to: Carnegie Gallery, Hobart; Coffs Harbour Regional Art Gallery, New South Wales; Caloundra Regional Art Gallery, Queensland

A Century of Collecting 1901–2001, Ivan Dougherty Gallery, College of Fine Arts, University of New South Wales, Sydney

Rendezvous mit Gitte, Gitte Weise Gallery, Sydney

low-down, Monash University Gallery, Melbourne

2000 *art at work: Photography and Moving Image*, International Terminal, Sydney (Kingsford Smith) Airport, Sydney

Zeitgenössische Fotokunst aus Australien (Contemporary Photographic Art from Australia), Neuer Berliner Kunstverein, Berlin; traveled to: Museum Schloß Hardenberg, Velbert, Germany; Kunstsammlungen, Chemnitz, Germany; Kulturzentrum der Stadt, Stuttgart, Germany; Monash University Museum of Art, Melbourne as *Lightness of Being* (2001)

Mjesto Na Kojem Nisam Bio/A Place I've Never Been To, Umjetnički Paviljon, Zagreb, Croatia

Images of Women by Women, Monash Gallery of Art, Wheelers Hill, Victoria

Sporting Life, Museum of Contemporary Art, Sydney

Body Language, Ivan Dougherty Gallery, College of Fine Arts, University of New South Wales, Sydney

Das Lied von der Erde/The Song of the Earth, Museum Fridericianum, Kassel, Germany

1999 *Moral Hallucination: Channeling Hitchcock*, Museum of Contemporary Art, Sydney

Something for above the couch, Gitte Weise Gallery, Sydney

National Photographic Purchase Award, Albury Regional Gallery, Albury, New South Wales

Contempora 5, Ian Potter Museum of Art in association with National Gallery of Victoria, Melbourne

Natural Disasters/Disasters Unnatural, Monash University Gallery, Melbourne

Passion for Wings, National Aviation Museum, Ottawa

1998 *The Seppelt Contemporary Art Award*, Museum of Contemporary Art, Sydney

Blue, Annandale Galleries, Sydney

After the Masters, 1993–1997 selected work, Ivan Dougherty Gallery, College of Fine Arts, University of New South Wales, Sydney

1997 *Sex-tet*, Ivan Dougherty Gallery, College of Fine Arts, University of New South Wales, Sydney

Fascination Street, Michael Milburn Gallery, Brisbane

1996 *RUN*, Michael Milburn Gallery, Brisbane

florescence, Ivan Dougherty Gallery, College of Fine Arts, University of New South Wales, Sydney; traveled to: Newcastle Region Art Gallery, Newcastle (1997); Campbelltown City Art Gallery, Campbelltown (1997); Tammworth City Art Gallery, Tammworth (1997)

Koncept, International Exhibition of Contemporary Photography, Umjetnički Paviljon and Galerija Gradska, Zagreb, Croatia

Digital Gardens: A World in Mutation, Power Plant, Toronto

Beyond the Sublime, Australian Centre for Photography, Sydney

Photography is Dead! Long Live Photography!, Museum of Contemporary Art, Sydney

Perception and Perspective, Next Wave Festival, National Gallery of Victoria, Melbourne

View of the New, National Gallery of Australia, Canberra

1995 *New Orientation: The Vision of Art in a Paradoxical World, 4th Istanbul Bienniala—International Exhibition of Contemporary Art*, Antrepo, Istanbul

Australian Contemporary Photography: From the Moet & Chandon Art Acquisition Fund, Art Gallery of Western Australia, Perth

The Artists Garden, Gallery 7, National Gallery of Australia, Canberra

Decadence: 10 Years of Exhibition at 200 Gertrude Street, 200 Gertrude Street, Melbourne

Alternative Realities: Australian artists working with technology, University of Science and Technology, Hong Kong; traveled to: Ian Potter Gallery, University of Melbourne Museum of Art, Melbourne; Zhu Qizhan Gallery, Shanghai; Wang Fun Art Gallery, Beijing; Gallery Artbeam, Seoul, Korea; Pacific Cultural Centre, Taipei, Taiwan (1996); Tamsui Centre of Art, Tamsui, Taiwan (1996); Mountain Art Gallery, Kaohsiung, Taiwan (1996); Karnataka Chitrakala Parishath Gallery, Bangalore, India (1996); Government Museum and Art Gallery, Chandigarh, India (1996)

Birds Eye View, New Media Network, Melbourne

Girls! Girls! Girls!, Orange Regional Art Gallery, Orange & Annandale Gallery, Sydney

Interlude, Ivan Dougherty Gallery, College of Fine Arts, University of New South Wales, Sydney

1994 *E-Topia*, New Media Network, Melbourne

Don't Stop, Geelong Regional Art Gallery, Geelong, Victoria

Horizons, Annandale Gallery, Sydney

Media Lounge International Symposium for Electronic Arts, Helsinki

Don't Stop, Linden Gallery, Melbourne

1993 *Perspecta*, Art Gallery of New South Wales, Sydney

Benefactors Exhibition, Art Gallery of New South Wales, Sydney

Virtu, Ivan Dougherty Gallery, College of Fine Arts, University of New South Wales, Sydney

March, Michael Milburn Gallery, Brisbane

Looking at Seeing and Reading, Ivan Dougherty Gallery, College of Fine Arts, University of New South Wales, Sydney

1992 *Strangers in Paradise: Contemporary Australian Art to Korea*, National Museum of Contemporary Art, Seoul; traveled to: Art Gallery of New South Wales, Sydney (1993)

Manu et Mente, Ivan Dougherty Gallery, College of Fine Arts, University of New South Wales, Sydney

but never by chance, Experimental Art Foundation, Adelaide; traveled to: Canberra College of Art Gallery, Canberra Institute for the Arts, Canberra; Museum of Contemporary Art, Sydney; Institute of Modern Art, Brisbane; Ian Potter Gallery, University of Melbourne (1993)

1991 *First Draft West 1985–1991*, First Draft West, Sydney

Industry, First Draft West, Sydney

Over East, Lawrence Wilson Art Gallery, University of Western Australia, Perth

1990 *Amore*, Artspace, Sydney

10 x 10, Milburn + Arte, Brisbane

Real Art, Institute of Modern Art, Brisbane

SELECTED COMMISSIONED PROJECTS

2005 *bulletproofglass #2*, architectural light box, Deutsche Bank, Sydney
2002 *flight research #5*, billboard, Socrates Sculpture Park, New York
  flight research #4, billboard, Yarra's Edge Urban Art program, Mirvac, Melbourne
2000 *airport #3 stART*, Museum of Contemporary Art, Sydney
  "The Game." *Visionaire*, no. 30 (January 2000).
  flight research #5 and *brownwork #9*, light boxes, Sydney Airport Corporation, Sydney

SELECTED PUBLICATION REFERENCES

2012 Broadfoot, Keith. "The Australian Tableau." *Eyeline*, no. 75 (2012).
  Littley, Samantha. "Rosemary Laing: The Moving Image." In *New Volume 2: Selected Recent Acquisitions 2009–2011*. Exh. cat. Brisbane: The University of Queensland Art Museum, 2012.
2011 Ahrens, Prue, and Michele Helmrich. *Asylum: Waiting for Asylum. Figures from an Archive/ Collaborative Witness: Artists' Responses to the Plight of the Asylum Seeker and Refugee*. Exh. cat. Brisbane: University Queensland Art Museum, 2011.
  Allen, Christopher. "In The Frame." Review. *The Weekend Australian* (April 30–May 1, 2011).
  Annear, Judy. *Photography and Place. Australian Landscape Photography: 1970s Until Now*. Exh. cat. Sydney: Art Gallery of New South Wales, 2011.
  Broadfoot, Keith, and Rex Butler. *Rosemary Laing: leak*. Exh. cat. Mebourne: Tolarno Galleries, 2011. http://www.archive.tolarnogalleries.com/archive/Rosemary%20Laing%20leak%202011/.
  Geczy, Adam. "Photography and Place. Australian Landscape Photography: 1970s until now." *Art Monthly*, no. 240 (June 2011).
  Images: The Collection Catalogue. 21st Century Museum of Contemporary Art. Ishikawa: 21st Century Museum of Contemporary Art, Kanazawa, 2011.
  Nelson, Robert. "World Turned Upside Down." *The Age* (March 2, 2011).
  Wake, Caroline. "The Victim Seen and Seeing." *Realtime* (September 6, 2011). http://www.realtimearts.net/article/105/10416.
2010 Allen, Christopher. "Are You Experienced?" Review. *The Weekend Australian* (June 5–6, 2010).
  Barlow, Geraldine, Max Delany, and Kyla McFarlane, eds. *Change: Monash University Museum of Art*. Exh. cat. Melbourne: Monash University Museum of Art, 2010.
  Crombie, Isobel. "Timelines (II)." In *Timelines: Photography and Time*. Exh. cat. Melbourne: National Gallery of Victoria, 2010.
  Marsh, Anne. *Look: Contemporary Australian Photography since 1980*. Melbourne: Macmillan Art Publishing, 2010.
  Meister, Helga. "Schmerz, der aus allen Poren dringt. Rosemary Laing widmet sich dem Leid der Menschen." *Westdeutsche Zeitung* (January 22, 2010).
  North Carolina Museum of Art: Handbook of the Collections. Raleigh, N.C.: North Carolina Museum of Art, 2010.
  Pia, Laura. "a dozen useless actions for grieving blondes: A New Series of Works by Rosemary Laing." *Look* (May 2010).
  Thompson, Cynthia. *Anguish*. Exh. cat. Memphis, Tenn.: Downtown Gallery, Memphis College of Art, 2010.
2009 Adolphs, Volker. *Ferne Nähe: >Natur< in der Kunst der Gegenwart* [Remote Proximity: >Nature< in Contemporary Art]. Exh. cat. Köln: Wienand Verlag, 2009.
  Clark, Suzanne. "A Long Road to *weather*." *The Courier Mail* (October 3–4, 2009).
  Daley, Linda. "Rosemary Laing: a dozen useless actions for grieving blondes." *Flash*, no. 2 (2009).

French, Blair, and Daniel Palmer, "Rosemary Laing." In *Twelve Australian Photo Artists*. Sydney: Piper Press, 2009.
  Helmrich, Michele. *prostrate your horses: weather and then some; Rosemary Laing at The University of Queensland Art Museum*. Brisbane: The University of Queensland Art Museum, 2009.
  Les nuages… là-bas… les merveilleux nuages. Exh. cat. France: Somogy, 2009.
  Manipulating Reality: How Images Redefine the World. Exh. cat. Florence: Palazzo Strozzi, 2009.
  Moore, Ross. "Rosemary Laing." *The Age* (April 29, 2009).
  Peterson, Tanya. "Dead Loss." *Art World*, no. 8 (April/May 2009).
  Regan, Margaret. "Disasters Deconstructed." *Tucson Weekly* (April 23, 2009).
  Sansom, Anna. "Rosemary Laing: *a dozen useless actions for grieving blondes*." *Eyemazing*, no. 3 (2009).
  Sasse, Julie, and Emily Handlin. *Trouble in Paradise: Examining Discord between Nature and Society*. Exh. cat. Tuscon: Tucson Museum of Art and Historic Block, 2009.
2008 Alexander, George. "Biennale of Sydney 2008: Revolutions—Forms That Turn." *ArtAsiaPacific*, no. 59 (July/August 2008).
  Annear, Judy. "Photography and Place." *Broadsheet* 37, no. 3 (2008).
  Art & Australia, ed. *Current: Contemporary Art from Australia and New Zealand*. Sydney: Dott Publishing, 2008.
  Capon, Edmund, ed. *Art Gallery of New South Wales: Highlights from the Collection*. Sydney: Art Gallery of New South Wales, 2008.
  Christov-Bakargiev, Carolyn, ed. *Revolutions—Forms That Turn: 16th Biennale of Sydney*. Exh. cat. Sydney: Biennale of Sydney, 2008.
  Marx, Jonathan. "Ideas take flight in Laing's photography." *The Tennessean* (January 6, 2008).
  Paparoni, Demetrio. *Surreale 08: Objective Images Not Found in Nature*. Exh. cat. Milan: Mimmo Scognamiglio Artecontemporanea, 2008.
  Peterson, Tanya. "Hallucinations." In *to walk on a sea of salt*. Exh. cat. Adelaide: Contemporary Art Centre of South Australia, 2008.
  Pugliese, Joseph. "The Tutelary Architecture of Immigration Detention Prisons and the Spectacle of Necessary Suffering." *Architecture Theory Review* 13, no. 2 (2008).
  Teale, Penny. *FX in Contemporary Photography*. Exh. cat. Melbourne: McClelland Gallery and Sculpture Park, 2008.
  Tello, Veronica. "Monument to Memory: Woomera in Australian Contemporary Art." *Art Monthly Australia*, no. 208 (2008).
2007 Bond, Anthony, and Wayne Tunnicliffe, eds. *Contemporary: Art Gallery of New South Wales Contemporary Collection*. Sydney: Art Gallery of New South Wales, 2007.
  Budick, Ariella. "Harrowing Bridal Images that Peek Behind the Veil." *Newsday* (June 29, 2007).
  Bullock, Natasha. "Time-Memory-Place." In *Photography: Art Gallery of New South Wales Collection*, edited by Judy Annear. Sydney: Art Gallery of New South Wales, 2007.
  Butler, Rex. "The Art of Rosemary Laing." *Art & Australia* 44, no. 4 (2007).
  Coleman, Catherine. "Intervened Landscape." In *Janus. Photography's Double Face: Works from the Permanent Collection*. Exh. cat. Madrid: Museo Nacional Centro de Arte Reina Sofía, 2007.
  Delmez, Katie. *Rosemary Laing: Flight*. Exh. cat. Nashville, Tenn.: Frist Center for the Visual Arts, 2007.
  Ennis, Helen. *Photography and Australia*. London: Reaktion Books, 2007.
  Forsyth, Graham. "Flying." *COFA Magazine*, no. 19 (2007).
  Gellatly, Kelly. "Pure Transit." In *Brought to Light II: Contemporary Australian Art 1996–2006*, edited by Lynne Seear and Julie Ewington. Brisbane: Queensland Art Gallery, 2007.
  Genocchio, Benjamin. "Rosemary Laing: *weather*." *New York Times* (March 2, 2007).
  Korotkin, Joyce. Reviews. *Tema Celeste*, no. 121 (May–June 2007).
  Lacayo, Richard. "And a Bit More on Storr." *Time* (June 8, 2007).

Meyers, William. "Transgression and Transformation." *New York Sun* (August 9, 2007).

Moran, Clarice. "Recent Photography at the N.C.M.A." *The Independent Weekly* (March 21, 2007).

Ohlsen, Nils. *Garten Eden: Der Garten in der Kunst seit 1900*. Exh. cat. Emden: Kunsthalle Emden; Köln: Dumont Buchverlag Gmbh, 2007.

Page, Beatrice, and Robert Leonard. *Grey Water*. Exh. cat. Brisbane: Institute of Modern Art, 2007.

Storr, Robert, ed. *Think with the Senses, Feel with the Mind: Art in the Present Tense*. Exh. cat. New York: Rizzoli International, 2007.

Tunnicliffe, Wayne. "You can not get past the fence." In *Think with the Senses, Feel with the Mind*, vol. 3, *Pages in the Wind: A Reader; Texts Chosen by the Artists of the 52nd International Art Exhibition*, edited by Robert Storr. Marsilio: La Biennale di Venezia, 2007.

2006 Block, René, Barbara Heinrich, and Svetlana Petrovic, eds. *Art, Life & Confusion: 47th October Salon*. Exh. cat. Belgrade: Belgrade Cultural Center, 2006.

Darwent, Charles. "Art at the Extremes." *ArtReview* (June 2006).

Jocks, Heinz-Norbert. "Rosemary Laing: Insider and Outsider der Wahrnehmung." *Kunstforum International* 182 (October/November 2006).

Slade, Lisa. *Strange Cargo, Contemporary Art as a State of Encounter*. Exh. cat. Newcastle: Newcastle Region Art Gallery, 2006.

Solomon-Godeau, Abigail. "Urolige landskaber" [The Unquiet Landscapes]. *blikfang*, no. 4 (2006).

Webb, Vivienne. *The Unquiet Landscapes of Rosemary Laing*. Exh. cat. Odense: Kunsthallen Brandts, 2006.

2005 Alexander, George. "Remembering Forwards*." ArtAsiaPacific*, no. 46 (Fall 2005).

Angeloro, Dominique. "Off with their heads." *Sydney Morning Herald* (Metro) (March 18, 2005).

Boecker, Susanne. "Rosemary Laing." *Kunstforum International*, no. 174 (January–March 2005).

Couacaud, Sally. *After Nature*. Exh. cat. Booragul: Lake Macquarie City Art Gallery, 2005.

Fischer, Peter. "Rosemary Laing: Floating." In *A Kind of Magic: The Art of Transforming/Die Kunst des Verwandelns*, edited by Peter Fisher and Brigitt Burgi. Exh. cat. Luzern: Kunstmuseum Luzern, 2005.

Fortescue, E. "Burning Desires: The Unquiet Landscapes of Rosemary Laing." *Sydney Daily Telegraph* (March 2005).

Goncharov, Kathleen. *The Forest: Politics, Poetics and Practice*. Durham, N.C.: Nasher Museum of Art/ Duke University Press, 2005.

Hill, Peter. "On a High for the People." *The Age* (May 28, 2005).

Kalina, R. "Down Under No More." *Art In America* (April 2005).

Martin-Chew, Louise, "Rosemary Laing: A collaboration with Stephen Birch." *Art & Australia* 42, no. 4 (Winter 2005).

Meacham, Steve. "Diving Right in Without a Parachute." *The Sydney Morning Herald* (March 17, 2005).

Meagher, David. "The Bride Stripped Bare." *Australian Financial Review Magazine* (April 2005).

McFarlane, Robert. "Red Carpet Treatment, But Not for the Bride." *Sydney Morning Herald* (April 5, 2005).

Palmer, Daniel. "Towards a Technocultural Aesthetic." In *A Short Ride in a Fast Machine: Gertrude Contemporary Art Spaces 1985–2005*, edited by Charlotte Day. Melbourne: Gertrude Contemporary Art Spaces, 2005.

Solomon-Godeau, Abigail, and Vivienne Webb. *The Unquiet Landscapes of Rosemary Laing*. Exh. cat. Sydney: Museum of Contemporary Art, 2005.

Spring, Tracey. "Rosemary Laing Story." *Sunday Afternoon*, ABC, 2005.

Tunnicliffe, Wayne. *one dozen unnatural disasters: a collaboration with Stephen Birch*. Exh. cat. Sydney: GrantPirrie Gallery, 2005.

Waltener, Shane. "Rosemary Laing: Domus Artium." *Modern Painters* (February 2005).

Wise, Kit. "Living Together Is Easy." *Frieze*, no. 90 (April 2005).

2004 Alexander, George. "Rosemary Laing." In *2004 Busan Biennale: Chasm–NET*. Busan: N-SIK HUR, 2004.

———. "Rosemary Laing." In *2004 Adelaide Biennale of Australian Art: Contemporary Photo-media*, edited by Penelope Curtin. Exh. cat. Adelaide: Art Gallery of South Australia, 2004.

———, and Javier Panera Cuevas. *Rosemary Laing*. Exh. cat. Salamanca: Domus Artium 2002, 2004.

Apparement léger: Semaines européennes de l'image (Apparently Light). Exh. cat. Dudelange: Galerie Nei Liicht, 2004.

Barragan, Paco. *Arquitecturas Urbanas*. Exh. cat. Madrid: Centro Municipal de las Artes de Alcorcón, 2004.

C. P. "La australiana Rosemary Laing expone su obra en el DA2." *Tribuna de Salamanca* (October 15, 2004).

Chillida, Alicia, ed. *Paisaje & Memoria/Landscape & Memory*. Exh. cat. Madrid: La Casa Encendida, 2004.

Femina. Exh. cat. Paris: Galerie Les Filles du Calvaire, 2004.

Fitzgerald, Michael. "Not dying, changing." *Time Pacific Magazine* (March 22, 2004).

Green, Charles, ed. *2004: Australian Culture Now*. Exh. cat. Melbourne: National Gallery of Victoria, 2004.

Mizuki, Takahashi, and Ericko Osaka, eds. *Living Together is Easy*. Exh. cat. Tokyo: Contemporary Art Centre, Art Tower Mito, 2004.

Pulido, Natividad. "Un Genero revisado con neuvos lenguajes." *Guia De Madrid ABC* (April 22, 2004).

Rees, Simon. "At the Galleries: Sydney – Rosemary Laing at Gitte Weise Gallery." *Flash Art* 37, no. 234 (January–February 2004).

Sánchez, C. "La obra de Rosemary Laing reinventa el paisaje australiano." *el Periódico el Adelanto de Salamanca* (October 22, 2004).

Solomon-Godeau, Abigail. "The Unquiet Landscapes of Rosemary Laing." *Aperture*, no. 175 (Summer 2004).

2003 Alexander, George. "*groundspeed*." *Monografias: Room*, no. 2/3 (2003).

———. "Rosemary Laing." In *Face Up: Contemporary Art from Australia*, edited by Britta Schmitz. Exh. cat. Berlin: Hatje Cantz Verlag and Autoren, 2003.

———, Graham Forsyth, Blair French, and Annemarie Jonson. *Rosemary Laing: A Survey, 1995–2002*. Exh. cat. Sydney: Gitte Weise Gallery; Brisbane: Brisbane City Gallery, 2003.

Boriani, G. "arts australia berlin 03." *Tema Celeste*, no. 100 (November–December 2003).

Dannatt, Adrian. "Rosemary Laing: *bulletproofglass*." *Art Newspaper*, no.132 (January 2003).

Dougherty, Linda Johnson, and Huston Paschal. *Defying Gravity: Contemporary Art and Flight*. Exh. cat. Raleigh, N.C.: North Carolina Museum of Art; New York: Prestel, 2003.

Eggebert, Anne, and Polly Gould, eds. *Nature and Nation: Vaster than Empires*. Exh. cat. Hastings: Hastings Museum and Art Gallery, 2003.

Hagedorn, Ingeborg. "Australischer Kunstmonat Oktober in Berlin." *Blattgold* (October 2003).

Hoeps, Reinhard, Alois Kölbl, Eleonora Louis, and Johannes Rauchenberger, *Himmelschwer. Transformationen der Schwerkraft*. Exh. cat. Munich: Wilhelm Fink Verlag, 2003.

Imdahl, Georg. "Auf der Fährte der Malerei trifft man auch schon mal den Computer." *Frankfurter Allgemeine Zeitung* (March 1, 2003).

Jocks, Heinz-Norbert. "Etwas anderes als die Realitat." *Süddeutsche Zeitung* (February 19, 2003).

Johnson, Ken. "Rosemary Laing." *New York Times* (January 3, 2003).

Louis, Eleonora. "Fri af tyngden." In *Himmel Falden*. Exh. cat. Odense: Kunsthallen Brandts Klædefabrik, 2003.

Mackenzie, Janet. "Face Up." *Studio International* (December 2003). http://www.studio-international. co.uk/reports/face_up.asp.

Martin-Chew, Louise. "Rosemary Laing and Jay Younger." *Art and Australia* 41, no. 1 (Spring 2003).

———. "Suspended in Uncertain Skies." *Weekend Australian* (February 8–9, 2003).

Meister, Helga. "Performance für die Kamera." *Westdeutsche Zeitung* (March 3, 2003).

Murphie, Andrew, and John Potts. *Culture and Technology*. New York: Palgrave Macmillan, 2003.

Palazzoli, Daniela, Pinacoteca Giovanni, and Marella Agnelli al Lingotto, eds. *L'attimo fuggente fra fotografia e cinema*. Exh. cat. Milan: Bompiani, 2003.

Stanhope, Zara. *Hothouse: The Flower in Contemporary Art*. Exh. cat. Melbourne: Monash University Museum of Art, 2003.

Trappschuh, Elke. "Auszug, Umzug, Aufbruch." *Handelsblatt* (March 8, 2003).

2002 Alexander, George. *bulletproofglass*. Exh. cat. Sydney: Gitte Weise Gallery, 2002.

Barragán, Paco. "The Art to Come." *Madrid: Subastas Siglo*, no. 11 (2002).

Giardino, Ariel. "Rosemary Laing." *H.*, no. 37 (October 2002).

Foster, Alasdair. "Rosemary Laing." In *Blink*, edited by Antonia Carver. London: Phaidon, 2002.

Hart, Deborah. "Rosemary Laing: *flight research*." In *Tales of the Unexpected*, edited by Alistair McGhie. Exh. cat. Canberra: National Gallery of Australia, 2002.

———. "Tales of the Unexpected." *artonview*, no. 30 (Winter 2002).

Johnson, Ken. "Rosemary Laing: *bulletproofglass*." *New York Times* (December 27, 2002).

Kaufman, Jason Edward. "Fair Report: ARCO, Madrid–International Trade Show or Cultural Festival?" *Art Newspaper: International Edition* 13, no. 123 (March 2002).

Koo, J. "Rosemary Laing." *Monthly Photographic Art Magazine, Sajinyesul*, no. 164 (December 2002).

Marsh, Anne. "Rosemary Laing." In *Monash University Collection: Four Decades of Collecting*, edited by Jenepher Duncan and Linda Michael. Victoria: Monash University Museum of Art, 2002.

Meagher, David. "Take Off." Art Market. *Australian Financial Review Magazine* (August 2002).

Nigrosh, Leon. "*Staged*; Contemporary Photography at WAM." *Worcester Magazine* (January 10, 2002).

O'Hehir, Anne. "Art Now 1900–2002." In *Australian Art in the National Gallery of Australia*, edited by Anne Gray. Canberra: National Gallery of Australia, 2002.

Temin, Christine. "In 'Staged,' Photographers Make the Scene." *Boston Globe* (January 2, 2002).

Smith, Roberta. "The Armory Show, Grown Up and in Love With Color." *New York Times* (February 22, 2002).

Wimmer, Elga. *Sahte/Gerçek (Faux/Real)*. Exh. cat. Istanbul: Borusan Art Gallery, 2002.

2001 Alexander, George. *groundspeed*. Exh. cat. Sydney: Gitte Weise Gallery, 2001.

———. "Post Natural Nature: Rosemary Laing." *Artlink* 21, no. 4 (2001).

Duckett, Richard. "Deliberate Images." *Time Out: Worcester Telegram & Gazette* (Worcester, Mass.; December 20, 2001).

Feinstein, Roni. "Art and Sport Down Under." *Art in America*, no. 5 (May 2001).

Hill, Peter. "Reviews: Rosemary Laing—*groundspeed*." *Eyeline*, no. 47 (Summer 2001/2002).

James, Bruce. "Soaring Laing Hears Call of the Wild." *Sydney Morning Herald* (Metropolitan) (October 10, 2001).

Martin, Melinda. "The Advantages of Being a Woman Artist." *Photofile*, no. 64 (December 2001).

Stoops, Susan L. *Staged!: Contemporary Photography by Gregory Crewdson, Rosemary Laing and Sharon Lockhart*. Exh. cat. Worcester, Mass.: Worcester Art Museum, 2001.

2000 Barragan, Paco. "Down Under: 15 fotografos australianos." *Lapiz* (July 2000).

———. "Ulttimas maniobras del arte austrliano." *ABC Cultural* (September 16, 2000).

———. "Visiones urbanas: Michael Raedecker, Rosemary Laing, Paul Nobl, Aitor Ortiz." *Subastas Siglo* 21, no. 12 (2000).

Brezovecki-Bidin, Iva. "Socijalna Sezibilnost I Eticki Angazman." *Vijenac* (2000).

Fitzgerald, Michael. "Suspension of Disbelief." *Time Magazine* (June 12, 2000).

Forsyth, Graham. "Gradience." *Art Monthly Online*, 2000.

French, Blair. "Rosemary Laing." In *Mjesto Na Kojem Nisam Bio/A Place I've Never Been To*, edited by Tihomir Milovac. Exh. cat. Zagreb: Croatian Photographic Union, Zagreb, 2000.

Heckmann, Stefanie. "Biennalen der Welt, vernetzt Euch!" *Berliner Zeitung* (2000).

Hynes, Victoria. "Quiet Achievers." *Art and Australia* 37, no. 4 (2000).

James, Bruce. "Arts Today." *ABC Radio National* (transcript) (June 1, 2000).

Kent, Rachel. *Sporting Life*. Exh. cat. Sydney: Museum of Contemporary Art, 2000.

Kis, Patricia. "Vrhunac sezone u Paviljonu." *Cetvrtak* (September 21, 2000).

Lynn, Victoria. *gradience*. Exh. cat. Sydney: Australian Centre for Photography, 2000.

Michael, Linda. "Rosemary Laing." In *Das Lied von der Erde/The Song of the Earth*. Exh. cat. Kassel: Museum Fridericianum, 2000.

Murphy, Bernice. *Zeitgenössische Fotokunst aus Australien* [Contemporary Photographic Art from Australia]. Exh. cat. Berlin: Neuer Berliner Kunstverein (NBK); Heidelberg: Edition Braus, 2000.

Muster, Anna. *Body Language: Art, Sport and the Cyber Conversation*. Exh. cat. Sydney: Ivan Dougherty Gallery, College of Fine Arts, University of New South Wales, 2000.

Peterson, Tanya. "Rosemary Laing." *Artlink* 20, no. 3 (2000).

Snell, Ted. "Surprise and Engagement." *Art and Australia* 38, no. 1 (2000).

Sorrento, Aureliana. "Schatten an der Wäscheleine." *Der Tagesspiegel*, Berlin (2000).

Unattributed author, "Letzte Handgriffe für: Das Lied von der Erde." *Hessische Niedersachsische Allgemeine* (2000).

Unattributed author, "Das Lied von der Erde." *DPict Magazine*, no. 2 (June/July 2000).

1999 Clabburn, Anna. *Natural Disasters/Disasters Unnatural*. Exh. cat. Melbourne: Monash University Gallery, 1999.

French, Blair. "Rosemary Laing." In *Contempora 5*. Exh. cat. Melbourne: National Gallery of Victoria, 1999.

Kahn, Douglas. "High Speed Nature: Rosemary Laing." In *Photo Files: an Australian Photography Reader*, edited by Blair French. Sydney: Power Foundation and Australian Centre for Photography, 1999.

King, Natalie. *aero-zone*. Exh. cat. Osaka: The National Museum of Osaka, 1999.

Kingwell, Mark. "Playing in the Digital Garden: Getting Inside by going Outside." *Descant*, no. 105 (1999).

Nelson, Robert. "Flights of Fancy for Some." *The Age* (September 1, 1999).

Rooney, Robert. "Calm Tribute to a Topsy-turvy World." *The Australian* (June 25, 1999).

Williamson, Clare. "Digitalis Australis: The Recent Hybrid in Australian Photography." *History of Photography* (Australia issue) 23, no. 2 (Summer 1999).

1998 French, Blair. *brownwork: Rosemary Laing*. Exh. cat. Sydney: Annandale Galleries, 1998.

Jonson, Annemarie. "Rosemary Laing/Stall Fall." *Art & Text*, no. 63 (November 1998–January 1999).

Michael, Linda. *Seppelt Contemporary Art Awards*. Exh. cat. Sydney: Museum of Contemporary Art, 1998.

1997 Marsh, Anne. "Rebecca Cummins and Rosemary Laing: Envisioned." *Eyeline*, no. 35 (Summer 1997/1998).

Millner, Jacqueline. "Beyond the Sublime 2." *Art & Text*, no. 56 (February–April 1997).

———. "Rosemary Laing: Pure Transit." *Globe*, no. 6 (1997). http://www.artdes.monash.edu.au/non-cms/globe/issue6/rltxt.html.

Stanhope, Zara. *Envisioned*. Exh. cat. Melbourne: Monash University Gallery, Monash University, 1997.

1996 Bachrach, Sanja, ed. *Koncept: International exhibition of Contemporary Photography*. Exh. cat. Zagreb: Hrvatski Fotosavez, 1996.

Dault, Gary Michael. "Cybernetic Horticulture." *Globe and Mail* (Toronto; October 26, 1996).

Dompierre, Louise. *Digital Garden: A World in Mutation.* Exh. cat. Toronto: The Power Plant Contemporary Art Gallery, 1996.

Fortesque, Elizabeth. "The Great Art Debate." *Daily Telegraph* (November 2, 1996).

Jonson, Annemarie. *Next Wave: Art & Technology.* Exh. cat. Fitzroy: Next Wave Festival Inc., 1996.

Kent, Rachel. *Alternative Realities.* Exh. cat. Parkville: University of Melbourne Museum of Art and The Asialink Centre Pacific, 1996.

McDonald, John. "Pictures of Banality." *Sydney Morning Herald* (Spectrum) (August 31, 1996).

McDonald-Crowley, Amanda. "Electronic Art in Australia: Do We Have Critical Mass?" *ArtLink* 16, no. 2/3 (1996).

Michael, Linda, ed. *Photography Is Dead! Long Live Photography!* Exh. cat. Sydney: Museum of Contemporary Art, 1996.

Morgan, Margaret. "Photography Is Dead! Long Live Photography!" *Art & Text,* no. 55 (October 1996).

Newton, Gael. "View of the New." *artonview—Australian National Gallery, Canberra,* no. 5 (Autumn, 1996).

1995 Jonson, Annemarie. *greenwork.* Exh. cat. Sydney: Annandale Galleries, 1995.

Khan, Douglas. "High Speed Nature: Rosemary Laing." *Photofile,* no. 45 (August 1995).

Vogel, Sabine, ed. *New Orientation: The Vision of Art in a Paradoxical World; 4th Istanbul Biennial.* Exh. cat. Istanbul: Istanbul Foundation for Culture & Arts, 1995.

1994 Coulter-Smith, Graham. "Exploring the Technological Other: Robyn Stacey & Rosemary Laing." *Continuum: Electronic Arts in Australia* 8, no. 1 (1994).

Forsyth, Graham. "Australian Perspecta: 1993." *Art & Text,* no. 47 (January 1994).

1993 Jonson, Annemarie. "Rosemary Laing: Blow Out." *Agenda,* no. 34 (1993).

Lumby, Catharine. "Rosemary Laing." In *Australian Perspecta 1993,* edited by Victoria Lynn. Exh. cat. Sydney: Art Gallery of New South Wales, 1993.

1992 Adams, Jude. "Something Borrowed Nothing Blue Some Old Nothing New." *Artlink* 12, no. 2 (1992).

Anderson, Peter. "Rosemary Laing." *Art & Text,* no. 42 (May 1992).

Davidson, Christina. "Rosemary Laing." In *Strangers in Paradise: Contemporary Australian Art to Korea,* edited by Victoria Lynn. Exh. cat. Seoul: National Museum of Contemporary Art, Korea, 1992.

———. *Travels in Paradise.* Exh. cat. Brisbane: Queensland Art Gallery, 1992.

Fenner, Fecility. "Erotica Blooms." *Sydney Morning Herald* (August 13, 1992).

Jackson, Beth. "essence and difference issues: arising from … but never by chance …" *Eyeline,* no. 20 (Summer 1992).

Pierce, Julianne. "Another Side of Eroticism." *Broadsheet* 21, no. 2 (June 1992).

Walker, Linda Marie, ed. *… but never by chance … (eroticism).* Exh. cat. Adelaide: Experimental Art Foundation, 1992.

Zurbrugg, Nicholas. "Travels in Paradise." *Photofile,* no. 36 (August 1992).

1991 Hutchings, Peter. "Not Far from Roses." *from Paradise work.* Exh. cat. Melbourne: 200 Gertrude Street; Adelaide: Experimental Art Foundation, 1991.

Steffensen, Jyanni. "Rosemary Laing, *from Paradise work.*" *Broadsheet* 20, no. 3 (1991).

1990 Butler, Rex. "A Love That Cannot Speak its Name." *Agenda,* no. 15 (December 1990).

Colless, Edward. "That's Amore." In *Amore.* Exh. cat. Sydney: Artspace, 1990.

Coulter-Smith, Graham. *Real Art.* Exh. cat. Brisbane: Institute of Modern Art, 1990.

Lumby, Catharine. "Dino Puts His Finger on It." *Sydney Morning Herald* (November 23, 1990).

———. "Rosemary Laing: Natural Disasters." *Eyeline* no. 11 (Autumn 1990).

1988 Butler, Rex. *Natural Disasters.* Exh. cat. Sydney: Artspace, 1988.

PUBLIC COLLECTIONS

Albury Regional Gallery, New South Wales

ARCO Foundation, Madrid

Artbank, Sydney

Art Gallery of New South Wales, Sydney

Art Gallery of South Australia, Adelaide

Art Gallery of Western Australia, Perth

Art Museum of Western Virginia, Roanoke, Virginia

Bendigo Art Gallery, Victoria

Buschlen Mowatt Foundation, Vancouver

Domus Artium 2002, Salamanca, Spain

Fonds national d'art contemporain, Puteaux, France

Foundation Belgacom, Brussels

Gippsland Art Gallery, Victoria

Griffith University Collection, Brisbane

Harvard Art Museum, Cambridge, Massachusetts

Kunstmuseum Luzern, Lucerne

Lyon Housemuseum, Melbourne

McClelland Gallery and Sculpture Park, Langwarrin, Victoria

Modern Art Museum of Fort Worth, Texas

Monash Gallery of Art, Wheelers Hill, Victoria

Monash University Museum of Art, Caulfield East, Victoria

Museo Nacional Centro De Arte Reina Sofia, Madrid

Museum of Contemporary Art, Sydney

National Gallery of Australia, Canberra

National Gallery of Victoria, Melbourne

National Museum of Women in the Arts, Washington, D.C.

Newcastle Regional Art Gallery, New South Wales

North Carolina Museum of Art, Raleigh

Norton Family Foundation, Santa Monica

Parliament House Art Collection, Canberra

Queensland Art Gallery, Brisbane

21st Century Museum of Contemporary Art, Kanazawa, Japan

The University of Queensland Art Museum, Brisbane

University of Canberra Collection, Canberra

University of Technology Collection, Sydney

Wadsworth Atheneum Museum of Art, Hartford, Connecticut

William Benton Museum of Art, University of Connecticut, Storrs

Rosemary Laing especially thanks Abigail Solomon-Godeau, Mary Sabbatino, and Jan Minchin. Thank you to Tanya Peterson, Sandra Barnard, and Ioulia Terizis in Sydney; Ryan Newbanks, Laura Lindgren, and all the contributors at Prestel, as well as Christopher Lyon, formerly of Prestel; John Dunn and Margaret Bishop of Piper Press; and Daniel Burns at Galerie Lelong. For supporting Abigail's Australian travel, thank you to Lynne Roberts-Goodwin, College of Fine Arts, University of New South Wales; Sherman Contemporary Art Foundation; Art Gallery of New South Wales; and Power Institute, University of Sydney. Rosemary Laing gratefully acknowledges the support over the years from Helga Weckop-Conrads and Walter Conrads, Michelle and Patrick Holmes, Stephen Grant and Bridget Pirrie, Mark Hughes, and Geoff Kleem.

Rosemary Laing is represented by Tolarno Galleries, Melbourne, and Galerie Lelong, New York.